European Thought and Culture in the Twentieth Century
Part II

Professor Lloyd Kramer

THE TEACHING COMPANY ®

PUBLISHED BY:

THE TEACHING COMPANY
4151 Lafayette Center Drive, Suite 100
Chantilly, Virginia 20151-1232
1-800-TEACH-12
Fax—703-378-3819
www.teach12.com

Copyright © The Teaching Company Limited Partnership, 2002

Printed in the United States of America

This book is in copyright. All rights reserved.

Without limiting the rights under copyright reserved above,
no part of this publication may be reproduced, stored in
or introduced into a retrieval system, or transmitted,
in any form, or by any means
(electronic, mechanical, photocopying, recording, or otherwise),
without the prior written permission of
The Teaching Company.

ISBN 1-56585-824-7

Lloyd Kramer, Ph.D.

Professor of History, University of North Carolina, Chapel Hill

Lloyd Kramer was born in Maryville, Tennessee, and grew up in Benton, Arkansas, and Evansville, Indiana. He received a B.A. from Maryville College and an M.A. in history at Boston College before going to Hong Kong to teach for two years at Lingnan College. After traveling widely in Asia and studying French in Paris, he pursued graduate studies in European intellectual history at Cornell University, where he received his Ph.D. in 1983.

Following completion of his graduate work, Professor Kramer taught for one year in the history department at Stanford University and for two years in the history department at Northwestern University. Since 1986, he has been a history professor at the University of North Carolina, Chapel Hill, teaching courses on European intellectual history, the history of Western civilization, and modern global history. He has received two awards for distinguished undergraduate teaching at the University of North Carolina.

Professor Kramer's historical research has focused mainly on French intellectual history after 1800, with particular emphasis on cross-cultural intellectual exchanges. He has written numerous articles and books, including *Threshold of a New World: Intellectuals and the Exile Experience in Paris, 1830–1848* (1988), *Lafayette in Two Worlds: Public Cultures and Personal Identities in an Age of Revolutions* (1996), and *Nationalism: Political Cultures in Europe and America, 1775–1865* (1998). His book on Lafayette received the Gilbert Chinard Prize from the American Society for French Historical Studies and the Annibel Jenkins Biography Prize from the American Society for Eighteenth-Century Studies.

Professor Kramer has also edited or co-edited several books, including one on historical education in America and (with Sarah Maza) the Blackwell *Companion to Western Historical Thought* (2002). He is also co-author (with R. R. Palmer and Joel Colton) of the ninth edition of *A History of the Modern World* (2002).

He has been a member of the School of Historical Studies at the Institute for Advanced Study in Princeton and has served as president of the Society for French Historical Studies.

Professor Kramer lives in Chapel Hill, North Carolina, with his wife, Gwynne Pomeroy, and their two children.

Table of Contents

European Thought and Culture in the Twentieth Century
Part II

European Thought and Culture in the Twentieth Century

Scope:

This course of 24 lectures examines major intellectual themes and debates in 20th-century European culture. Our discussion will draw on the methods of intellectual history and refer to the evolving contexts in which leading writers and theorists developed their ideas. This approach to the history of ideas rests on the assumption that ideas shape and influence all other aspects of the historical process, but it also stresses the importance of social, political, and economic realities in the formation and diffusion of all ideas.

We will interpret 20th-century European thought as an ongoing dialogue between advocates of different philosophical or theoretical perspectives and as an intellectual response to complex cultural traditions and disturbing European events, including: (1) rationalist scientific forms of knowledge and the optimistic belief in progress; (2) classical realist representations and accounts of the external world; (3) the traumatic violence and massive costs of two destructive world wars; (4) the political history and conflicts of fascism, communism, and liberalism; (5) the social and economic changes that resulted from urbanization, imperialism, warfare, the Great Depression, and late 20th-century globalization.

The course does not provide detailed descriptions of these contexts, but it suggests that all these historical realities (and others) affected the changing themes of European literature, social science, philosophy, psychology, art, political theories, and intellectual identities. Important texts or artistic creations do not simply reflect the contexts in which they appear, but this course will argue that creative thinkers are always interpreting, redefining, criticizing, and influencing the historical world in which they live.

The lectures look at three general chronological periods or cultural eras in modern European history, and each era is discussed in roughly eight lectures: (1) the cultural innovations during the three decades before 1914, (2) the responses to World War I and the new cultural themes of what historians call the "interwar" era, and (3) the responses to World War II and the new forms of thought that emerged in the decades after 1945.

We begin the first section of the course with two lectures on the dominant ideas and cultural institutions of the late 19th century, because modern intellectual movements evolved out of the cultural assumptions and urban "culture industry" of this era. We then devote two lectures to the contrasting literary movements of naturalism and symbolism, noting that both these movements would influence later novels and poetry. The following two lectures look at new departures in philosophy, science, and art that would contribute to a general 20th-century trend toward relativism and subjectivism in European thought. We conclude this pre-1914 section of the course with two lectures on the emergence of modern sociology and social theory in France and Germany.

The next section of the course starts with a lecture on how the First World War contributed to a new cultural pessimism and made Europeans more receptive to psychological theories that stressed human irrationality. We examine the ideas and diverging schools of psychoanalysis in the next two lectures before turning to postwar literary themes in three lectures on pessimistic poets, surrealist writers, and influential authors who developed the narrative style and psychological themes of modernist novels. We then conclude the discussion of interwar European culture with two lectures on philosophy and social theory, stressing the new interest in language and the political anxiety about fascism, communism, and the economic crisis of the 1930s.

The final section of the course begins with a lecture on different intellectual responses to Nazism in Germany. We will then look at other responses to the events of World War II in a lecture on postwar existential philosophy and a lecture on literary attempts to remember or interpret the horrors of the Holocaust and totalitarianism. The next four lectures describe new "isms" that gained wide cultural influence in the period between 1950 and 1990, including feminism, structuralism, poststructuralism, and postmodernism. We conclude with a lecture on the revival of various Enlightenment themes among late 20th-century intellectuals who criticized cultural "isms," such as postmodernism, and rejected political "isms," such as fascism and communism.

Our objective throughout this course is to understand the ideas of influential 20th-century European thinkers, to reflect on the interactions between ideas and historical contexts, and to think critically about how the ideas of creative 20th-century writers continue to raise questions for our own time. Intellectual history analyzes the evolving dialogues among the people of other places and times, but it also emphasizes the importance of sustaining a critical dialogue between the present and the past. This course seeks to expand our dialogue with the intellectual world of 20th-century Europe and to show how the challenging ideas of that historical era are still vital components of the world's contemporary cultural life.

Lecture Thirteen
The Modern Novel—Joyce and Woolf

Scope:

New conceptions of psychology and the human mind reshaped 20th-century novels, as well as poetry and social theories. This lecture looks at the exploration of the "inner life," time, and art in the modern novel and discusses the influential work of James Joyce and Virginia Woolf. "Modernist" writers emphasized the internal experiences of time and space, thus suggesting that the internal world of psychology and personal experience was more real than the external world of public events. Joyce and Woolf felt separated from their own societies, and both experimented with a stream-of-consciousness style to represent the complexity of human thought, language, and memory. These innovations contributed to a widespread 20th-century literary interest in the internal workings of human consciousness and emotions.

Outline

I. The pervasive impact of the First World War extended from politics and economics into the cultural spheres of psychology, poetry, art, and social theory. We have seen how poets responded to the horrors of war, but the war also affected novelists.

   A. The war did not simply create a new approach to literature; as in other areas of the arts and social theory, it seemed to accelerate trends that emerged earlier.

      1. It made the new experimental forms of fiction more acceptable to a wider audience that had become disillusioned and disoriented.

      2. Like the poetry and art of the era, the postwar novel tended to question the possibility of a stable external reality.

      3. The recurring theme in much postwar fiction suggested that external social and political realities did not conform to traditional languages that described them; reality had to be portrayed in new ways.

   B. This literary theme is comparable to the revolt against positivism in social theory; it emphasized internal attempts to make sense of the world.

1. Most postwar novelists expressed a skepticism about official truths and the whole system of national politics and public life.
2. Critics of public life in the 1920s argued that the Great War had shown the bankruptcy of the public sphere in European societies.
3. In this period of political disillusionment, the consolation for creative people came through art rather than public involvement.
4. The truths of art were described as internal truths and often linked to the unconscious. This theme resembled Freud's themes, but Freud preferred classical literature and science to the cultural avant-garde.

C. The modern novel, however, sought to challenge realistic modes of representation and to defamiliarize the familiar external world.
1. This modernist literary pattern appeared on the Continent in such writers as Marcel Proust and Franz Kafka and in the English novelists James Joyce and Virginia Woolf, whom we will discuss in this lecture.
2. The new postwar English novels reshaped much 20th-century literature.

II. To challenge or rethink the meaning of the "familiar" world, modern novels redefined time and space. The goal for many novelists was to alter the empirical view of social reality and the logical order of events.

A. Empiricism stresses logical cause-and-effect relations.
1. The classical realist novel usually narrated stories in an empirical mode by using horizontal narratives: beginning, middle, end.
2. This is the classical narrative pattern in Western literature, and it assumes a coherent external reality of time and space.

B. Modernist novels, by contrast, explore events vertically rather than horizontally; events in these novels do not happen in simple sequential order.
1. The characters often encounter an external world of random or repetitious events; their thoughts move backward and forward in time.

2. The most important events usually take place inside the individual and are described with narratives about the internal world.
3. The narrative of external events is fragmented; it also focuses on individual internal experience and develops multiple voices or perspectives—in contrast to earlier novels, such as the work of Balzac.
4. The inner event may not last very long in terms of external time, but an inner event may be so complex that it requires extended narration.

C. Time, therefore, is portrayed as unstable or diverse (as Bergson had suggested in his philosophical arguments); the novelist examines the inner time and space of characters rather than the time and space of classical science.
1. In describing this inner space, many modern novelists also suggest that the human "self" has no stable center or absolute identity.
2. This view could be compared to themes in Dadaism or surrealism, but the novelists provided more sustained explorations of time and space.
3. Narrators in modern novels describe subjective inner realities, but unlike Dada poems, the novels rarely lapse into nonsense.
4. At the same time, though, many modern novels are not easy to read; they differ from the linear style of popular novels and they challenge the desire for a commonsense understanding of experience.

D. The new narrative techniques and the attempt to defamiliarize both the external and personal world can be seen in James Joyce and Virginia Woolf.
1. T.S. Eliot said that Joyce's novel *Ulysses* created a new artistic language for the modern world and made previous novels obsolete.
2. Critics at the time and later said that Joyce's work was obscure, vulgar, and confusing, yet critics also noted that it changed literature.

III. James Joyce (1882–1941) was born into a family of 10 children near Dublin; he was educated in Jesuit schools and at University College in Dublin, but he was unhappy in Ireland.

A. After meeting Nora Barnacle in 1904, he and Nora left for the Continent; they lived together in Italy, Switzerland, and after 1920, in Paris. They did not officially marry until 1931.

1. Joyce was determined to be a writer, but he could not get his early works published. He and Nora soon had two children and lived in poverty while he struggled to write.

2. Joyce became a bitter critic of Ireland. He made several trips back to Dublin as he tried to publish his early stories, but after 1912, he never again visited his native country—he was the permanent exile.

B. The image of the struggling exile artist became part of the cultural legend that gradually accumulated around Joyce; he faced great hardships.

1. He had problems with his vision and underwent more than 10 operations on his eyes; his daughter was mentally ill and was placed in a sanitarium.

2. Joyce himself was often self-absorbed and obsessed with his own literary reputation, but his work was embraced by literary modernists, such as Eliot and Ezra Pound. He became famous in Paris.

3. Excerpts from *Ulysses* began to appear in literary journals at the end of World War I; the whole novel was published in 1922 by Sylvia Beach, an American who owned a bookstore in Paris.

4. The book was banned as pornographic in America until 1933. Joyce meanwhile worked for 18 years on his final book, *Finnegans Wake*, which was published in 1939, but generally left readers baffled.

C. Joyce tried to portray the complex connection between interior life and external events in *Ulysses*. The novel focused on three main characters: Leopold and Molly Bloom and Stephen Dedalus.

   1. The meaning of time is transformed in the novel; the book's 800 pages describe events and thoughts of the three main characters on June 16, 1904 (the date Joyce met Nora).

   2. The story has the structure of Homer's *Odyssey*, but this is the day-long "odyssey" of unexceptional people in a modern city.

   3. Stephen Dedalus is an artist, Leopold Bloom is a Jewish businessman, and Molly is his wife, who is having an extramarital affair.

   4. Stephen and Bloom move around Dublin, encounter various random events, meet each other, and talk, but much of the action consists of internal reflections on bodily functions, death, and tedious daily life.

D. There is nothing heroic about the characters, but Joyce tried to portray how people actually think; he used indirect interior monologues and showed how thought processes skip around from subject to subject.

   1. As Joyce shows in the style of his novel, thought is neither logical nor chronological; it skips around in time and moves between complex ideas and the most mundane bodily processes.

   2. The novel culminates in a long interior monologue in which Molly Bloom's thoughts flow in a famous "stream of consciousness."

   3. Joyce filled his novel with literary and cultural allusions and various forms of humor that were not easy for readers to understand.

E. But his experiments with stream of consciousness and interior monologues became an innovative, distinctive narrative style in 20th-century literature. This style had wide influence, because it offered a new way to portray interior life.

IV. This style of writing was also used by Virginia Woolf (1882–1941), who was not an exile. She criticized much of Joyce's work but felt separated from various aspects of British life and wrote modernist narratives with interior monologues.

    A. Woolf was born into an upper-class English family with two strong-willed parents: Leslie and Julia Stephen. Her father was a prominent author and editor, and young Virginia Stephen seemed to have a happy early childhood.

        1. But her mother died when she was 13, her father went into prolonged mourning, and he died when Virginia was twenty-two.

        2. Her older brother died two years later. Virginia began to suffer from manic depression, which caused mental breakdowns and depression at repeated intervals throughout her life.

    B. She married Leonard Woolf in 1912; he was part of her brothers' social and intellectual circle at Cambridge University.

    C. She was also part of the famous Bloomsbury circle in London—a term that referred to writers and artists who lived in the Bloomsbury neighborhood; it also attracted political and economic thinkers, such as John Maynard Keynes.

    D. In Woolf's novels, the external events typically receive less attention than the complex inner thought processes; like Proust, Woolf wrote about memory. She said that there are only a few essential hours in life, crucial moments of self-recognition, that are a kind of shock on the mind and emotions. Identities emerge from these rare moments.

    E. These themes appear in *To the Lighthouse* (1927), a novel that explores the meaning of time, memory, and language. It is also a portrait of Woolf's parents in the fictional characters of Mr. and Mrs. Ramsay.

        1. The interior monologues in the novel refer to the rare moments of insight that come amid the long stretches of daily routine.

        2. "The great revelation perhaps never did come. Instead there were little…miracles, illuminations, matches struck unexpectedly in the dark."

F. Woolf often felt inadequate to describe these little "illuminations," ("words fluttered sideways and struck the object inches too low"), and her own mental anxieties led her finally to commit suicide by drowning in a river.

    1. Yet she succeeded in creating a literary style that conveyed the complex thoughts and emotions of the human mind.

    2. This kind of writing was one of the great modern literary innovations.

Essential Reading:

Virginia Woolf, *To the Lighthouse*.

Supplementary Reading:

Richard Ellmann, *James Joyce*, revised edition, pp. 485–552.

Quentin Bell, *Virginia Woolf: A Biography*, vol. 2, pp. 109–140.

Questions to Consider:

1. Do you think that your own thought processes could be described as a stream of consciousness?

2. Do you agree with Virginia Woolf's idea that self-recognition or knowledge comes only at rare moments over a lifetime?

Lecture Thirteen—Transcript
The Modern Novel—Joyce and Woolf

We've noted in the last several lectures that the pervasive impact of the First World War extended from politics and economics into the cultural spheres of psychology and poetry, art and social theory, and many other aspects of European thought. And we've seen how the poets responded to the horrors of the First World War. But also affected were the novelists. And it promoted developments within other forms of literature that also, I think, reflected the response to the disorientation of the war.

Now, the war simply did not create a new approach to literature. There were many important literary patterns in the novel that had begun to emerge before the war, and so as in other areas of the arts and social theory, the war seemed mainly to accelerate trends that had emerged earlier. It made the new experimental forms of fiction that writers had begun to develop before 1914—it made these experimental forms of fiction more acceptable to a wider audience—an audience that had become, in many ways, disillusioned or disoriented by the First World War.

And like the poetry and art of the era, the post-war novel tended to question the possibility or the existence of a stable, external reality. The recurring theme in a great deal of the post-war fiction—the novels published in the 1920s especially—the recurring theme in a lot of this literature suggested that external social and political realities did not conform to traditional languages that had described them. And so, reality had to be described or portrayed in new ways. And this literary theme among the novelists is comparable in some ways to the revolt against positivism in social theory. It emphasized internal attempts to make sense of the world.

Now, most post-war novelists expressed some kind of skepticism about the official truths of the societies in which they live, or they were skeptical about the whole system of national politics and public life. The critics of public life in the 1920s argued that the Great War had shown the bankruptcy of the public sphere in European societies. These critics argued that the terrible events of the war showed that the political leaders and political systems didn't know what to do—didn't know how to function in a proper way. And so there was a widespread political disillusionment with the main governments in

Europe. This is particularly pronounced among certain writers. And so for creative persons in this period, the main consolation came through the arts rather than through public involvement. And you see it especially in the first decade after World War I, a kind of retreat into the personal—the realm of personal literary and artistic exploration. And in this exploration of the arts, the truths of the arts were described as internal truths and often linked to the unconscious. And in this respect, we see the continuation of certain patterns that had already begun to emerge among symbolist poets and writers before the Great War. But in the period after the First World War, this emphasis on the unconscious or on the complexity of the mind drew often on some of the ideas of Sigmund Freud, and Freud's description of the unconscious was important not only for Surrealist poets and artists but also for a new generation of writers and novelists.

But Freud himself—although he had a strong interest in literature—Freud himself always preferred Classical literature and the sciences over the avant-garde cultural and literary movements of the early 20th century.

Now, as the modern novel evolved in the period around 1920 and afterwards, it sought to challenge the classical, realistic mode of representation. It sought to de-familiarize the familiar external world—to take what was familiar and to make it unfamiliar. And this is one of the most important patterns in modernist literary work throughout the European continent. And we can see this modernist literary attempt to de-familiarize the familiar. Continental writers such as Marcel Proust and Franz Kafka—and I want to talk about them somewhat later—in the next lecture, in fact. But you can also see those patterns in the English novelists—James Joyce and Virginia Woolf, whom we will discuss in this lecture. And I want to argue that these new post-war English novels helped to reshape much of 20th-century literature.

But before I turn to the specific examples of Joyce and Woolf, I want to say a few things about the general patterns of modernist literature—the modernist novel—patterns that made this kind of writing different from what had existed before. In order to challenge or re-think the meaning of the familiar world, modern novels tended to redefine the meaning of time and space—very important redefinition in this kind of literature. The goal for many novelists was to alter the empirical view of social reality and the logical order of events. The classical, empirical account of reality stresses a logical cause and effect relationship—that a certain cause produces a clear effect—that you can analyze it, describe it, observe it—and this is the way in which an empirical account of these relations unfolds. And in many ways, the classical, realist novel of the 19th century often narrated stories in this empirical mode. It provided a horizontal narrative—a beginning, a middle, and an end—a clear set of events in which a certain cause produces an outcome. You can see patterns, relationships. And this is in fact the classical narrative pattern in Western literature. You can trace it back all the way to antiquity. It assumes a coherent external reality of time and space, which can then be described in a coherent narrative, and there is a kind of overlap between the narrative and a reality outside the narrative—or outside the text—that is being described.

Now, modernist novels, by contrast—instead of exploring events horizontally, tended to explore events vertically. That is, the events that are narrated or described in the modernist novel don't always happen in simple, sequential order. In fact, they are often out of order—they are fragmented. And they don't simply go from point A to point B to point C. They may go very, very deeply into point A— into a kind of in-depth analysis. That's why I say it's a kind of vertical exploration of a problem or a phenomenon, rather than a horizontal narrative.

And the characters in these modernist novels often encounter an external world of random or repetitious events. And as they reflect on these events, their thoughts move backward and forward in time. In fact, the most important events in a modernist novel usually take place inside the individual and are described with narratives about the internal world or the internal psychological processes of the character—so we can go vertically or deeply into a character without extensive narratives about the character's actions in the external world. In fact, the narrative of external events is often fragmented. It focuses on the individual—the internal, the complex—psychological. And it often narrates events from multiple voices or perspectives. In this respect, we might describe a modernist novel to the Cubist paintings that we talked about in an earlier lecture, where you have the same event or experience described from multiple perspectives or with multiple voices. There is no stable narrator—no stable point of observation—just as we might say there's no stable point of view in a Cubist painting. We have multiple perspectives.

Now, in the narration of these inner events, the narrative of an inner event may go on for a long time, even though the event itself is brief. An inner event may not last very long in terms of external time. But it is so complex that it requires extended narration. You might find a novel giving many pages to a series of thoughts that happened within five or 10 minutes of a character's life, rather than five or 10 days or five or 10 weeks. It's an extensive narrative of very limited periods of time. So time, in the modernist novel, is often portrayed as unstable or diverse. Or the meaning of time depends on the position of the person who's experiencing it. And here, too, we might compare the position of the modernist novel to the philosophical ideas of Henri Bergson, who we discussed earlier. Bergson had suggested that time does not have a permanent or stable meaning. And this is what often novelists tried to portray in their works—the novelist examines the meaning of inner time and inner space rather than the time and space of classical science. So we have a redefinition of both time and space.

Also, in describing the inner space, many modern novelists suggest that the human self has no stable center or absolute identity. There is no simple way to say this is who someone is. There's a kind of a floating identity. And this view of the identity of the self can be compared to various themes in Dadaism or Surrealism. But the modernist novels usually provided more sustained explorations of time and space than we see in a Dada poem, for example. The narrator in a modern novel may describe subjective inner realities much like a Surrealist poet or a Dada poet, but unlike Dada poems, the novels rarely lapse into complete nonsense. They continue to tell a story in some way, unlike those nonsensical poems that the most extreme Dada writers were trying to produce.

But it's also true that many modern novels are not easy to read. They differ from the linear style of popular novels—or classical novels. And they always in some way challenge the desire for a common sense understanding of experience. They challenge our desire to simply know that one thing follows another or one event follows another. Instead, the narration will problematize—will create a complex relationship between various events and thoughts. And so these new narrative techniques and the attempt to de-familiarize both the external and the personal world can be seen in a great deal of post-World War I writing—in Europe and eventually in the United States—in North America—we see these patterns in much modernist literature. And in order to describe a little more about how this works, I want to turn now to a couple specific examples and look at James Joyce and Virginia Woolf.

The poet T.S. Eliot once said that Joyce's novel, *Ulysses*, created a new artistic language for the modern world and made all previous novels somehow seem obsolete. He had somehow redefined the meaning of the modern novel. In scientific language, we could almost say he created a new paradigm for what a writer might do. But despite the enthusiasm from some critics and writers like Eliot, there were always critics at the time and later who said that Joyce's work was obscure—or that it was confusing, or that it was simply vulgar—that somehow this great breakthrough in literature was not so valuable as it was made out to be. So Joyce has always been a controversial figure in modern literature.

But even those who attacked Joyce's work tended to agree that somehow his writing had changed the parameters of modern literary work. Even if you attacked him, you tended to concede that something important was going on there.

James Joyce lived from 1882 to 1941. He was born into a large family in Ireland—he was one of 10 children. He was born very close to Dublin. And he was educated in Jesuit schools and at University College in Dublin. He lived his entire youth in Ireland. But he was unhappy there. It was difficult to find the kind of niche that he wanted to pursue his interests. He decided fairly early on that he had literary interests, but he was restless and somewhat unhappy. And after meeting a woman named Nora Barnacle in 1904, he and Nora left Ireland for the Continent. And over the next few years, they lived together in Italy and in Switzerland. They lived in Switzerland during the First World War. And finally, after 1920, Joyce moved to Paris. He and Nora lived in Paris. They did not officially marry until 1931, but they lived together after 1904.

Now, Joyce was determined to become a writer. He began to write a number of short stories, and working on novels, but he could not get his early works published. He and Nora soon had two children, so they had a number of financial problems, because he could not get his writings published. They were living in poverty while he struggled to write and to produce his early works. And during these years, Joyce became a bitter critic of Ireland. He was disillusioned with Irish culture and Irish politics. He made several trips back to Dublin in the period between 1904 and 1912. He was trying to find publishers who would publish his early stories. But after 1912, he never again visited his native country. He was the permanent exile. And the image of the struggling exile artist true to his literary calling became part of the cultural legend that gradually accumulated around Joyce. He faced great hardships, and yet this gave his life as well as his work a kind of romantic literary reputation. He also had personal problems with his vision. He had more than 10 operations on his eyes—had great problems reading. Then his daughter became mentally ill and had to be placed in a sanitarium. There were a lot of personal problems. Joyce himself was often self-absorbed and obsessed with his own literary reputation. But his literary work was embraced by literary modernists such as T.S. Eliot, who I mentioned earlier, and Ezra Pound, the American Poet. And Joyce became famous in Paris in the 1920s.

The first excerpts from his novel, Ulysses, began to appear in literary journals at the end of World War I. And then the whole novel was published in 1922 by Sylvia Beach, an American woman who owned a bookstore in Paris—a famous bookstore called Shakespeare and Company. Sylvia Beach was the first publisher of *Ulysses*. But the book was banned in America. It was deemed to be pornographic. It was banned in America until 1933. Joyce, meanwhile, in the 1920s and 1930s continued to live mostly in Paris. And for the next 18 years, he worked on his final book, *Finnegans Wake*, which was published in 1939. But that book generally baffled readers and did not have the impact that *Ulysses* had when it appeared in the early 1920s.

Now, in all of his work, and particularly in *Ulysses*, Joyce tried to portray the complex connection between the interior life and external events—somehow the link between the internal and the external. And this is something that we see in *Ulysses*. This novel focused on three main characters—Leopold and Molly Bloom, husband and wife, and another character, Stephen Dedalus. The meaning of this novel operates on many levels. But one of the key elements in the meaning of the novel is the exploration of time. Because the meaning of time is transformed. The novel's 800 pages describe the events and thoughts of the three main characters on one day. The day is actually June 16, 1904, which was the date that Joyce had met Nora—this had great significance in his life. So all the events of this story take place on one day. And this story has the structure of Homer's *Odyssey*. But this is a day-long odyssey instead of over years, and it's an odyssey of unexceptional people in a modern city.

Stephen Dedalus is an artist. Leopold Bloom is a Jewish businessman, and Molly is his wife who, we find out, is having an extramarital affair. And as the novel unfolds, Stephen and Bloom move around Dublin. They encounter various random events. They actually meet each other and talk. There are a number of encounters with other people in places, taverns, and so forth, pubs. But much of the action consists of internal reflections—reflections on things like bodily functions or death or simply the tedious aspects of daily life. There's nothing heroic about the characters in this novel. But Joyce tried to portray how people actually think. He used a very famous method of interior monologues to show how our thought processes skip around from subject to subject—that you never simply think in a straight line. Your mind is always moving around in a kind of interior monologue. And as Joyce shows in the style of his novel, human thought is neither logical nor chronological. It skips around in time. It moves between complex ideas and the most mundane bodily processes. And this is the way that interior thought process works. You know this experience from your own life. Even now as you listen to me talk, you think for a while about modernist novels, and then maybe your mind drifts to what you did yesterday or how you're getting hungry and would like to get something to eat, or maybe your mind drifts off to who you're going to see later today or tomorrow or what you really need to do over your summer vacation. And then it comes back to what I'm talking about when I'm describing these novels. So, your mind—all of our minds—operate in some way that moves from very important or high thoughts to the most practical problems about 'well, time to fix lunch' or whatever.

And in this case—in Joyce's *Ulysses*—the novel culminates in a very long interior monologue in which Molly Bloom's thoughts flow in a very famous stream of consciousness—unpunctuated narrative of the thoughts that go through her mind at the end of the novel. But through the novel, Joyce included literary and cultural allusions that were difficult for people to understand. He had allusions to Classical literature. He threw in various forms of humor—you kind of had to be an insider to understand. And at the time, many people were baffled by many aspects of the novel. In fact, his novel, *Ulysses*, has remained one of the most challenging novels for readers ever since.

But his experiments with stream of consciousness and interior monologues became an innovative, distinctive narrative style in 20th century literature. And this style has had enormous influence. It offered a new way to portray the interior life of the human being—and to do so in writing.

Well, this style of writing was also used by Virginia Woolf, and I want to turn now to a couple of things about her life and work. Virginia Woolf was born in 1882, and she lived until 1941—very interesting overlap with the years of Joyce's life. But she was not an exile. She lived her life in England. She did not live abroad—she traveled a lot abroad, but she did not go into exile. She criticized much of Joyce's work. She had critical things to say about it. And she was not simply following in any particular style. But she felt separated from many aspects of British life. She didn't move away from Britain, but she felt in some ways like an outsider. And she wrote modernist narratives with extensive interior monologues.

Woolf was born into an upper class English family. She had two very strong-willed parents, Leslie and Julia Stephen. Her father was a prominent author and editor and a well-known writer. And young Virginia Stephen seemed to have a happy early childhood. But all that changed when she was 13 years old. Her mother died when she was thirteen. He father went into a kind of prolonged period of mourning and depression, and then he died about nine years later, when Virginia was about twenty-two. And then her brother died a couple of years later. And around this time of her brother's death, Virginia began to suffer from a mental illness—manic depression—which caused her to have mental breakdowns at various points in her life. She would go into depression at repeated intervals throughout her life—when she would be unable to work or she would fall into a deep depression. And then it would pass, and she would have period of extremely energetic activity.

In 1912, she married a man named Leonard Woolf—hence becoming Virginia Woolf. And Leonard Woolf was part of her brother's intellectual and social circle at Cambridge University. But Virginia Woolf did not go to the university, because she was a woman—who couldn't go to Cambridge like her brothers. And she, in fact, criticized the restrictions on women in many of her works—and particularly in her famous short book, *A Room of One's Own*, which was published in 1929 and which critically examined the position of women in modern cultural society. She described in that book the search for independence and autonomy that women had to struggle with as they made their way in modern societies.

She was also part of the famous Bloomsbury circle in London, a term that referred to the writers and artists that lived in the Bloomsbury neighborhood in London—a circle that include political and economic thinkers as well as writers. The economist, John Maynard Keynes, was also part of this group. But in general, the members of the Bloomsbury group focused on art more than politics, and they saw art as a path towards transcendental good. They wanted art to express the truth of emotions and experience. And Virginia Woolf and her husband also ran a small press that published fiction and non-fiction works, including the English editions of Freud.

Well, in Woolf's novels, the external events typically received less attention than the complex inner thought processes. In this respect, she was a lot like Marcel Proust. She wrote a great deal about memory. She once said, "The past is beautiful, because one never realizes an emotion at the time. It expands later and thus we don't have complete emotions about the present, only about the past." We have our most complete emotions when we reflect on what has happened to us. We can't fully understand that experience when we're in the middle of it. And she said that there are only a few essential hours in your entire life. These moments in time are crucial moments of self recognition—moments which provide a kind of shock on the mind and emotions—Those moments when those things you thought you understood suddenly change, and our identities, she said, our identities emerge from these rare moments—these isolated moments when suddenly all the tedious aspects of life fall away, and we encounter some truth about ourselves.

Now, these themes appear in a number of her works, including what I think is her most important novel, *To the Lighthouse*, which was published in 1927—a novel that explores the meaning of time, memory, and language. It's also a portrait of her parents, who appear in this novel in the characters of Mr. and Mrs. Ramsay. And the novel includes a number of interior monologues. These monologues refer to those rare moments of inner insight that come amid long stretches of daily routine. As she says in the novel, "The great revelation perhaps never did come. Instead there were little…miracles, illuminations, matches struck unexpectedly in the dark." This is the way she understand life. There are these moments of illumination, like matches struck unexpectedly in the dark. But it's very difficult to capture these, and she often felt that in her own writing, she really didn't achieve this. She said, the "words fluttered sideways and struck the object inches too low"—you didn't quite get it. And she always felt that perhaps she didn't fully explain perhaps what she set out to explain.

Now, Woolf's own mental anxieties finally led her to commit suicide by drowning in a river in 1941. And yet, she succeeded in creating a literary style that conveyed the complex—often disjointed—thoughts and emotions of the human mind. And this kind of writing that Woolf produced was one of the great modern literary innovations. And it was also a kind of writing that appeared among a new generation of writers on the Continent, and I want to discuss them in the next lecture.

Lecture Fourteen
The Continental Novel—Proust, Kafka, Mann

Scope:

The new literary interest in memory, identity, and personal experience could be found in all European cultures. This lecture continues the discussion of the modern novel with examples from French and German literature, focusing specifically on the work of Marcel Proust, Franz Kafka, and Thomas Mann. All these writers sought to portray the complexity of personal lives and desires in modern Europe. Proust explored the isolation of the self, often stressing a personal alienation from the social world and examining the nature of memory and time. Franz Kafka described the anonymity and the nightmarish impersonal experiences of modern society. Thomas Mann portrayed the personal struggle to survive the "illness" of the modern social world. Like most modern writers, these authors all wrote about the individual's separation from other people.

Outline

I. Cultural and intellectual historians often note that literary modernism emerged at about the same time in numerous European cultures; we have seen how "modernist" themes emerged in the English-language works of Joyce, Woolf, and various poets.

   A. Meanwhile, the typical modernist ideas—emphasis on inner experiences, memory, time, and the ambiguity of language— were also influencing the work of writers on the Continent, and Freud's ideas spread across Europe.

   1. The First World War did not create the literary fascination with the complex inner self, but it suggested that the external world was ill.

   2. The writers who gained the greatest cultural influence in the decades after 1920 all analyzed the "self" in relation to a disorienting world.

   B. They wanted to portray the psychology of human desire, but they also stressed the "strangeness" of the social world; they had little interest in, or hope for, political solutions to the alienating experiences of modern life.

1. These literary themes can be seen most notably in the influential works of Marcel Proust, Franz Kafka, and Thomas Mann.
2. I want to discuss each of these authors and emphasize their common modernist tendency to "defamiliarize" personal and social experience.
3. This is the modern literary pattern that made 20th-century European literature both difficult and emblematic of the era in which it appeared.

II. Marcel Proust's novel *Remembrance of Things Past* has frequently been described as the first great modern novel; it has attracted endless attention from literary critics.

A. Although Proust (1871–1922) wrote his most famous work in the 20th century, he emerged from the late 19th-century context of upper-class French culture; his own family reflected different strands of that culture.
1. His father was a successful doctor from a Catholic family with deep roots around the old cathedral city of Chartres. His mother was from a well-to-do Jewish family in Paris. Marcel grew up in a "mixed" world.
2. He was closer to his mother, who had strong interests in music and literature. He suffered from asthma throughout his life.

B. He began to write as a young man, but he was at first mostly interested in the social life of upper-class Parisian salons; he gradually withdrew from society, especially after his mother died in 1905.
1. He settled into a Parisian apartment in which his bedroom was lined with cork to keep out noise, distractions, and germs.
2. His most intense emotional relations were with men, yet these relationships were stymied in various ways, leaving him emotionally frustrated. The theme of frustrated love appeared often in his novel.
3. He was deeply attracted to a man named Alfred Agostinelli, for example, but Agostinelli was married and refused to stay with Proust. He was killed in a plane crash while learning to fly (1914).

C. Working in his isolated environment (he rarely went out of his apartment during the day) and supported by inherited money, Proust wrote his huge novel, which was translated into English as *Remembrance of Things Past*.

   1. The first volume was published in 1913 at his own expense; by the time of his death in 1922, Proust had written six volumes.

   2. While France suffered through the horrors of World War I, Proust sat alone in his cork-lined room, exploring his personal memories and describing the social world that he had known in his youth.

   3. Although the novel included long descriptions of social events and even public conflicts, such as the Dreyfus Affair, the book's main theme stressed the isolation of the self and the difficulty of communication.

D. Proust described the mysteries of "involuntary memory"— the experience in which an encounter with some object or place in the present provokes a vivid memory of a past experience, object, or person.

   1. This is the experience of the narrator who remembers his childhood yearning for his mother when he eats a small *madeleine* biscuit.

   2. He describes the way that memories come involuntarily into one's mind and how this inner experience changes the meaning of time; a brief moment's encounter in the present carries the mind to the past.

   3. This past becomes part of the present; time is not just "here and now." This was the theme in Proust's depiction of how time is experienced.

E. Proust also tried to show how human interactions (and love) are blocked by the inability to communicate feelings or share reciprocal feelings.

   1. There is a deep loneliness or isolation at the heart of human life; yet this isolation gives art its special role, because only through art can isolated persons recognize some part of themselves in others.

2. "The book is only a sort of optical instrument which the writer offers to the reader to enable the latter to discover in himself what he would not have found but for the aid of the book"; art leads people to themselves.
3. The artist who offers portraits of the self offers a vehicle for human communication and a means for moving beyond solitude. In this view, art is a private act rather than a public or political act.

F. Proust began to be famous in the early 1920s (he did not have to pay for publication of later volumes); however, he died before he could play any kind of public intellectual role, which in any event, he was too reclusive to pursue.
1. His work told the story of inner anxieties, memories, and obsessions, and some critics would always find it too self-referential and obscure.
2. Yet Proust helped to create a new style of modern writing that used first-person narration, "flashbacks" in time, and endless exploration of selfhood, desire, or social disorientation.

III. This sense of disorientation can also be found in the German literature of the postwar era, much of which portrayed a crisis in modern life.

A. Nobody developed this vision of a decentered world more starkly than Franz Kafka (1883–1924), who grew up in a German Jewish family in Prague.
1. Kafka's father was a merchant whom his son came to view as tyrannical and deeply hostile to Franz's cultural and literary interests.
2. The young Kafka was part of a small minority (German Jews) in a large Czech city and was aware of his own marginal position.
3. He studied law and, after receiving his law degree, worked in the Prague offices of a large Italian insurance company. He hated the work and began to write novels and short stories in his limited spare time.

B. Kafka felt alienated from his professional life and was unhappy in his relations with women. He became engaged three times (twice to the same woman) but always broke off the relationships.

    1. He also developed tuberculosis and died at the early age of 40; later, his three sisters and two of his close women friends died in Nazi camps.

    2. Drawing on his personal experiences, his problems with his father, and his social and professional life in Prague, Kafka wrote stories in which the characters seem to be totally alone or in uncontrollable situations.

C. Like Proust, Kafka suggests that solitude is an inescapable part of the human condition, yet Kafka's social world seems to be even more threatening.

    1. Kafka's name has been turned into an adjective—Kafkaesque—that conveys a specific cultural meaning: people (like the characters in his stories) live in a social world that has lost meaning.

    2. People who live in this world experience neither order nor coherence.

    3. Everyone has become alienated, and the lifeless, bureaucratic world that Weber described has taken over all of life.

    4. Social and political processes seem to operate without meaning; they have no discernable goals or purpose.

D. The official world seems to exist mainly as a mechanism for keeping people permanently frustrated or for turning them into objects to control.

    1. Such themes appear in Kafka's novel *The Trial* (1925), which tells the story of Joseph K., who is arbitrarily arrested, put on trial, and put to death for no discernable reason—though he feels inner guilt.

    2. The theme of guilt might be compared to Freud's concept of how people feel guilty in their families and in civilized life, but Kafka places this theme in a social context that denies people their humanity.

E. This theme seems to anticipate all kinds of 20th-century horrors (which is why some view Kafka as a writer who anticipated the worst features of modern history).

1. The nightmare is perhaps best summarized in "The Metamorphosis."
2. This story (published in 1916) describes a person who wakes up to find himself transformed into a large bug. He has no way to control or even to understand the external world, including the office where he works.

IV. Kafka's work had a major influence on 20th-century literature, but the nightmarish vision was not as extreme in the work of the German writer Thomas Mann (1875–1955). Nonetheless, Mann believed that Europe was in a crisis.

A. His father was a grain merchant and young Thomas was at first destined for this career. The father died when Thomas was 15 years old and the son moved toward writing.

B. Unlike Proust and Kafka, Mann got married as a young man (to Katia Prinsheim) and had six children; yet Mann was also interested in the problems of frustrated desire and social crisis.

C. His short prewar novella, *Death in Venice* (1911), suggested that European traditions faced exhaustion and decline.

D. Mann believed that official cultures and governments had stripped away the vital sources of modern Europe's creativity.
   1. At first, Mann seemed to view World War I as an opportunity to renew German society and culture, but he later changed his mind.
   2. He believed that the war destroyed Europe's confidence in its past and faith in its future.

E. He analyzed all of these ideas symbolically in his great novel *The Magic Mountain* (1924), which is set in a sanitarium for tuberculosis patients in Switzerland.

F. Mann himself seemed to believe that the West had embraced death, and some scholars think he wanted to defend aspects of the Enlightenment.

G. Mann did not share the modernist emphasis on the internal mind, but he shared literary pessimism about social relations and clichéd language.

Essential Reading:

Marcel Proust, *Swann's Way*, translated by G.K. Scott Moncrieff, pp. 3–36.

Franz Kafka, "Metamorphosis," in *Metamorphosis and Other Stories*, translated and edited by Malcolm Pasley, pp. 76–126.

Supplementary Reading:

Anthony Heilbut, *Thomas Mann: Eros and Literature*, pp. 401–434.

Jean-Yves Tadié, *Marcel Proust*, translated by Euan Cameron, pp. 563–599.

Questions to Consider:

1. Do you have "involuntary memories" that are set off by encounters with certain smells, sights, objects, or people?

2. What meanings do you associate with the word "Kafkaesque"?

Lecture Fourteen—Transcript
The Modern Novel—Proust, Kafka, Mann

Cultural and intellectual historians often note that literary modernism emerged in numerous European countries at about the same time—that it was not simply in France and in England, but it was in many different cultures. And we've seen how modernist themes emerged in the English languages works of Joyce and Woolf and various poets in Britain, but in these same years, the typical modernist ideas with emphasis on inner experiences, the emphasis on memory and time, the interest in the ambiguity of language—these themes were all influencing the work of writers on the Continent. And it was also in this period—the 1920s—of course, that Freud's ideas were spreading across Europe, giving added interest to that emphasis in the unconscious that we were talking about.

Now, the First World War did not create the literary fascination with the complex inner self. I've been stressing that many of these themes were there before the war. But I think the war gave a great deal of emphasis to the belief that the external world had somehow fallen ill—that there was some kind of disease in Europe. And this image—this metaphor of illness—is something that appears often in the literary and philosophical works of the 1920s. And the writers who gained the greatest cultural influence in the decades after 1920, all analyzed the self in relation to a disorienting world—that the world was somehow out of joint, that people could not somehow assume an easy relationship with the world around them.

And writers wanted to portray the nature of this disorientation. They also wanted to show the psychology of human desire. They wanted to show how human beings desired things and found themselves frustrated in their desires. And in this process, human beings encounter the external world, and they encounter the strangeness of the external world. There's something about that world that frustrates or stymies desire.

Now, most writers in the 1920s have little interest in or hope for political solutions to the alienating experiences of modern life. They wrote a lot about alienation—about the problems of modern social life—but they didn't see a political solution to those problems. And we can see this in the literary works of some of the most influential Continental writers, including the works of Marcel Proust, Franz

Kafka, and Thomas Mann. And I want to discuss each of these authors in this lecture, and I want to emphasize their common modernist tendency to de-familiarize personal and social experience.

I was discussing in the last lecture how modernist writers are always trying to de-familiarize—to make strange—the world in which we live. And that's a pattern we can see again in the Continental writers as much as we can see it in the British poets and novelists.

This de-familiarization of the familiar is the modern literary pattern that made 20th century European literature both difficult to read and emblematic of the era in which it appeared. You can learn a great deal about the world of these writers, because somehow the complexity of their writing suggests the ambiguity of that social world.

So let's turn first to Marcel Proust. Proust's novel, *Remembrances of Things Past*, has frequently been described as the first great modern novel. And it has attracted endless attention from literary critics ever since it appeared. Since the 1920s, critics and literary historians have been writing about this book.

Although Proust wrote his most famous work in the 20th century, he actually emerged from a late 19th-century cultural context in Paris—or in France. He was born in 1871, and he lived until 1922. He didn't have a long life. He had a lot of health problems. He died at a relatively young age. His own family reflected various strands in French culture—that late 19th-century French culture. His father was a successful doctor—a physician—from a Catholic family—a family with deep roots around the old Cathedral city of Chartres, outside of Paris where the great cathedral was located. His mother, on the other hand, was from a well-to-do Jewish family in Paris. And so, young Marcel grew up in a mixed world—a world that was Catholic and Jewish, rural and urban, a world that was part of the 19th century in tradition but also a world of modern commerce and social relations. In many ways, he was closer to his mother. His mother had strong interest in literature and music. His father, as I said, was a doctor who had an interest in medicine—was often away from the child. So he was close to his mother, and he was also close to his mother because of his health problems. He suffered from asthma throughout his life, and apparently his mother was protective of him and tried to help him with these problems.

He began to write as a young man, but in his early years, he was more interested in the social life of upper class Parisian salons than the rigors of literary life. But gradually, he withdrew from this salon society. He became increasingly withdrawn into his own writing, and this pattern appeared especially after his mother died in 1905. And after that, he settled into a Parisian apartment in which his bedroom was lined with cork in order to keep out noise and distractions and also germs. He was always sort of obsessed with germs and with the threat of illness—a very interesting pattern in his life. And his most intense emotional relations were with men. He had a number of close relations with men, and yet these relationships which would tend to be romantic—they would be stymied in various ways, leaving him emotionally frustrated. And in fact, the theme of frustrated love appears frequently in his novels—that somehow relationships are locked. They are unable to be completely satisfying.

He was deeply attached to a man named Alfred Agostinelli, and this was an example of how he would be close to a man. But Agostinelli was married, and he refused to stay with Proust. In fact, Agostinelli was killed in a plane crash while learning how to fly airplanes in 1914. And this event had a devastating effect on Proust. He had these kinds of frustrating personal experiences.

But working in his isolated environment, he was beginning to write his great novel, *Remembrances of Things Past*. He rarely went out of his apartment during the day, and he was supported by inherited money—the wealth of his family—so he didn't have to have a job. And he worked on this novel. The novel was published in French *A la Recherche du Temps Perdu*—but translated into English as *Remembrances of Things Past*, and that's how it's usually known in English.

The first volume was published in 1913 at his own expense. And there were six volumes by the time of his death in 1922. So while France was suffering through the horrors of World War I, Proust sat alone in his cork-lined room exploring his personal memories and describing the social world that he had known in his youth. And although the novel included long descriptions of social events and even long descriptions of public conflicts, such as the politics of the Dreyfus Affair, the book's main theme stressed the isolation of the self and the difficulty of communication. This is at the heart of the book.

Also in this book, Proust described the mysteries of what he called involuntary memory. This is the experience in which an encounter with some object or place in the present provokes a vivid memory of a past experience or object or person. And we've all had this experience where you see someone who looks a bit like someone you knew years ago and sets you to thinking about a certain relationship or a friendship or a romance or a family member. Or maybe you had an experience of a certain smell that reminds you of being in your grandmother's house. Or maybe you had an experience of a certain sound or some kind of experience that involuntarily provokes in your mind a memory of being in another place in another time. And this is the experience of the narrator in this novel, who remembers his childhood yearning for his mother. You have memories of being in the countryside or in a house—in this case, eating a small madeleine, a little biscuit, a petite madeleine, which reminds you of something far away, a childhood yearning for closeness with your mother.

And Proust describes the way memory comes involuntarily into the mind and how this inner experience changes the meaning of time. A brief moment encounter in the present carries the mind to the past. And this past becomes part of the present, so time is not just here and now, time is always both in the past and in the present. It comes back and forth. We're living now, but we're in some sense always linked to our own past—our own memory, and we can't simply control this. This memory will come into our mind involuntarily. And Proust was one of the first writers—perhaps the first—to fully describe this process of involuntary memory. And this was the theme in his depiction of how we experience time.

But Proust also tried to show how human interactions and love are blocked by the inability to communicate feelings or share reciprocal feelings. And throughout his novel, there is a portrayal of the deep loneliness or isolation at the heart of human life—that we are all ultimately alone, unable to fully communicate who we are or how we feel. And yet it's precisely this isolation which gives art this special role in human life, because only through art can isolated persons recognize some part of themselves in others. We see in a work of art something that speaks to that sense of our self, and in that moment, we are not entirely alone. As he said in one of the passages in his writing, "The book is only a sort of optical instrument which the writer offers to the reader to enable the reader to discover in himself what he would not have found but for the aid of the book." That is to say, that in reading a book, we encounter some part of ourselves. Art leads people to themselves. And this would be true not only of literature but all great art. There is a moment where there is an act of great communication. It pulls the isolated self into communication with someone or some idea outside the self which in turn links back to the self—a moment of exchange. And so the artist who offers portraits of the self offers a vehicle for human communication and a means for moving beyond solitude. When an artist reveals something of himself or herself, other people find parts of themselves in what the artist has revealed.

But art in this view is a private act. It is an act of personal exploration and memory—self-recognition—rather than a public or political act. And Proust was not concerned with the public, political acts of art or of public life.

Now, Proust began to be famous in the early 1920s. His books began to attract attention. He didn't have to pay for publication for later volumes—one sure sign of his breakthrough. However, he died before he could play any kind of public intellectual role, which in any case, he was too reclusive to pursue. He wouldn't have wanted to be a public intellectual. But he was an example of a writer that was focused on the interior experience or the social experience of the self rather than of the public political world, although he had a certain interest in these things. He would read the newspapers and so forth, but his work is not ultimately about politics. His work told the story of inner anxieties, memories, and obsessions, often with long, long passages about very brief moments in time.

Some critics would always find it too self-reverential and too obscure. And yet Proust helped to create a new style of modern writing that used first-person narration, that would flash back in time, move backwards and forwards in time, that would provide endless exploration of self-hood, of childhood memories, of desire, of social disorientation. And in these ways, Proust had an enormous influence on modern literature.

The sense of disorientation that Proust often portrayed can also be found in German literature of the post-war period, and I want to turn now to a couple of examples from German literature. The German writers also portrayed a crisis in modern life. And nobody developed this vision of a crisis—of a de-centered world—more starkly than

Franz Kafka. Kafka lived from 1883 to 1924, and he grew up in a German-Jewish family in Prague, surrounded by a large Czech community, of course, but always feeling himself in a minority—a kind of double minority: German and Jewish in a Czech city.

Kafka's father was a merchant who his son came to view as a tyrannical and deeply hostile figure. He felt that his father was his enemy, because he couldn't accept young Franz's cultural and literary interests. And the young Kafka felt himself alienated from his father but also in many ways from his environment—part of a minority, a German-Jew in a Czech city; part of a family in which he felt abused and unable to be himself. So, in various ways, he felt himself to be in a marginal position.

He studied law as a young man, and after receiving his law degree, he worked in the Prague offices of a large insurance company. But he hated the work. He did the work because he needed the money, but he found insurance work a dreadfully boring job, so his real work was his writing. He began to write novels and short stories in his spare time—at night or during vacations, or on the weekends. And he felt alienated from his professional life. He was also unhappy in his relationships with women. He became engaged three different times to be married. Twice, he was engaged to the same woman, but always he broke off these relationships. He never could bring himself actually to the point of marrying. He also developed tuberculosis, and he died at the very early age of forty. It's interesting to try to speculate what might have happened to Kafka if he might have lived to a normal age. His three sisters were later arrested by the Nazis and sent to a death camp. They died during the Second World War. Also, two of his close women friends died in Nazi death camps. So, he came from a community that was, in a way, decimated by what would happen later in the century.

And yet, his writing, in a sense, almost anticipates the horrors that would befall his own family and his own community. He drew on his personal problems, his personal experiences, his encounters with his father, his social and professional life in Prague. He drew upon all of this to write stories in which the characters seem to be totally alone or in uncontrollable situations. Like Proust, Kafka suggests that solitude is an inescapable part of the human condition. And yet, Kafka's social world seems to be—if anything—more threatening than the social world that Proust describes. That for Kafka, there's endless danger all around. In fact, Kafka's name has been turned into an adjective—one of those rare writers that become an adjective, so that even now, we talk about a Kafkaesque experience—and an adjective that conveys a specific cultural meaning—an experience in which things are totally estranged or threatening or bizarre or unexpected. And the term Kafkaesque has this meaning. It would suggest people living in a social world that has lost its meaning. And this is the way his characters in his stories seem to live their lives. There is neither order nor coherence for the people who live in this world. Their personal and social lives are fragmented. They live an experience of fragmentation and alienation. Everyone has become alienated, and everyone is living in a lifeless, bureaucratic world—the kind of world that Max Weber had described in his sociology; a world in which there is a kind of iron cage in which bureaucracy and the tedium of modern rationalizing social life has taken over all aspects of personal experience or social life.

So in Kafka's world—the world he describes in his writing—social and political processes seem to operate without meaning. They have no discernible goals or purpose. And the world seems to exist mainly as a mechanism for keeping people permanently frustrated or for turning them into objects to control. You can't get the bureaucracy to respond. You're somehow being persecuted by forces beyond your reach—a Kafkaesque moment—maybe the kind of experience you've had trying to get your insurance claims settled. This is the problem Kafka is trying to understand but in a much more complex way than simply in daily life.

Now, these themes appear in Kafka's novels, including his great novel, *The Trial*, which was published shortly after his death. It was published in 1925. It tells the story of a man, Joseph K.—he doesn't even have a last name—a man who is arbitrarily arrested, put on trial, and put to death for no apparent reason. K is somehow simply caught up in this system. He is accused of something he doesn't understand. He feels some kind of inner guilt, like maybe he's done something, but he can't quite identify anything. But the point is that he's caught up in a system that he can't control. And this theme of guilt in Kafka's characters can, in some ways, be compared to Freud's concept of how people feel guilty in their families or in civilized life. But Kafka went beyond Freud in various ways in that he places these themes in a social context. The social context itself denies people their humanity. The social context makes them feel guilty. And I think that this theme—this theme of being caught in a world beyond your control—anticipates all kinds of 20th-century horrors. We have the image of the 20th century as the century of terrible wars, of the century of concentration camps, the century of arbitrary imprisonment. And for Kafka, this is already somewhat anticipated in his greatest novels. And this is why some critics view Kafka as a writer who is maybe the most representative writer of the 20th century—the person who anticipates the worst features of modern history.

And this nightmare that he describes is perhaps best summarized in the story, *The Metamorphosis*—a story published in 1916, which describes a man who wakes up to find himself transformed into a large bug. And he has no way to control or even to understand the external world, including the office where he works, his boss, the world around him. But this experience of being a kind of play thing of forces beyond your control—the alienation that comes with that experience—that is at the heart of the Kafkaesque conception of literature and of personal and social experience.

Kafka's work had a major influence on 20th-century literature—not only in the German world but as it was translated, influence spread throughout the world. But the nightmarish vision he had was not quite as extreme as in the work of the other German writer I want to discuss, Thomas Mann. Mann lived from 1875 to 1955. And he was from Germany, but he would live for many years in the United States—during the Nazi period.

Thomas Mann believed that Europe was in a state of crisis. This was a theme that would appear often in his writing. A few things about his personal life: his father was a grain merchant. And young Thomas was at first destined for this career. But the father died when young Thomas Mann was only 15 years old, and so the son gradually moved away from this whole business and commerce and turned toward writing. He claimed later that his mother's family tended to art, his father's family tended to business, and it was art that ultimately attracted his interest.

Unlike Proust and Kafka, Thomas Mann married as a young man. He married a woman named Katia Prensheim, and he had six children. So he had an extended family life—in direct contrast to both Proust and Kafka. And yet, Thomas Mann was also interested in the problems of frustrated desire and the problems of social crisis—the kinds of problems that interested Proust and Kafka. His short, pre-war novella, *Death in Venice*, which appeared in 1911, had suggested that European traditions faced exhaustion and decline. And in this novel—it's a fascinating short novel—Thomas Mann describes a scholar who becomes obsessed with a young boy—a man who had always been a rigorous, disciplined, intellectual scholar. He goes to Venice on a holiday, and he discovers a young boy, he becomes obsessed with him as if he's almost a young, Greek god. And he remains—the scholar remains—in Venice during a plague—an epidemic breaks out, but he cannot leave, and then he dies. And it's a curious metaphor for crisis, for death, for something that has gone wrong. And Thomas Mann is already writing in these terms before the First World War.

And he used the metaphor of illness to convey in many of his writings to convey personal and cultural themes. Illness was one of his favorite metaphors. And he would feel this all the more acutely in Europe in 1933, when the Nazis came to power and he would then flee into exile to the United States to escape from the Nazis. For him, they were the symbol and expression of this illness in Europe.

Mann believed that official cultures and governments had stripped away the vital sources of modern Europe's creativity. And in this respect, he was very much influenced by Nietzsche. He believed that Nietzsche had shown the problems in Europe—this kind of illness. And so for years, Mann looked for ways to get beyond this. At the beginning of World War I, he saw the war as perhaps an opportunity to renew German society and culture. But later, he changed his mind, and he saw the war as representing simply another example of the illness in Europe. He believed the war destroyed Europe's confidence in its past and its faith in its future.

And he went on to explore the whole meaning of this illness or this crisis in Europe in his great novel, *The Magic Mountain*, which appeared in 1924. And this novel is set in a sanitarium for tuberculosis patients in Switzerland. It's like a hospital clinic which is a meeting place for people from all over Europe, and they come from many different cultural traditions. They're all in this same center. They're all ill. The main character is a man named Hans Castorp, who is unclear about his own values. And he listens to the debates and the discussions of the people at the clinic. The main debating characters that he listens to are characters named Naphta and Settembrini. Settembrini advocates the Enlightenment. He defends Voltaire, the meaning of reason. Naphta, his opponent, represents religion, the Jesuits, and claims that violence and terror are the characteristics of the post-Enlightenment world.

Well, Thomas Mann himself seemed to believe that the West had embraced death, and many scholars believe that he was seeing perhaps the Enlightenment as a way to oppose that death. Perhaps it's significant in the novel that Naphta, the defender of the Jesuits, ultimately kills himself, and Settembrini, the defender of the Enlightenment survives. But the main character, Castorp—young Hans Castorp—goes down the mountain at the end of the novel. He's cured of tuberculosis, but then he goes off and dies in the Great War, which is a bigger illness. The Great War is a bigger illness than the tuberculosis of the sanitarium. And Mann's novels seem to suggest that Europe must find a way to embrace life in order to challenge its illness and its death.

So although Thomas Mann did not share some of the modernist emphasis on the internal psychological exploration of the mind, he shared in that general, modern, literary pessimism about social relations and clichéd languages. And it is this interest in language that also entered into philosophy. And we're going to turn now to the philosophical exploration of language in our next lecture.

Lecture Fifteen
Language and Reality in Modern Philosophy

Scope:

Modern philosophers moved in two new directions. One group focused on the linguistic foundation of human knowledge and developed ideas that became known as logical positivism or analytic philosophy. Another group emphasized human consciousness and the encounter with phenomena in the material world, thus developing a philosophy called phenomenology. This lecture discusses these two trends in European philosophy with special reference to Ludwig Wittgenstein and Edmund Husserl. Wittgenstein influenced the linguistic turn in Austrian and English philosophical circles, though he differed from many of the logical positivists. Husserl, by contrast, influenced German and French philosophers who examined the relation between consciousness and the material world.

Outline

I.   Philosophers in 20th-century Europe generally challenged philosophical traditions; like the writers, poets, artists, and scientists, the philosophers looked for new ways to describe human knowledge and the human mind.

   A. In most general terms, philosophers rejected the systems of earlier "metaphysical" philosophers; the metaphysical tradition went back to Plato in ancient Greece and remained important through most of the 19th century.

   1. For example, Hegel had developed a comprehensive metaphysical theory about the unfolding Idea in human history.

   2. Metaphysical philosophies often proposed a comprehensive system for explaining human knowledge or existence, and they often assumed that reality existed on dual levels (e.g., body and mind, material and spiritual).

   B. Most 20th-century philosophers, by contrast, wanted to make philosophy more scientific by getting beyond metaphysical dualisms.

   1. They decided that metaphysical systems did not provide a reliable basis for truth, a theme that also appeared in modern social sciences, psychology, historical studies, and even literary studies.

    2. Yet this search for new forms of philosophical knowledge led in two different directions during the first half of the century.

C. Some philosophers argued that language was the foundation for all true statements about the world; therefore, language should be the object of analysis.

    1. Language could be studied objectively, in the same way that scientists studied nature.

    2. This form of thought evolved into the movements of logical positivism or the related school of analytical philosophy.

    3. The Austrian philosopher Ludwig Wittgenstein contributed to this new linguistic approach to philosophy, which became influential in both Vienna and England; it analyzed what language could truthfully say.

D. Other philosophers, however, argued that a new scientific philosophy must examine the human consciousness and how it encounters the world.

    1. This second trend in philosophy became known as phenomenology.

    2. The key early figure in this group was Edmund Husserl, a German philosopher who tried to explain the interaction of consciousness and objects in the world.

    3. Husserl's theories had wide influence in Germany and France and became important for existential philosophers, such as Jean-Paul Sartre.

E. This lecture discusses the themes of logical positivism and phenomenology by summarizing the ideas of Wittgenstein and Husserl.

    1. Although their approaches to philosophy differed, they both wanted to give philosophy a more reliable foundation for what might be called post-metaphysical truth claims.

    2. But philosophy had less cultural influence than literature or the arts.

II. Intellectual historians have often located the emergence of logical positivism among Viennese philosophers in the 1920s, but the movement also had links to England.

    A. One of these links was Ludwig Wittgenstein (1889–1951), who studied with Bertrand Russell in Cambridge before the First World War.

        1. Wittgenstein was born into a wealthy Viennese family, the youngest of eight children; his father was an engineer in the steel and iron industry.

        2. The elder Wittgenstein was one of the richest people in Vienna, and he put great pressure on his children to pursue similar careers. Young Ludwig at first studied engineering and long had an interest in machines.

        3. But the pressures on the children were difficult; three of Ludwig's brothers committed suicide, and he had to fight his own depressions.

    B. He eventually left Vienna to study in Germany, then at Cambridge, where he was influenced by Bertrand Russell's interest in mathematics and logic.

        1. Wittgenstein met a number of creative thinkers at Cambridge (the economist John Maynard Keynes was one of his friends), but he also liked to withdraw from social contacts; he built a hut in Norway.

        2. During the First World War, he went back to Austria and served throughout the war in the Austrian army; he also read philosophy.

        3. He was captured in the last months of the war and sent to an Italian prison camp. In this camp, he wrote his only philosophical text that was published in his lifetime: *Tractatus Logico-Philosophicus* (1922).

    C. He sent the manuscript to Russell, who arranged for it to be published; then Wittgenstein became a high school teacher in Austria for about six years.

        1. During that time, he met occasionally with members of the "Vienna School"—the philosophers who were developing logical positivism.

        2. He eventually returned to Cambridge (1929) and lived in England for the rest of his life (with sojourns in Ireland and Norway).

3. He taught small classes at Cambridge University, worked in medical centers during World War II, and wrote numerous texts that were finally published after his death as *Philosophical Investigations.*

D. Throughout his career, Wittgenstein criticized traditional philosophy; he said that philosophers used language in nonrigorous or imprecise ways.

    1. He wanted philosophical language to follow the most precise, logical structure to give logical, truthful pictures of reality.

    2. But most philosophical statements did not provide this kind of truth; they expressed opinions or feelings or propositions that lacked meaning because they were not grounded in reality (as true science should be).

    3. Wittgenstein, therefore, ended the *Tractatus* with the sobering claim that philosophers should recognize their clear linguistic limits.

    4. "What we cannot speak about," he said, "we must pass over in silence."

E. This statement meant that because philosophy did not have the language to speak truthfully about the world, it really could not say much. Wittgenstein thought he proved his case by not publishing more philosophy.

    1. He said that his philosophy was like a ladder that carried him up to a truth about philosophical language, then the ladder had to be thrown away. After 1929, however, he began to write philosophy again.

    2. He became more interested in the uses of ordinary language; he wanted to show how philosophical meaning was part of a linguistic system.

    3. He disliked abstract theorizing, but he also developed an almost mystical interest in how languages and linguistic systems could achieve meaning. He moved away from the theme of verifiable language uses.

III. Meanwhile, the development of logical positivism and analytical philosophy pushed some of Wittgenstein's earlier themes in even more radical directions.

A. Writers such as A.J. Ayer (1910-1989) argued that philosophy should deal only with issues that can be verified through empirical observation; this theme of 19th-century positivism was now carried into philosophy.

1. Such ideas meant that philosophers could not deal with metaphysical questions (e.g., "Do humans have souls?" "Is there a God?") because there is no meaningful, truthful way to establish truth or falsehood.

2. This view also eliminated all questions about ethics, morality, or aesthetics. For logical positivists, the answers to these kinds of questions simply expressed feelings, not philosophical truths.

B. Ayer said that philosophers who tried to answer these questions went beyond "the limits of all possible sense-experience" and, thus, their work was "devoted to the production of nonsense."

1. Philosophy for the logical positivists had the task of analyzing precise claims about the world to see if they could be verified.

2. The goal was to clarify linguistic confusions and to support the claims of science; there was no interest in moral questions or "higher truths."

IV. The linguistic emphasis of logical positivism or analytical philosophy had wide influence on English (and American) academic philosophy.

A. But a number of Continental philosophers took a different, phenomenological approach to the quest for a new scientific philosophy.

1. The key figure in early phenomenology was Edmund Husserl (1859–1938), who was born in Moravia in what is now the Czech Republic.

2. Husserl was from a liberal German Jewish family; he became a Protestant at age 27 and studied mathematics in Germany.

3. Husserl's real interest, however, was philosophy, especially after he also studied psychology; he wanted to make philosophy scientific.

B. He taught philosophy at several German universities. After 1916, he was at the University of Freiburg, but after 1933, he was barred from the university.

C. Husserl laid out his theory of phenomenology in various works and lectures, including a concise summary in *The Idea of Phenomenology* (1907). Husserl was more concerned with the structure of human consciousness than with specific problems of language.

D. For Husserl, meaning emerged from the ways in which a conscious subject responded to daily life in what he called the "life-world." His philosophy emphasized the intentions or the actions of active, conscious persons, as compared to the linguistic structures that analytic philosophers described.

E. Husserl argued that the consciousness and the experience of the knowing human subject makes the world meaningful.

V. The themes of phenomenology, like the main ideas of logical positivism or analytical philosophy, thus contributed to a wider cultural rejection of metaphysical traditions.

A. In this view, human beings had no recourse to a transcendent realm or higher being that would give a secure foundation to knowledge and ethics.

B. Philosophy could examine language or human consciousness, both of which gave meaning to the world, but it could not show any other meaning in knowledge or history (as Hegel found in the Spirit).

C. Linguistic philosophers saw limits on what philosophy could know; phenomenology soon found limits in communicating consciousness.

Essential Reading:

Edmund Husserl, *The Idea of Phenomenology*, translated and introduced by Lee Hardy, pp. 15–55.

Norman Malcolm, *Ludwig Wittgenstein: A Memoir*, 2nd ed., pp. 23–81.

Supplementary Reading:

Barry Smith and David Woodruff Smith, editors, "Introduction," in *The Cambridge Companion to Husserl*, pp. 1–37.

Allan Janik and Stephen Toulmin, *Wittgenstein's Vienna*, pp. 13–32, 167–201.

Questions to Consider:

1. Did the "linguistic turn" in analytical philosophy destroy the classical philosophical aspiration for transcendent wisdom?

2. Do you think consciousness gives meaning to the objects of the world?

Lecture Fifteen—Transcript
Language and Reality in Modern Philosophy

We've been talking about how a great deal of 20th-century thought and culture represented a challenge to European traditions, and we can see some of these same patterns in the development of 20th-century philosophy. Philosophers in 20th-century Europe generally challenged philosophical traditions. And in this respect, they were like the writers, the poets, the artists, and the scientists, because the philosophers were looking for new ways to describe human knowledge and the human mind. And in the most general terms, I think we can say that the philosophers rejected the systems of earlier metaphysical philosophers.

The metaphysical tradition in philosophy goes all the way back to Plato in ancient Greece, and it remained very important through most of the 19th century. It was the dominant philosophical tradition. It was a tradition that tried to develop comprehensive accounts of reality and knowledge. For example, Hegel had developed a comprehensive metaphysical theory about the unfolding idea in human history—the way in which all of history is given meaning by a transcendent idea which enters into the physical and historical world. And metaphysical philosophies over human history had often proposed this kind of comprehensive system. They wanted to explain the meaning of human knowledge or existence, and they usually assumed there were dual levels of reality. There was a physical level and there was a metaphysical—something beyond the physical. Or to put it another way, there was the body and the mind or the material world and the spiritual world. There was something beyond this physical world, and that's at the heart of much of the metaphysical tradition, which, of course, is also related to theology and the other strands of Western thought.

But in the 20th century, most of the leading philosophers wanted to make philosophy more scientific by getting beyond the metaphysical tradition, by getting beyond this metaphysical dualism that described the material world and then a higher spiritual world—a world of the ideal, that platonic world beyond the physical. And these 20th-century philosophers decided that metaphysical systems did not provide a reliable basis for truth. This is the same kind of theme that appeared in many forms of 20th-century thought—the desire to avoid metaphysical claims. You can see this in modern social science, in psychology, in historical studies, in literary studies—the desire not to claim that these forms of human activity are given meaning by some transcendent being or transcendent reality but have to be studied only in the material world—the world that we encounter with the senses.

And yet this search—this philosophical search—for new forms of philosophical knowledge led in two rather different directions during the first half of the 20th century. There was a shared desire to get beyond the metaphysical tradition, but the desire evolved in different forms. Some philosophers argued that language for all true statements about the world. So, language analysis should be the basic element of philosophy. Or to put it another way, language should be the object of philosophical study, because all truth claims about the world—all knowledge and understanding of reality—all of these things are embedded in language. And language could be studied objectively, much like scientists study nature. You have a structure, you have a system, you have claims in language that can be analyzed. And this form of thought—this linguistic thought—evolved into the movements—the philosophical movements—of logical positivism or the related school of analytical philosophy. Logical positivism and analytical philosophy are often linked. They're overlapping elements or trends in 20th-century philosophy.

And the Austrian philosopher, Ludwig Wittgenstein contributed a great deal to this new linguistic approach to philosophy. And this kind of kind of linguistic philosophy became influential in both Vienna and in England. It analyzed what language could truthfully say.

There were many other philosophers, however, who argued that a new scientific philosophy must examine the human consciousness and how the consciousness of human beings encounters the world—the material world, the phenomena of the material world. And this second trend in philosophy became known as phenomenology. And the key early figure in this group, the phenomenological movement, was a philosopher named Edmund Husserl, who was from Germany and who tried to explain the interaction of consciousness and objects in the world. Husserl's theories had wide influence in Germany and France. And they became important for a number of later philosophical movements, including the existential philosophers, such as Jean-Paul Sartre. So, you can see the echo of phenomenology coming down in later philosophy.

In this lecture, I'm going to discuss the themes of both the logical positivists and the phenomenologists by summarizing the ideas of Wittgenstein and Husserl. I'm going to use them as examples of these two contending philosophical movements. And although their approaches to philosophy differed, they both wanted to give philosophy a more reliable foundation for what might be called post-metaphysical truth claims. They believed that there could be certain forms of philosophical truth, but these had to be based on something beyond the metaphysical tradition.

In general, these philosophical movements—although they were important—they had less cultural influence than the literary and artistic movements that we talked about earlier. Philosophy tended to become more of an academic enterprise and to have less general resonance in the culture at large—in part, because philosophy became so technical that few people outside the university and outside academic philosophy could understand it.

Now, intellectual historians have often located the emergence of logical positivism among Viennese philosophers in the 1920s. But the movement also had strong links to England. There are really two centers for this—Cambridge, for example, the Cambridge group in England and the Viennese philosophers in Austria. And these links between these two centers of philosophy can be seen in part in the life and career of Ludwig Wittgenstein.

Wittgenstein lived from 1889 to 1951. He was from Austria, but he studied with Bertrand Russell, the British philosopher Bertrand Russell, at Cambridge before the First World War. So he was in many ways a key bridge between these two centers of philosophical thought. Wittgenstein was born into a wealthy Viennese family. He was the youngest of eight children. His father was an engineer who was in the steel and iron industry in Vienna, and he was in fact one of the richest people in Vienna—made a great deal of money in his business. And he put great pressure on his children to pursue similar careers. He wanted his sons to be in the same kind of work. And young Ludwig at first studied engineering—was heading in this direction—and in fact throughout his life, he had an interest in machines. But the father's pressure on the children created a very difficult psychological situation for the whole family. In fact, three of Ludwig's brothers committed suicide—an amazing problem in this family of depression and anxiety, and Ludwig himself had to fight his own depression throughout his life. There was a complex psychological dynamic going on there.

Perhaps to get away from his father—to get away from this pressure, young Wittgenstein left Vienna before the First World War. He went to Germany to study, and then he went on to Cambridge, where, I mentioned earlier, he worked with Bertrand Russell. And he was very much influenced by Russell's interest in mathematics and logic. This was the direction Russell was taking his philosophical work. And after Cambridge, Wittgenstein met a number of important creative thinkers—not only philosophers but also economists and social theorists. So, for example, the economist, John Maynard Keynes, was one of his friends at Cambridge. But he also had a tendency to withdraw from social contact. Wittgenstein always wanted to have a private space for himself. Eventually, he built a small hut in Norway where he would retreat from time to time just to get away from the social and intellectual world that he was involved in in Cambridge.

When the First World War broke out, Wittgenstein went back to Austria and then served throughout the war in the Austrian army. But he used this time also to read philosophy while he was in the army. He pursued a project of study. And in the last months of the war, he was captured and sent to an Italian prison camp. And amazingly enough, while in this Italian prison camp, he wrote the only philosophical text that was to be published during his lifetime—the important work, the *Tractatus Logico-Philosophicus*, which appeared in 1922 and was written in an Italian prison camp. This was sort of an inspiring story. Whatever the situation, you have a vision of what you want to do, I suppose you can pursue it. So you can write philosophy in a prison camp or like Kafka, you can write short stories after a long day at the insurance company.

Well, in this case, Wittgenstein sent his manuscript to Russell after he got out of the prison camp, and Russell arranged for it to be published. And then Wittgenstein became a high school teacher in Austria for about six years. He withdrew from the elite philosophical circles. And during this time, he occasionally met with philosophers in Vienna who were forming what would be known as the Vienna School—philosophers who were developing logical positivism—new approaches to philosophy. But Wittgenstein did not fully embed himself in that community. He was teaching in a high school.

But he eventually decided he wanted to return to Cambridge. He felt most at home in England. So, in 1929, he left Austria, he moved back to Cambridge, and he lived in England the rest of his life, except for these various sojourns or periods when he would withdraw from Cambridge and go and live in Ireland or in Norway in this kind of secluded environment that I noted before.

He taught very small classes at Cambridge University. He did not have a lot of students. He worked also in medical centers during World War II, though he supported the British war effort during the Second World War by working in hospitals. And he wrote numerous philosophical texts that were finally published after his death in another book called *Philosophical Investigations*. But these were texts that were not published during his lifetime.

Now, throughout his career, Wittgenstein criticized traditional philosophy. He was a philosopher who was very skeptical about the whole philosophical tradition. He said that philosophers had always used language in non-rigorous or non-precise ways, and he wanted philosophical language to follow the most precise, logical structure in order to give logical, truthful pictures of reality. He wanted philosophical language to be more precise. But he said most philosophical statements did not provide this kind of truth. They expressed opinions or feelings or they were simply some sort of attitude of the philosopher. They were not grounded in reality as a true science should be. And as he studied these philosophies, he became more skeptical about what philosophy could achieve. In fact, he ended his famous book, the *Tractatus*, which is a short book, he ended that book with the silvering claim that philosophers should recognize their clear linguistic limits. He stressed that there's a very clear limit to what we can actually know, and this could create a certain kind of modesty. And he had a very famous line in the *Tractatus*, "What we cannot speak about, we must pass over in silence." And for Wittgenstein, what we must pass over in silence turned out to be quite a bit, because there's a lot we can't know, and if we can't know for sure, we shouldn't make philosophical claims about it.

This myth that philosophy, since it didn't have the language to speak truthfully about the world—it really couldn't say a great deal. In fact, maybe Wittgenstein proved his case by not publishing more philosophy during his life. He sort of had worked out his philosophical position that there's not a lot we can say, and then he sort of stopped publishing. He said his philosophy was like a ladder—a nice metaphor—he said his philosophy was like a ladder that carried him up to a truth about philosophical language—the philosophical truth that there's a great deal we can't say. And then the ladder had to be thrown away. You climb up there with a ladder, and there you are, and you set the ladder aside.

In fact, when he went back to Cambridge, he did begin to write philosophy again, but as I said, he didn't publish these works. His later writings were published by his friends after he died. He also in later years became more interested in the uses of ordinary language. He wanted to show how philosophical meaning was part of a linguistic system. And what he disliked was abstract theorizing. And he wanted to somehow make sure that language had a precision that some kind of abstractions in philosophy didn't provide.

But he felt that in some ways, there was almost a mystical approach to language. He became more philosophically drawn to the mystery of language as he went on. And he began in his later work to move away from the theme of precise, verifiable language uses. So, Wittgenstein was a very complex thinker who was both looking for precision, but was also fascinated by the almost unknowability of language and the problematic claims that language makes.

Now, meanwhile, as Wittgenstein was exploring his later work but not publishing very much, the development of logical positivism was taking place in Britain—this kind of dual movement of positivism and analytical philosophy. And it pushed many of Wittgenstein's earlier works in more radical directions. And one representative author here was the British philosopher, A.J. Ayer, who argued that philosophy should deal only with issues that could be verified through empirical observation. And this was a theme of 19th-century positivism—that only observation yields positive knowledge. And now, with people like A.J. Ayer, the idea was carried into philosophy. This idea meant that philosophers could not deal with metaphysical questions. For example, classic questions, like "Do humans have souls?" or "Is there a God?" These are classical metaphysical and theological questions that have been debated, of course, for centuries and centuries, but the logical positivists and people like A.J. Ayer said, 'no, we cannot even talk about those questions, because there is no meaningful, truthful way to establish whether such claims about these ideas are true or false, so we don't talk about them.' And this view also eliminated all questions about ethics, about morality, or even about aesthetics.

For the logical positivists, the answers to these kinds of questions simply expressed feelings, not philosophical truths, and philosophy had to establish itself on the basis of rigidly provable truths. Ayer, in fact, said that philosophers who tried to answer these questions, went beyond "the limits of all possible sense-experience". So for Ayer, if a philosopher was trying to analyze this, they were involved in what he called the production of nonsense. That was his level of contempt for this kind of work. And Ayer was a very outspoken positivist philosopher.

So philosophy for the logical positivist had the task of analyzing precise claims about the world to see if these claims could be clarified. And the goal was to clarify linguistic confusions. And by clarifying confusion, the assumption was that you would have the reliability of a science. But there couldn't be in this kind of thinking—there couldn't be any interest in moral questions or what they called higher truths. This was an impossible task—to get to these metaphysical truths.

Now, the linguistic emphasis of logical positivism or analytical philosophy—this had a very wide influence on English and American academic philosophy. Throughout much of the 20th century this was the approach—this linguistic philosophical approach—was the dominant method in British and American university departments of philosophy. But on the Continent, a number of philosophers were pushing their thought in another direction. They were developing a phenomenological approach to the quest for a new scientific philosophy. And I want to turn now to the emergence of phenomenology.

As I mentioned before, the key figure in early phenomenology was Edmund Husserl. Husserl lived from 1859 to 1938. He was born in Moravia in what is now the Czech Republic. He came from a liberal German-Jewish family, but he became a Protestant at age 27. And he went on to…he studied mathematics at the beginning. He was very interested in mathematical problems, but gradually, his interests turned to philosophy. And this interest became even stronger when he took up the study of psychology. So, he was a philosopher who was also very interested in human psychology. He wanted to make philosophy scientific. And this may have been part of what he drew from the example of psychology.

He taught philosophy at several German universities, but after 1916, he was at the University of Freiburg, and this is where he ended career. In fact, after 1933—after the Nazis came to power—he was barred from the university. He had retired from teaching by this time, but the Nazi laws against Jews were used to exclude him from even using the library. He was blocked even from that kind of work. After his death in 1938, his late works were sent to Belgium to avoid their destruction in Germany. So, he was in a difficult position in his last years.

Now, Husserl laid out his theory of phenomenology in various works and lectures, including a concise summary in a work called *The Idea of Phenomenology*, which was published as early as 1907. And this was a place in which he began to lay out his mature theory. Husserl was more concerned with the structure of human consciousness than with specific problems of language. This is where he differed from Wittgenstein and the linguistic philosophers.

Husserl said that consciousness is the essence of being, but it cannot be studied simply as a physiological problem of the brain—you can't understand consciousness just as something that we look at as a medical problem. It has to be analyzed as a process of active engagement with objects in the world. This is what consciousness is—it's becoming aware of objects and people around you.

So Husserl, like other philosophers, rejected metaphysical explanations for thought. He wanted to show how consciousness evolves through interactions with experiences in the world of phenomenon. This concept of phenomenon is very important, and of course, this is where the whole term phenomenology comes from.

For Husserl, meaning emerged from the ways in which a conscious thinker or conscious person encounters objects in daily life—in what he called the life world—different ways in which experience evolves, but there is a very practical life world in which human beings interact hour by hour. And so, unlike the linguistic philosophers, he gave much more emphasis to the intentions or the actions of active, conscious persons. And this is what makes phenomenology different from the linguistic philosophy. Linguistic philosophers stressed the structures—the underlying structures of language that one has to work with. Husserl, by contrast, stressed the processes of consciousness itself. And he said it is the consciousness of the knowing subject of the experience of the knowing subject that makes the world meaningful—that objects in themselves do not have meaning. They're simply there, including the human body or any other object. But these objects take on meaning as they are experienced by the human consciousness. And so, Husserl's phenomenology carried the scientific goal of describing both consciousness and the material world without any reference to metaphysics. This consciousness is in the mind, but this comes out of the materiality of the human body. The essence of being a reality for Husserl lay in the human consciousness rather than in any higher, transcendent realm. All that we have to understand if we're going to think philosophically is how consciousness works.

But some critics argued that this conception of consciousness led to either subjectivism or to forms of idealism. The complaint was that subjectivism—that every individual simply experiences the world with his or her own consciousness. There is no objective reality. That was one critique. The other critique was that it lapses into idealism of the kind that existed in the work of philosophers like Fichte at the beginning of the 19th century—an idealist philosophy that made the world a creation of the mind—that the consciousness simply creates the world. Husserl rejected these critiques. He claimed that phenomenology did not deny the essence of objects. He said it doesn't say that it's only created by the mind. He said that it just offers a way—phenomenology offers a way—to understand how consciousness comprehends the object—that there is always a kind of exchange between the object and consciousness. We might think of it as a kind of dialectical relationship. For consciousness to work, there has to be an object to which it responds. But for that object to have meaning, there must also be a consciousness. This is the dialectic or the dialogue that phenomenology emphasized.

So, the themes of phenomenology were very different from the linguistic themes of logical positivism or analytical philosophy. But the themes of phenomenology resemble the positivist and analytical philosophers in contributing to a wider cultural rejection of metaphysical traditions. In this view, human beings had no recourse to a transcendent realm or a higher being—a higher being that would give a secure foundation to knowledge and ethics. This had been the essence of the metaphysical tradition, and this is what modern philosophy rejected. According to these 20th-century philosophers, philosophy could examine language or it could examine human consciousness—both of which gave meaning to the world. But it could not show any other meaning in knowledge or history, as, for example, Hegel had found in the spirit. It could not appeal to a spirit beyond the physical world to make sense of what people encountered in their daily lives.

So, linguistic philosophers saw clear limits to what philosophy could know. You could not know many things. And phenomenology also described many limits in what consciousness could communicate. There were limits in language, limits in experience, there were limits in consciousness. So there's a rather modest claim in all of these philosophies. And yet, this fascination with both language and consciousness forced people to rethink the meaning of inherited languages and theories. And we could see this same kind of thinking in the limits of language emerging in new forms of political and social theories in the 1930s. And in the next lecture, I want to turn to the emergence of new social theory in the period around 1930.

Lecture Sixteen
Revisiting Marxism and Liberalism

Scope:

The rise of Stalinism, the development of fascism and Nazism, and the worldwide economic depression of the 1930s pushed many writers toward a new engagement with public issues. In this lecture, we look at several theoretical responses to the crises that had become so apparent by the 1930s: the emergence of (1) a revisionist (less economic) Marxist theory in the works of writers such as Theodor Adorno and Antonio Gramsci and (2) a revisionist liberal (less laissez-faire) theory in the works of John Maynard Keynes and his critic Friedrich Hayek. Both the Marxists and the liberals challenged important aspects of their respective theoretical traditions, but they held very different views about how Europeans might best move beyond the crisis of the 1930s.

Outline

I. We have discussed the cultural effects of World War I, especially the war's impact on literature and the arts, but the war also transformed the social and political world.

   A. The Bolshevik Revolution in Russia led, by the early 1930s, to a new kind of Marxist state—the dictatorial communism of Joseph Stalin.

       1. Meanwhile, in response to the war, Russia's communist revolution, and economic problems, the Fascist and Nazi movements gained power in Italy (1922) and Germany (1933).

       2. The dictatorships of Benito Mussolini and Adolph Hitler forced European intellectuals to rethink liberal political and economic ideas.

   B. These political events in Russia, Italy, and Germany coincided also with the great economic crisis that began in 1929 and continued throughout the 1930s.

       1. The political and economic problems of the 1930s pushed many intellectuals toward a new concern with social issues.

2. The postwar literary and artistic fascination with the internal life did not completely disappear in the 1930s; for example, Joyce was writing *Finnegans Wake* during the 1930s.
3. But the 1930s have generally been portrayed in intellectual history as a time of intense political engagements; writers chose sides among fascism and communism and liberalism.

C. Classical liberalism was on the defensive. Liberalism had always stressed the autonomy of individuals and the role of individual rights in modern societies.
   1. By the 1930s, these ideas had been widely challenged by World War I and by the rise of communism and fascism.
   2. Intellectuals in the 1930s were, thus, concerned with the relation between individuals and society.
   3. Most intellectual critics challenged traditional liberalism, or fascism, or communism—or they supported one of these political doctrines; they felt obliged to take more political positions.
   4. Although many intellectuals criticized classical liberalism, they also could not fit easily into fascism or communism; they often stressed individual creativity in ways that challenged fascism and communism.

D. The challenge for intellectuals was to work out a new analysis of the relations between individuals and society in the conditions of the modern world.
   1. This kind of social analysis required a theoretical response to Stalinism, fascism, and the Great Depression.
   2. In many cases, intellectuals had no choice but to make political choices in the 1930s: Would they support or oppose fascism; would they leave Russia or Italy or Germany?
   3. Ideological conflicts of the era forced people to take sides.

E. The influence of this new context appears most notably in the new Marxists and the new liberal theorists of the 1930s.

1. Although some intellectuals, such as the poet Ezra Pound and the philosopher Martin Heidegger, were attracted to fascism, most writers (outside Italy and Germany) became hostile to fascism.

2. Fascism tended to be strongly anti-intellectual and to celebrate action over thought and the crowd over the ideas of individuals.

F. Yet many social theorists were also disenchanted with orthodox Marxism, especially as they learned about the Stalinist repression in the Soviet Union.

    1. One common intellectual response was to work out a new kind of Marxism or liberalism that rejected both Stalinism and fascism.

    2. Classical Marxism and liberalism stressed the rationality of human beings and economic knowledge, but this was revised in the 1930s.

    3. Some Marxists wanted to combine Marx and Freud or to rethink the role of culture in social and political life. We can see these themes in the German "Frankfurt School" and in the works of Antonio Gramsci.

    4. At the same time, liberals debated the value of classical laissez-faire economic theory—a debate that divided John Maynard Keynes and Friedrich Hayek in England.

G. We will discuss both of these "revisionist" patterns and emphasize the idea that the revision of "classical" social or economic theories was as important as the revisions in all other intellectual fields; it was also a response to the context.

II. One important strand of Marxist social theory attempted to revise Marx by analyzing the influence of Hegelianism on Marx's early work and by linking Freud to Marx.

A. Such themes emerged among theorists at the Frankfurt Institute of Social Research; this group, known in intellectual history as the Frankfurt School, eventually included such theorists as Theodor Adorno and Max Horkheimer.

    1. The Institute was founded in 1923, but it was dissolved after the Nazis came to power in 1933; its members fled into exile (most to the United States).

2. The thinkers wanted to create a new kind of critical Marxism or critical theory that rejected Stalinism and classical liberalism.

B. The leaders of the Frankfurt School often stressed the Hegelian origins of Marxism; they believed that the Hegelian view of historical change was lacking both in Stalinism and liberal political theories.

1. Frankfurt School theorists criticized the excessive positivism of modern communism and criticized Marxists for losing sight of noneconomic aspects of human activity and culture.
2. Adorno (1903–1969), for example, wrote about music and the nonrational aspects of human identity. Marx had not understood the unconscious, and Freud had not understood economics.
3. The goal was to link psychology and economics, and Nazism offered plenty of material to analyze. What was the appeal of such movements?

C. The critical theory of the Frankfurt School drew on the young Marx's *Economic and Philosophical Manuscripts* (rediscovered in the early 1930s).

1. These texts were more Hegelian than his later work; they stressed the problem of alienation in mass societies, which seemed as relevant for conditions in the Soviet Union as for conditions in capitalist factories.
2. How could alienation and repression be overcome in both capitalist and communist societies? Freud could be useful for answering this question because he showed how repression shaped civilization itself.

D. For Frankfurt School theorists such as Adorno, social reformers had to deal with economic institutions *and* with the influence of the unconscious mind.

III. The problem of alienation and the influence of culture were also important to the Italian Marxist theorist Antonio Gramsci (1891–1937); he was a member of the communist party who was jailed by the fascists and died in prison.

  A. His most important writings were collected in a work called *Prison Notebooks*, which was published after World War II.

    1. Gramsci criticized fascism and orthodox Marxism; his goal was to develop a nontotalitarian communism based on broad local social movements and on intellectuals who supported the lower classes.

    2. He thought the "economism" of most Marxists blinded them to the reciprocal relation between culture and political or economic life.

    3. Culture created the "hegemony" of ruling ideas and groups; therefore, Marxists should challenge the cultural hegemony of capitalism—a task that required a cultural movement that differed from Lenin's Bolshevism.

    4. Instead of top-down communism, Gramsci wanted intellectuals and the masses to be "organically" connected in popular social movements.

  B. Gramsci's objective (like the goal of Frankfurt School theorists) was to find a nontotalitarian form of socialism; this would resist new oppressions.

    1. It also emphasized an open-ended dialectical process in which individuals would continue a critical analysis of culture and society.

    2. These new Marxisms, however, still called for a new socialist system.

IV. The liberals had a different response to the economic and social crisis of the 1930s; the ideas of John Maynard Keynes (1883–1946) revised classical liberalism.

  A. Keynes was the son of an economist; he grew up in Cambridge and became a close friend of writers and artists in the Bloomsbury circle.

    1. He married a Russian ballerina (Lydia Lopokova) in 1925; he was also well known for his journalism, and his investments made him wealthy.

      2. Keynes became famous after writing a short book about the dangers of demanding excessive reparations from Germany in 1919.

      3. He said that Germany needed to participate equally in Europe's economy.

B. Keynes strongly opposed socialism, but he began to argue that the capitalist market system needed to be managed by government interventions.

      1. This was his response to the crisis of the 1930s; he explained his ideas in *The General Theory of Employment, Interest and Money* (1936).

      2. This book rejected the classical laissez-faire view of the economy and argued that people did not invest enough money during economic downturns; the market could not guarantee employment or stability.

C. Keynes thus revised classical economics by calling for governments to provide the investments that private capital alone would not produce.

D. Keynes's theory quickly became the dominant approach to economics and government policy; economists at Cambridge promoted these ideas.

E. This theory did not call for government ownership of the means of productive enterprises, but it assumed that government must play an active role in the economy, especially to deal with unemployment.

V. Keynes's revision of classical liberal economic theory also elicited strong criticism from economists at the London School of Economics.

A. The most important critic was Friedrich Hayek (1899–1992), who was from Vienna. In such works as *Prices and Production* (1931) Hayek argued that the market itself could resolve economic problems; even unemployment would be overcome if the economy were able to "unwind" freely.

B. More generally, Hayek argued that government planning of the economy would lead to the demise of democracy. This was the argument of his famous book *The Road to Serfdom* (1944).

C. Hayek stood apart from the leading social and economic theories of the 1930s; he condemned all forms of Marxism and Keynes's revised liberalism. He shared the widespread theoretical interest in relations between the individual and society but defended older liberal economic ideas.

Essential Reading:

Antonio Gramsci, *The Antonio Gramsci Reader: Selected Writings, 1916–1935*, edited by David Forgacs, sections on "Hegemony, Relations of Force, Historical Bloc" and "Intellectuals and Education", pp. 189–221, 300–322.

Friedrich A. Hayek, *The Road to Serfdom*, pp. 1–71.

Supplementary Reading:

Robert Skidelsky, *Keynes*, pp. 1–12, 70–90.

Martin Jay, *The Dialectical Imagination*, pp. 86–112.

Questions to Consider:

1. Can the economic theories of Marx and the psychological theories of Freud be combined in a coherent social theory?

2. Whose economic ideas have greater influence today—those of Keynes or Hayek?

Lecture Sixteen—Transcript
Revisiting Marxism and Liberalism

We've discussed the cultural effects of World War I and the ways in which various writers and artists interpreted the meaning of the war. We especially looked at the war's impact on literature and on the arts. But it's important to remember that the war also transformed the social and political world. And that social transformation and political transformation had an enormous impact on the post-war generation of European intellectuals.

In the first place, the Bolshevik Revolution in Russia, which had begun in 1917, had developed, by the early 1930s, a new kind of Marxist state. And this was the dictatorial communism of Joseph Stalin. And the very presence of this communist state on the margins of Europe had an enormous impact on intellectual life in the 1920s and 1930s.

Meanwhile, in response to the war, in response to Russia's communist revolution, and in response to various economic problems in the 1920s and '30s, the new fascist and Nazi movements gained power in Italy and in Germany. The fascists came to power in Italy as early as 1922. And the Nazis came to power in Germany in January 1933. And the dictatorships of Benito Mussolini and Adolph Hitler forced European intellectuals to rethink liberal political and economic ideas. In fact, the very presence of these new fascist and communist regimes called into question a whole series of assumptions that had dominated 19th-century political thought and social theory.

Now, these political events in Russia, in Italy, and in Germany, coincided also with the great economic crisis that began in 1929 and continued throughout the 1930s—the Great Depression—which was, of course, a worldwide event, had great impact in North America as well as in Europe. It was the combination of the political and economic problems of the 1930s that pushed many intellectuals toward a new concern with social issues. The 1920s had been a period of great literary experimentation—the rise of Surrealism, various forms of modernism, a whole series of experiments in literary life.

Now, this post-war literary and artistic fascination with the internal life and the unconscious did not entirely disappear in the 1930s, and there were plenty of writers still concerned with the problem of language or the meaning of literary traditions. For example, James Joyce was writing *Finnegans Wake* in the 1930s, exploring the most intricate linguistic experiments—the meaning of literary language. So that process didn't entirely disappear.

But in general, the 1930s have been portrayed in intellectual history as a time of intense political engagements—a time when writers could not simply think about the meaning of memory in their personal lives, but a time when writers had to choose sides in a very complex political situation.

They had to choose between fascism and communism and the ideas of liberalism—classical liberalism. And classical liberalism was very much on the defensive in the 1930s. Liberalism had always stressed the autonomy of individuals. This was the classic idea coming out of the Enlightenment—the idea of individual rights, of individual thought, individual freedoms, and the idea that the individual was in some sense autonomous in the social world. But by the 1930s, these ideas had been very widely challenged—in part, by the experience of World War I, which as I noted in an earlier lecture, had weakened many of the liberal traditions. But also, liberalism had also been undermined by the arrival of communism and fascism, which for all their differences, were both staunchly anti-liberal. So, intellectuals in the 1930s were concerned in new ways with the relationship between individuals and the society. They couldn't ignore the social dimension. And most intellectual critics challenged—in one way or another—the ideas of these various ideologies. Some critics were very critical of traditional liberalism. Some critics were very critical to fascism, others were very hostile to communism. They were critical of these different traditions. Or, in one way or another, they supported these political doctrines. They would choose to become a communist, or they would identify with liberal political parties. They felt obliged to take political positions.

Now, many intellectuals criticized classical liberalism—the ides of the totally autonomous individual. But they also had a hard time of fitting easily into communism or fascism. Because for intellectuals or writers or intellectual critics, there was always a stress on individual creativity or on the autonomy of the individual critic. And this interest in the individual—individual creative writer or critic— challenged basic assumptions of both fascism and communism. Both fascism and communism identified identity in terms of groups—you're part of a nation, or you're a part of a social class, and that is the essence of your social identity. But for intellectuals, that was a difficult step to take.

So, the challenge for intellectuals was to work out a new analysis of the relations between individuals and society—an analysis that would conform to the conditions of the modern world—that might challenge the assumption that individuals are totally autonomous beings—the classical liberal idea—but would also remain a skepticism toward the more universalizing claims of fascism and communism.

So, the kind of social analysis that emerged in the 1930s required a theoretical response to Stalinism, fascism, and the Great Depression. And in many cases, intellectuals themselves had no choice but to make a political decision. They were living in a society where every day their lives were affected by these political realities. Would they support or oppose fascism? Would they leave Russia? Would they leave Italy or Germany and go into exile? These were the kind of very difficult personal questions that the ideological conflicts of the era posed...if these ideological conflicts forced people to take sides.

Well, the influence of this new context appears most notably in the new Marxist theories of the 1930s and the new liberal theories of the 1930s. And I want to focus on those elements of intellectual life in this lecture. Although some intellectuals were attracted to fascism, most writers became hostile to fascism. There were some exceptions. The poet, Ezra Pound, for example, was attracted to Italian fascism. And the famous German philosopher, Martin Heidegger, was drawn to Nazism and the ideas of the Nazi movement. But most writers outside of Italy and Germany remained critical of fascism, in part, I think, because fascism tended to be strongly anti-intellectual. It tended to celebrate action over thought and to emphasize the crowd over the ideas of the individual. So they—in a sense—these fascist movements downplayed the importance of intellectual work, stressing group identities.

But at the same time, many social theorists in these years became disenchanted with orthodox Marxism—especially as they learned about the Stalinist oppression in the Soviet Union. So, one common intellectual response was the attempt to work out a new kind of Marxism or a new kind of liberalism that would reject both Stalinism and fascism. The classical Marxists and classical liberals stressed that rationality. This is where both Marxism and liberalism were hostile to fascism, because they stressed the rationality of human beings and the rationality of economic knowledge. And it was these rational traditions of Marxism and liberalism that were revised in the 1930s.

Some Marxists wanted to combine Marx and Freud or to rethink the role of culture in social and political life. And we can see these themes in the Marxism of the German Frankfurt School. And this is what I'm going to talk about in just a minute. You can see this kind of Marxism in the Frankfurt School and also in the work of the Italian theorist, Antonio Gramsci. So there was a new kind of Marxism that looked at culture and at psychology.

At the same time, the liberals were debating the value of the classical laissez-faire economic theory, which had been an important part of liberalism throughout the 19th century. And there was a debate about the relevance of that in the 20th century—a debate that we can see very clearly in Britain in the works of John Maynard Keynes and Friedrich Hayek who were both working in England in the 1930s. And I want to say something also about the revision of classic liberalism. So, we're going to look at the revisionist patterns in social theory in the 1930s—revisions that revised classical Marxism and classical liberalism. And I think that these revisions of classical social or economic theories were as important as the revisions in all of the other intellectual fields. These revisions of classical Marxism and liberalism were a response to this very difficult social and political context of the 1930s.

So, let's look now briefly at a few of the themes in the new Marxism that emerged in the 1930s. One important strand of Marxist social theory attempted to revise Marx by the influence of Hegelianism on Marx's early work and also trying to link Freud to Marx—bring in Hegel and bring in Freud to try to revise Marx. And these themes could be seen especially among the theorists at the Frankfurt Institute of Social Research in Germany. It's a very important institute of social thought. There was a group of writers who became known in intellectual history recently as the Frankfurt School, and it included a number of famous social theorists—people such as Theodor Adorno and Max Horkheimer, who were the leaders of this institute in the late 1920s and throughout the 1930s. In fact, the institute was founded in 1923, but it was dissolved after the Nazis came to power in 1933. And its members fled into exile—mostly to the United States, but it retained this identity as the Frankfurt School. And so, intellectual historians always refer to this group as the Frankfurt School even during the years the Frankfurt School didn't exist as an institution in Germany. It was re-established after World War II.

Now these thinkers—the Frankfurt School thinkers—wanted to create a new kind of critical Marxism or a critical theory that rejected Stalinism but also a theory that challenged or rejected classical liberalism. And the leaders of this Frankfurt School often stressed the Hegelian origins of Marxism. They believed that the Hegelian view of historical change—the dynamic dialectical elements of Hegelianism were lacking in both Stalinism and in liberal political theories. And so they went back to the early Marx, and they began to criticize the excessive positivism of modern communism. They criticized Marxists for losing sights of the non-economic aspects of human activity and culture. They wanted it to be a form of social critique that went well beyond economics. And you can see this especially in the work of Adorno—a very important member of this school.

Adorno lived from 1903 to 1969, and in addition to writing a great deal about social and political problems, he wrote a great deal about music, for example. He was very interested in music, and he was interested in the non-rational aspects of human identity—about personality. And he complained that Marx had not understood the unconscious. That had never been part of classical Marxist theory. But Freud, on the other hand, had never understood economics. He didn't understand how important the material economic world was. So the great challenge for a critical new theory would be to link psychology and economics—to bring together the insights of Marx with the insights of Freud. And the example of Nazism offered these people a great deal of material to work with. What was the appeal of a movement like Nazism? If the Nazis gained mass support, why did that happen? And so the theorists of the Frankfurt School would sometimes look at the economic bases of various fascist movements but also try to understand the various psychological dimensions. You can see this, for example, with Erich Fromm who is one of the psychologists connected with the Frankfurt School, who tried to write about the psychological meaning of such movements. Or Herbert Marcuse who later became best known in America who tried to look at both the Hegelian and the psychological elements of social theory in order to understand how modern societies worked.

Well, the critical theory of the Frankfurt School often drew on the young Marx's economic and philosophical manuscripts. These had been rediscovered in the early 1930s, and these texts were much more Hegelian than Marx's later work. These texts stress the problem of alienation in modern societies. And this whole problem of alienation could be used to analyze conditions in the Soviet Union as well as conditions in capitalist factories. Alienation came back into the study of Marx's social theory. How could alienation and repression be overcome? This is the question the Frankfurt School theorists wanted to understand. And they said this is a problem in both capital and communist societies. Communism has not overcome the problem of alienation. And maybe Freud could be useful for answering these questions, because Freud had shown how repression shaped civilization itself. So in order to truly liberate people, you have to include something that goes beyond economics. You have to think about the psychological and social aspects of alienation as well as the economic.

So for the Frankfurt School theorists—people like Adorno—social reform had to take serious the influence of the unconscious mind as well as economic institutions. Adorno would be involved later on in the production of a study called *The Authoritarian Personality*, in which he is trying to understand how the elements of psychology also contribute to the processes of fascism and the appeal of authoritarian movements.

This problem of alienation and the influence of culture was also important to the Italian Marxist theorist, Antonio Gramsci. Gramsci lived from 1891 to 1937 and he would later be one of the most influential Marxist theorists in European thought—not so much in his own lifetime, but after he died. He became particularly important in the kind of revival of Marxist thought in the 1950s and 1960s in Western Europe when many intellectuals continued to be drawn to Marxism as an analytical tool.

Gramsci was a member of the communist party who had been jailed by the fascists in the 1920s and who had in fact lived almost all of the rest of his life in prison—he died in prison—a victim of the fascist regime. While he was in prison, he continued to write and to analyze social and economic and political processes. He was very interested in politics. He had been a journalist earlier in his life. And after his death, his writings were collected in a work called the *Prison Notebooks*, and his prison writings were eventually published after World War II and then translated into many other languages.

Gramsci criticized fascism. He was a great critic of fascism. But he also criticized orthodox Marxism. His goal was to develop a new kind of communism—a new kind of non-totalitarian communism that would be based on broad, local, social movements. And it would also depend on intellectuals who supported the lower classes. He thought that most Marxists had become too economic in their thinking. They had been blinded to what he called economism. They saw everything to be reduced to economic terms. But for Gramsci, it was very important to see the reciprocal relation between culture and political or economic life. And he said that culture was as important for maintaining power as for political and economic institutions. So, culture created what he called the hegemony of ruling ideas. Whatever group is in power has a kind of hegemonic control over the institutions of culture—the media, the schools, the universities. And so, in order to change a society, you can't simply attack the economic and political institutions, you have to challenge the cultural hegemony of capitalism. And this would be a task that would require a cultural movement—a cultural movement that went far beyond from anything that could be seen in Lenin's style of Bolshevism. Instead of a top-down communism, which was the hallmark of Bolshevism, Gramsci wanted a kind of popular movement in which intellectuals and the masses would be kind of organically connected in a popular social movement so that the political ideas flow up and not simply down. So, Gramsci's objective—like the goal of the Frankfurt School of theorists—was to find a non-totalitarian form of socialism—a form of socialism that would resist the new oppressions of the fascists system, which, for Gramsci, was also linked to capitalism. And Gramsci wanted a more open-ended dialectical process in which individuals would continue a critical analysis of culture and society. It would be a new form of Marxism that emphasized cultural critique, cultural dynamism, and cultural change as well as economic and political critique and transformation.

But these new Marxisms—the Frankfurt School and Gramsci—were still calling for a new socialist system. They said that socialism is the way to ensure greater progress and freedom in the world. This is how they differed from the liberals. And I want to turn now to the revision of liberalism that was taking place during this same period—during the crisis of the 1930s.

And here the key figure is John Maynard Keynes, who lived from 1883 to 1946. And Keynes played a major role in revising classic liberalism. Keynes was the son of an economist—he grew up in Cambridge. He came from an academic background. And as a young man, Keynes became a friend of writers and artists in that Bloomsbury group—that Bloomsbury circle that I talked about earlier when we were discussing Virginia Woolf. So, he was connected to writers and artists as well as to social theorists.

He married a Russian ballerina named Lydia Lopokova. He married her in 1925, and he was a well-known journalist by this time. He wrote often for the newspapers as well as the more technical economic journals. His investments also made him very wealthy. He was one of those rare academics that not only wrote about economics, he made a lot of money. So, he had an active role in public life.

He became famous in the early 1920s after writing a short book about the dangers of the Versailles Treaty. He said that the Versailles Treaty at the end of World War I had made excessive economic demands on Germany, and he said that the excessive reparations that had been imposed on Germany in 1919 could not be realistically paid. And he said that Germany needed to participate more equally in Europe's economy and that if it were not brought into the European economy, it would create resentment and problems in Germany's future—a point that many people came to accept, that maybe Germany had been treated too harshly at Versailles.

So Keynes was someone very involved in the public debates of his time. But he also strongly opposed socialism. He thought that socialism was not the way to deal with economic problems, even though he believed that there were problems in the capitalist market system. And it was this attempt to regulate the market system that Keynes developed in his writings. He argued that in the modern economy, the problems of the market had to be managed, to some extent, by government interventions. And this was Keynes' response to the conditions of the economic crisis in the early 1930s. He explained his ideas in an extremely influential book, a book called *The General Theory of Employment, Interest and Money*, which was published in 1936. But it brought together a number of ideas that he had been developing in articles over several years in the early 1930s.

Keynes, in this book, rejected the classical laissez-faire view of the economy, and he argued that people did not invest enough money during economic downturns—that the market itself could not guarantee employment or stability—that once you started into a slump, the market did not have the resources to get everybody back up and working. So, he revised the classical economic theory by calling for governments to provide investments that private capital alone would not produce. This was Keynes' most important idea— that governments, by using deficit spending—at least in the short run—governments could use deficit spending to put more money into the economy. Only the government could provide enough money to get the machine running again. And this public expenditure would have what he would call a multiplier effect. Because as you put money into the economy, you prime the pump, so to speak. You have brought about a higher level of employment. And as employment went up, people would spend more money. This money, in turn, would spread through the economy, as consumers would use their wages to purchase what companies produced, and this would lead to new employment, which in turn would lead to the end of the economic problem. This would be the ultimate outcome of deficit spending. You would have a revival of the economy. The market would then take off again.

And in fact Keynes' theory quickly became the dominant approach to economics and to government policies. The economists at Cambridge promoted these ideas widely. The ideas spread throughout Britain. They were picked up in the United States. Many of the advisors around Franklin Roosevelt and the New Deal embraced Keynesian economic theory. And in fact, for the next 30 or 40 years, the Keynesian theory was repeatedly used as a way to justify deficit spending in times of economic downturn.

This theory did not call for government ownership of the means of enterprise, but it assumed that government must play an active role in the economy—especially to deal with problems of unemployment. And the Keynesian model continues to have an influence throughout the rest of the 20th century.

But Keynes' revision of classical economic theory also elicited strong criticism from other economists in Britain—particularly economists who were based at the London School of Economics. And I want to say a word of this critique of the Keynesian position, because this was the other direction in which liberal thought went among some people in the 1930s. The most important critic of the Keynesian position was Friedrich Hayek, who lived from 1899 to 1992. Hayek was an Austrian. He was originally from Vienna. He studied law and economics in Vienna before moving to London, where he eventually ended up at the London School of Economics.

Hayek was also strongly opposed to socialism. Like Keynes, he had no sympathy for socialism. But in fact, he was even critical of Keynes' argument, because he said this call for government intervention through deficit spending was wrong. And in works such as *Crisis and Production*—a book published in 1931—Hayek argued that the market itself could resolve all economic problems—even unemployment would be overcome if the economy were simply able to unwind freely. Unwind was his term—you have an economy that gets into a jam, but then you can unwind through the market. And Hayek also argued that the only way to deal with economic problems would be to do certain kinds of monetary adjustments—that you cannot solve the economic problem by any kind of government intervention.

But more generally, Hayek argued that the government planning of the economy would lead to the demise of democracy. And this is the argument of his most famous book, which is called *The Road to Serfdom*, published in 1944. And in that book, Hayek compared fascism and socialism and claimed that both of these forms of thought showed the dangers of government regulation of the economy. The left and the right both made the same mistake. Fascism and communism made the same mistake. They provided for government intervention in the economy.

So Hayek rejected Keynes' model of government spending as a solution to economic problems, and he reaffirmed the classical liberal model, though he added a new emphasis on the role of the money supply. Hayek stood apart from the leading social and economic theories of the 1930s. He condemned all of them. He condemned Marxism, he condemned fascism, he condemned Keynes' revised liberalism. But he shared in this widespread theoretical interest in the relation between the individual and society. He came down on the side of the older, liberal economic idea of individual autonomy in a market economy.

Lecture Seventeen
Responses to Nazism and the Holocaust

Scope:

The rise of Nazism created a new political context for European intellectuals and provoked a wide range of responses in the 1930s and 1940s. This lecture discusses three contrasting examples of the intellectual response to Adolph Hitler and the actions of Germany's Nazi regime. It first summarizes the ideas of Martin Heidegger and describes his support for the Nazi movement. It then notes the intellectual resistance to the Nazi regime, with special reference to the actions of the philosopher Hannah Arendt and the theologian Dietrich Bonhoeffer. Their lives and writings became eloquent statements of opposition to totalitarianism and to what Arendt called the "banality of evil." Both these writers described the struggle to resist totalitarian regimes and defend human morality against modern uses of power and technology.

Outline

I. We have seen how intellectuals responded to the First World War and to other political and economic problems of the 1930s. Some writers could perhaps ignore these problems, but almost nobody could avoid the consequences of Nazism.

   A. By the early 1940s, every major European nation was at war (except for Spain, and the Spanish had just gone through a devastating civil war).

   1. The question for all intellectuals came down to the issue of Nazism: How should one respond to this new totalitarian regime?

   2. Like other Europeans, the intellectuals were divided. This division offers a remarkable example of how every intellectual's life and work are connected to the historical context in which he or she lives.

   B. I'll discuss this relation between intellectuals and the political-military context of the 1930s and 1940s by looking at three notable German intellectuals: Martin Heidegger, Hannah Arendt, and Dietrich Bonhoeffer.

1. These people represent three different responses to Nazism: affiliation, exile, and internal resistance (leading to death).
2. Their actions exemplify the modern intellectual's struggle to deal with powerful, violent political regimes.

II. The history of Nazi Germany is a vast, much debated subject, but the key problems of opposition or support for the regime emerged quickly and remained in place from 1933 to 1945. Hitler came to power (legally) in late January 1933.

A. He almost immediately gained "emergency powers" and soon launched the persecution of Jews, outlawed all political parties and trade unions (except Nazi organizations), and established police control over the whole society.
1. The Nazis militarized German culture, established concentration camps for people they disliked, and prepared for a new war.
2. The war began in September 1939, and the Nazi conquests led to the systematic genocidal plan to create a "new European order."
3. The culmination of the Nazi campaign was, of course, the Holocaust, the deadly outcome of Nazism that led to the deaths of at least six million Jews and other so-called "non-Aryan" people.

B. Nazism was the unavoidable issue of the era, and its impact was felt in Europe and elsewhere long after the Nazis were finally defeated.

III. Martin Heidegger became one of the most well known intellectuals to embrace the Nazi regime; his actions remain a major blight on his intellectual reputation.

A. Heidegger (1889–1976) came from a pious lower-middle class Catholic family in southern Germany; he planned to become a priest.
1. He studied philosophy instead and became an assistant of Edmund Husserl at the University of Freiburg (1919–1923). He married Elfriede Petri, who was Protestant, and renounced his Catholicism in 1919.

2. He went to teach at the University of Marburg, where he worked on his most important book, *Being and Time* (1927). He then succeeded Husserl as a philosophy professor at the University of Freiburg.

B. Heidegger argued that Western philosophy did not give adequate attention to the problem of Being. Even Husserl, whose account of consciousness was important for Heidegger, did not explain how to be conscious of Being.

   1. Heidegger referred to the idea of Being as "*dasein*"; it is the core of human existence—the reality that enables one to say, "I am."

   2. Heidegger said most people do not want to think about Being or about the way in which one's Being is located in time.

   3. If one becomes aware of Being, then it is possible to see how others have imposed on this Being—and one can resist this imposition.

C. Heidegger challenged the Western scientific and positivist tendency to reduce Being to rigid categories or simple identities; he said that Being was more fluid.

   1. He became interested in more mystical forms of thought. His critique of Western philosophy, as well as his emphasis on Being, had a great influence on later thinkers, including existentialists, such as Sartre.

   2. But Heidegger also came to believe that the German people could find ways to revitalize their organic Being in the Nazi movement.

   3. He saw Nazism as an alternative to modern industrial society, which he condemned for its indifference to Being, and he praised the "inner truth and greatness of the [Nazi] movement."

D. His sympathy for the Nazi movement led to his appointment as rector at the University of Freiburg in April 1933. He revised the curriculum to serve the "organic unity" of the German spirit and linked his philosophy to Nazism.

   1. He also supported the removal of Jewish faculty and staff from the university; he joined the Nazi Party, remaining a member until 1945.

2. He resigned as rector of Freiburg University in 1934 (apparently unhappy with the delays in his proposed reforms).

3. He did not play an active role in the Nazi movement after this time, but he never renounced his actions or affiliations, even after 1945.

E. Heidegger's links with Nazism have been used to discredit his philosophy; others say that his ideas should be separated from those actions, but even those who defend his philosophy see his actions as an intellectual blindness.

IV. At the time Heidegger was promoting the Nazi program of national renewal at Freiburg, one of his most brilliant students, Hannah Arendt, was fleeing into exile.

A. Arendt (1906–1975) was born into a Jewish family in Hanover; her father died when she was only seven, but her mother encouraged her education.

1. She studied philosophy with Heidegger at the University of Marburg; they became lovers when she was 18, and she admired his work.

2. He was then 35 and played the role of an intellectual "father."

B. But the affair eventually broke off, Heidegger settled in Freiburg, and Arendt went to Berlin; she began to face the pressure of anti-Semitism.

1. She became active in Zionist political circles. After the Nazis seized power, she was arrested (she was doing research on anti-Semitism).

2. She was released from jail after eight days, but the experience convinced her that she must leave Germany (August 1933); she moved to Paris.

C. Arendt criticized intellectuals, such as her old mentor and lover Heidegger, who were supporting the Nazis; she believed that intellectuals must resist.

1. When the Germans occupied France, Arendt and her husband, Heinrich Blücher, managed to escape; they reached New York in May 1941.

2. From her exile base in New York, Arendt tried to understand why a totalitarian regime had gained absolute power in Germany.

D. This intellectual project led eventually to publication of *The Origins of Totalitarianism* (1951), an influential analysis of modern totalitarian systems. Arendt tried to explain how these systems held power.

   1. Arendt stressed that racism, imperialism, and anti-Semitism prepared the way for totalitarian movements, but she did not see this situation as a specific or unique aspect of German culture.

   2. She emphasized that people joined the "crowds" of a nationalist, racist movement because such crowds gave lonely people a place to belong.

   3. Totalitarian movements were not simply dictatorships; they had strong support from much of the population, who embraced the "leader."

   4. Such regimes also sustained their power by the use of terror.

E. Where Heidegger had seen Nazism as an expression of revitalized national Being, Arendt saw the movement as a terrorizing form of modernity.

   1. She also analyzed the peculiar modernity of the Holocaust in *Eichmann in Jerusalem: A Report on the Banality of Evil* (1963), which discussed the trial of a bureaucratic manager of genocide.

   2. This book became controversial because critics said that Arendt ignored Eichmann's own guilt; she portrayed him as a vacuous cog in a system.

   3. This is what she meant by the banality of evil—ordinary people doing murderous work that was simply a job in a modern office building.

F. In this respect, Nazism and the Holocaust were part of a modern, impersonal process in which individuals abdicated moral and political responsibility.

   1. In other works, Arendt advocated a commitment to classical (Greek) ideals of a republican public sphere of political life.

   2. Her wider theme, however, suggested that intellectuals must act against totalitarian systems.

3. Arendt later reestablished a friendship with Heidegger, but the old friends would never come to a common understanding of Nazism.

V. While Arendt was developing her analysis of totalitarianism in New York, Dietrich Bonhoeffer was working for the German Resistance, then sitting in prison cells.

   A. Bonhoeffer (1906–1945) was part of a well-to-do German Protestant family. His father was a professor of psychiatry at the University of Berlin.

      1. Despite his father's objections, the young Bonhoeffer studied theology at the University of Berlin. After receiving a doctorate, he spent a year at Union Theological Seminary in New York.

      2. He became a friend of the theologian Reinhold Neibuhr in New York, then returned to teach theology at the University of Berlin.

   B. Bonhoeffer's career was advancing until the Nazis came to power in 1933. He said that Christians must support the Jews and argued that Nazism was completely at odds with Christian teachings.

   C. In 1939, Bonhoeffer decided to accept an invitation to return to New York, where he could teach some courses at Union Theological Seminary. After he arrived in America, however, he felt uncomfortable about his separation from Germany; he returned to Berlin in July.

   D. Soon after the war began, Bonhoeffer joined a secret resistance group and participated in a plan to get Jews out of Germany.

      1. He was arrested in April 1943 and was executed about a month before the end of the war (April 9, 1945).

      2. His prison letters and other writings became an eloquent testimony to the modern struggle against totalitarian violence.

Essential Reading:

Hannah Arendt, *The Portable Hannah Arendt*, edited with an introduction by Peter Baehr, excerpts in sections on "Totalitarianism," and "Banality and Conscience: Eichmann Trial and Its Implications," pp. 75–140, 313–365.

Dietrich Bonhoeffer, *Writings*, selected and with an introduction by Robert Coles, excerpts from "The Cost of Discipleship" and "Letters and Papers from Prison," pp. 53–64, 115–127.

Supplementary Reading:

Martin Heidegger, "The Self-Assertion of the German University," and Hannah Arendt, "For Martin Heidegger's Eightieth Birthday," both in Gunther Neske and Emil Kettering, editors, *Martin Heidegger and National Socialism*, pp. 5–13, 207–217.

Questions to Consider:

1. Why is it difficult for intellectuals to defy their national governments?

2. Do you think a writer's political actions and personal behavior can discredit his or her writings in other spheres, such as philosophy and literature?

Lecture Seventeen—Transcript
Responses to Nazism and the Holocaust

We've seen in earlier lectures how intellectuals responded to the First World War and also how they responded to some of the political and economic problems of the 1930s. And I've been stressing that intellectuals are involved in some way with their context. And some of the writers in the 1920s or 1930s might have been able to ignore economic problems or the rising political problems of the period, but by the early 1940s, there was no way to ignore what was happening in Europe. Nobody could ignore the consequences of the rise of Nazism and the beginning of World War II.

In fact, by the early 1940s, every major European nation was at war or had recently been occupied by the German army. All the nations were at war, except for Spain, and the Spanish had just gone through a devastating civil war that had resulted in the emergence of a new fascist regime in Spain. And so, the question for all intellectuals in Europe in this period came down to the issue of Nazism. How should one respond to this totalitarian regime? And like other Europeans, the intellectuals were divided. And I think that this division among the intellectuals offers a remarkable example of how every intellectual's life and work is affected—how every intellectual's life is affected by the historical context in which he or she lives. And in retrospect, it's easier for us to say, "Well, this person should have done this action or should have resisted in this way". Of course, when people are in the middle of it, they can't see where things are going. They can't see the outcome, and it's extremely difficult to know what choices to make.

And I want to discuss this problem—the problem of making political choices—by looking at the ways intellectuals responded to the political-military context of the 1930s and 1940s. And I want to look specifically at three notable German intellectuals, because, of course, it was the Germans who faced this problem most acutely. I'm going to discuss the examples of Martin Heidegger and Hannah Arendt and Dietrich Bonhoeffer, because these three people represent three very different responses to the rise and expansion of Nazism. They represent the example of affiliation or support, the example of exile, and in the case of Bonhoeffer, the case of internal resistance leading finally to death. And I think their actions exemplify the complexity of the modern intellectual's struggle to deal with violent and powerful political regimes—a problem that has repeatedly appeared in modern Europe and a problem that has appeared in many parts of the world in the last century.

Well, the history of Nazi Germany is a vast and much debated subject. But the key problem that I want to talk about—the problem of opposition or support of the regime—emerged very quickly and remained in place from 1933 down to 1945. Hitler and the Nazis came to power legally in late January 1933 when Hitler was appointed Chancellor of the German government. And almost immediately, Hitler declared and gained so-called emergency powers and soon launched the persecution of Jews, outlawed all political parties and trade unions—except the official Nazi organization. He established police control over society. The secret police became a major force in German life, including, of course, in German intellectual life. The Nazis militarized German culture. They soon established concentration camps for political opponents and people they disliked, and they began to prepare for a new war—began re-arming and expanding the German army.

The war that they so much wanted began in September of 1939, and the Nazi conquest soon led to the systematic, genocidal plan to create a new European order. The plan that they called the Final Solution, which was the culmination of the Nazi genocidal plan, which was of course the Holocaust which led to the deaths of at least six million Jews and other so-called non-Aryan people. So this was the deadly outcome of Nazism—the most devastating war in European history and the Holocaust.

So, Nazism was the unavoidable issue of the era. And its impact was felt in Europe and, in fact, around the world long after the Nazis were finally defeated. In fact, we're still invariably living with certain consequences of this period in European history. So I want to turn now to the specific ways in which certain German intellectuals responded to this event. And I'll begin with the case of Martin Heidegger.

Heidegger became one of the best-known intellectuals to embrace the Nazi regime. And his actions remain a major blight on his intellectual reputation. He's never finally overcome this choice he made in 1933 to identify with the Nazis. Heidegger was born in

1889. He lived until 1976. And he came from a pious lower-middle class Catholic family in southern Germany. In fact, as a young man, he planned to become a priest. But then he went to the university and studied philosophy and became interested in philosophy and later became an assistant to Edmund Husserl, who was at this time at the University of Freiburg. And this was in the period between 1919 and 1923 that Heidegger was working with Husserl.

He also married in this period. He married a woman named Elfriede Petri, who was Protestant. And it was at this period that Heidegger renounced his Catholicism—in 1919. He then went on to teach at the University of Marburg, where he worked on his most important philosophical work, the book Being and Time, which was published in 1927. And then he succeeded Husserl as a philosophy professor at the University of Freiburg.

Now, Heidegger's philosophy became some of the most influential philosophical work of the 20th century. He argued that Western philosophy did not give adequate attention to the problem of being— what philosophers call the ontological question—of being. And he said that even Husserl, whose account of consciousness had been very important for Heidegger, even Husserl did not explain how to become conscious of being. Heidegger referred to this idea of being as dassein. It is the core of human existence. It is that deep reality that enables one to say "I am" or "I exist" or "I think". In other words, before you can take any action in the world, before you can make any statement, you have to assume something about the nature of being, because it is being that makes possible all philosophical statements, all claims about the world.

But Heidegger said that most people don't want to think about being or about how one's being is located in time. He said if you think about it, though, it changes the way you think about yourself. It becomes possible to see how others have imposed upon one's own being. And when you're aware of the limits on one's own being, then you can resist these impositions. You can become aware of the impositions that restrict the development of your own being.

Now, in developing this concept of being, Heidegger challenged the Western scientific and positivistic tendency to reduce being to rigid categories or simple identities. He said that being is more fluid. It's moving. It can't be pinned down. And in fact, he became interested in various forms of mystical thought—forms of thought that stressed the fluidity of being. And this conception of being and his critique of Western philosophy had a great influence on later thinkers, including existentialists such as Sartre and many other later 20th-century philosophers.

But Heidegger also came to believe that the German people needed to find ways to revitalize what he called their organic being. And he believed they could find this revitalization in the Nazi movement. He saw Nazism as an alternative to modern industrial society. And he condemned modern industrial society for its indifference to being. So he plays Nazism. He said that there is something admirable in "the inner truth and greatness of the Nazi movement." He saw the Nazi movement as a way to give new life to that deep, organic being in the German people. And this sympathy for the Nazi movement led to his appointment as rector at the University of Freiburg in April 1933. The rector is like the chief administrative official of the university. And after receiving this appointment, he set about revising the curriculum of the university to serve what he called 'the organic unity' of the German spirit. And he linked this philosophy to Nazism.

He also supported the removal of Jewish faculty and staff from the university. This is one of the ironies—it was Husserl himself who was later barred from using the library at the university because of these kinds of policies—Husserl, who had been Heidegger's own advisor and mentor at one point.

Heidegger also joined the Nazi party and remained a member until 1945. While he resigned as rector at Freiburg—the university—in 1934. Apparently he was unhappy in the delays in his proposed reforms. But he did not play an active role in the Nazi movement after this time. And yet, he never renounced his actions or affiliations with the Nazi movement—even after 1945 and even after people explicitly asked him about his actions during the Nazi period.

Well, Heidegger's links with Nazism had been used to discredit his philosophy. People say, 'look, if this is where his ideas lead, they should be rejected.' Other people say that his ideas need to be separated from those actions. And this is one of the debates about many intellectuals. Can you separate an intellectual's political actions from the value of his ideas—or the ideas become discredited because of personal actions. This is a debate that goes on in intellectual history. But even those that defend his philosophy see Heidegger's actions during the Nazi period as a terrible intellectual blindness—as a flaw—in his career and in his personal life.

Now, at the time Heidegger was promoting the Nazi program of renewal at Freiburg, one of his most brilliant students, Hannah Arendt, was fleeing into exile. And I want to say now a few things about the case of Arendt. She represents a second example—a second model—of intellectual responses to the Nazi context.

Arendt was born in 1906. She lived until 1975. She was born into a Jewish family in Hanover, Germany. Her father died when she was only seven years old. She didn't know her father very well. But her mother encouraged her education and pushed her strongly to continue her studies. And so Arendt went to study philosophy at the University of Marburg. And there she met Heidegger who had come there as a professor. And soon after her arrival, she was working with Heidegger, and they became lovers. She was only 18 years old. She had great admiration for his philosophical work. He was then 35 years old. As I mentioned before, he was married. He had a family. But he was drawn to Arendt. I think these were the days before modern sexual harassment regulations, and so though he was her professor, he soon became her lover. And he played the role of a kind of intellectual father. They were very close at this time.

But the affair eventually broke off. Heidegger went back to Freiburg to take up a new position as professor of philosophy, and Arendt eventually moved to Berlin where she began to face the pressure of anti-Semitism in the early 1930s. She actually became active in various Zionist political groups—political circles—among people who were encouraging Jews to immigrate to Palestine. And after the Nazis seized power, she was arrested. She had been doing research on anti-Semitism. She was arrested, put in jail. She was released from jail after only eight days in prison. But this experience was so threatening and frightening that it convinced her she must leave Germany.

And so, in August of 1933, as I say just as Heidegger is rector at the University of Freiburg, Arendt moves to Paris. And she began to criticize intellectuals, such as her old mentor, Heidegger—intellectuals who were supporting the Nazis, because she believed intellectuals must resist, that this was a moment in which intellectuals must stand up against the government and not praise or support it.

When the Germans occupied France, Arendt and her husband, Heinrich Blücher, managed to escape. She had been in France since her escape from Germany. She eventually had married someone else. And she was living in France. She was able to get out, and she and her husband reached New York in May of 1941—part of a group of exiles that managed to escape from France.

And from her exiled base in New York, Arendt tried to understand why a totalitarian regime had gained absolute power in Germany. And this became the focus of much of her intellectual research and writing over the following decade. In fact, this intellectual project led eventually to publication of one of her most important books—a book called *The Origins of Totalitarianism*, which was published after the war in 1951. And this book became an extremely influential analysis of the modern totalitarian system. She tried to explain how such systems emerge and why they are able to hold power. And she used the example of Nazi Germany, but she referred to other totalitarian regimes as well, including regimes in communist societies. And Arendt stressed that racism, imperialism, and anti-Semitism prepared the way for totalitarian movements—that these are ideas that give credence to extremist political groups. But she did not see this kind of thought or this kind of movement as a unique aspect of German culture. She thought that many cultures could fall into the same pattern, because, she emphasized, people join the crowds of extreme nationalist and racist movements, because belonging to such a crowd gives lonely people a place to belong. That is, in the modern deracinated or uprooted life that people live in modern societies, they are looking for something they can identify with. And radical nationalist movements which feed into totalitarian or authoritarian political groups provide that sense of belonging. So, totalitarian movements were not simply dictatorships, they actually had strong support from much of the population who embraced the leader. And therefore, it was a mistake to try to understand totalitarian regimes as simply a seizure of power by a small elite. These regimes sustained their power and got into power, in part, because many people actually support what these regimes claimed to do.

Of course, once these regimes are in power, they also sustain their power by the use of terror. And she stressed that totalitarian regimes are always able to maintain their power by the threat of violence. They don't have to actually exercise the violence against most people—just an occasional exercise of violence or throwing some people into prison is enough to give everybody the message. You know if you live in such a state, the threat of violence is always there.

So while Heidegger saw Nazism as some kind of revitalized national being, Arendt saw the movement as a terrorizing form of modernity. Totalitarianism is kind of systematic terrorism, and it's very effective. Now, she also wanted to analyze the peculiar modernity of the Holocaust, because she saw this terrible event as something that was also distinctively modern. And she went on to write about the Holocaust in a famous book called *Eichmann in Jerusalem: A Report on the Banality of Evil*—a book that was published in 1963. It came out of a series of articles that she had written in the early 1960s. This was a book about the trial of a bureaucratic manager of the genocide that the Nazis had perpetrated in Europe.

Eichmann had been a bureaucratic official. He had organized the movement of the trains that carried the people to the death camps. After the war, he had fled to Argentina where he was arrested, eventually, by the Israeli secret police and brought back to Israel for trial and eventually executed. Now, this book, *Eichmann in Jerusalem*, became controversial, because critics said Arendt was ignoring Eichmann's own guilt. She portrayed him generally as a kind of vacuous cog in a big system—an almost mindless bureaucrat—a kind of careerist who was just trying to get on in the world. And this is what she meant by the term 'the banality of evil'. She said that in this kind of modern world, ordinary people can do murderous work simply by fulfilling a job in a modern office building. It's a banal life. They're not out there with guns or swords like some medieval warrior. They're simply going to work everyday and performing acts that lead to terrible destruction. And in this respect, Nazism and the Holocaust were part of a vast modern, impersonal process in which individuals abdicated moral and political responsibility. In this way, you can say this book extends the ideas that Max Weber had developed when he talked about the rationalizing process of modern bureaucracies. Someone like

Eichmann was just a bureaucrat trying to work as efficiently as he could to do his job. And that's the meaning of the banality of evil.

Now, Arendt herself said that intellectuals needed to take personal responsibility for their actions. And in a number of her later works, she advocated a renewed commitment to classical and Greek ideals of a republican public sphere of political life. But her wide themes suggested that intellectuals must act against totalitarian systems—that intellectuals must take a personal political stand, and they must resist the modern, totalitarian machine. And this is exactly what Heidegger and Eichmann didn't do.

Now, Arendt herself eventually re-established her friendship with Heidegger—a complicated and interesting personal story. And they continued to correspond and even to visit after the Second World War. But these old friends would never come to a common understanding of Nazism, and I think the Arendt-Heidegger relationship is one of the most complex places to explore the problem of the intellectual and the relation to the modern Nazi regime.

While Arendt was developing her analysis of totalitarianism in New York, Dietrich Bonhoeffer was working for the German resistance and then sitting in various German prison cells. And I want to turn now to the third example of an intellectual reaction to a totalitarian regime.

Bonhoeffer was born in 1906—the very same year as Hannah Arendt. And he died in 1945 in circumstances that I'll discuss in a minute. He came from a well-to-do German Protestant family—a well-established, well-educated family whose father was a professor of psychology at the University of Berlin—a very successful professional leader in his field. And there were seven children in the family. The family suffered a great trauma during World War I, because the oldest brother died in that war—one of the many places in Europe where you're going to see the personal impact of the terrible casualties of the First World War. And the Bonhoeffer family was very affected by this in young Dietrich's childhood.

Despite his father's objections, the young Bonhoeffer went on to study theology at the University of Berlin. He didn't follow his father in the study of medicine. And he actually received a doctorate in theology. And then, after completing his studies in Berlin, he spent a year in New York at Union Theological Seminary. And while he was in New York, he became a good friend of the theologian, Reinhold Neibuhr, who was teaching at Union Seminary. And Neibuhr and Bonhoeffer remained friends for many years after this.

But Bonhoeffer returned to teach theology at the University of Berlin. And his career was advancing quite nicely until the Nazis came to power in 1933. And at this point, Bonhoeffer's fortunes took a turn in a different direction. Bonhoeffer said that Christians—true Christians—must support the Jews. They must stand by the Jews as they were being persecuted in the 1930s. And he argued that Nazism was at odds with Christian teaching. You couldn't reconcile Christianity and Nazism. And so Bonhoeffer actually gave up his job at the university. He felt pressured. He felt alienated. He gave up his job and then he broke his links with the official Lutheran Church. And he taught thereafter at a seminary of an alternative church—the so-called Confessing Church, which created a seminary and was outside the Lutheran Church, which was generally aligned with the Nazi regime—or at least with not opposing it.

Meanwhile, Bonhoeffer began to write about these issues—about the relationship of the Christian and regime. He wrote an important book in 1937 called *The Cost of Discipleship,* talking about how you have to pay a price to be a disciple of Christ. And he condemned German Christians for supporting the Third Reich rather than the true Christian tradition. So he was increasingly alienated from the regime and the power in the German society.

In 1939, Bonhoeffer decided to accept an invitation to return to New York, where he had been invited to teach courses at Union Theological Seminary. He had maintained his friendship with people there, like Neibuhr. So he went back to America in 1939. But no sooner had he returned to New York, did he begin to feel uncomfortable about his separation from Germany. He felt he was not where he should be. So he returned to Berlin in July of 1939—barely a month before the beginning of the Second World War. And he wrote to Neibuhr after he went back—wrote a very moving letter that summarized he had chosen to leave the opportunity to be in New York and to go back to Berlin. He said, "I must live through this difficult period with the Christian people of Germany. I will have no right to participate in the reconstruction of Christian life in Germany after the way if I do not share the trials of this time with my people. I have to go back," he told Neibuhr, "because it is my moral obligation. I must be a part of this process."

Well, soon after the war began, Bonhoeffer joined a secret resistance group that was operating within the German military intelligence—a small, elite group that included some opponents of the Nazi regime. They were opponents—they were based within the military intelligence, and he was able to get a position there. And he participated in a plan to get Jews out of Germany—to smuggle Jews out of German society. But he was arrested in April of 1943, and then held in a series of prison. He was finally moved to Buchenwald—one of the concentration camps—in February of 1945. And then he was executed about a month before the end of the war—April 9, 1945.

Now, Bonhoeffer's prison letters and his other writings became an eloquent testimony to the modern struggle against totalitarian violence, and his life and his work became a model for the writer, the intellectual, and the religious person who resists oppression. And in the post-war era, when Bonhoeffer's actions and his fate became known, he came to represent the alternative to Heidegger's affiliation to the Nazis. He represents the extreme alternative to Heidegger's cooperation. And like Arendt's critique of totalitarianism and the banality of evil, Bonhoeffer's rejection of Nazism showed that intellectuals could make free ethical choices, even in the most dangerous and repressive situation.

And this theme—this theme of making choices in difficult situations—would remain an important idea throughout the post-war era. It would appear in a number of intellectual works after the war. And we can see it particularly in the rise of the new existential philosophy movement at the end of the Second World War. And I want now to turn to the subject of existentialism in our next lecture.

Lecture Eighteen
Existential Philosophy

Scope:

The horrifying, disorienting events of the Second World War influenced the postwar philosophical themes of existentialism. The existentialists wrote books that nonspecialist readers could understand, in part because they often used literature to portray their views of human experience, freedom, and personal choices. This lecture discusses existential philosophy in France, focusing on the lives and ideas of Jean-Paul Sartre and Albert Camus. Both these writers were affected by experiences in World War II, both wrote novels about the "absurdity" of existence, and both believed that individuals must use their freedom to take self-defining action in the social world. They took different political positions during the Cold War, however, and their emphasis on individual freedom elicited criticism from those who stressed the social constraints on personal actions.

Outline

I. The ideas and themes of 20th-century philosophy can never be explained as simply a "reflection" of the era's terrible military and political events, yet the philosophers (like everyone else) were forced to respond to the world in which they were living.

   A. We've seen how German philosophers and social theorists made difficult choices during the Nazi era, but their situation was not unique.
      1. Nazi armies and occupation forces took control of other European nations, forcing intellectuals in France and elsewhere to choose sides.
      2. If flight became impossible, writers (and everyone else) had to decide between collaboration, resistance, or the silence of "internal exile."

   B. This was the context in which French existential philosophy emerged during the early 1940s. Stressing the absurdity of human existence and the human freedom to make choices, existentialism seemed to fit in the postwar context.

1. The most important existentialist writers—Jean-Paul Sartre, Albert Camus, Simone de Beauvoir—responded to the German occupation of France and stressed the importance of taking personal action.
2. This lecture discusses existential thought with reference to this context and suggests why it gained so much attention in the decade after 1945.

C. The broad cultural interest in existential philosophy far exceeded the public interest in the technical linguistic themes of Britain's logical positivism.

D. The public response to existentialism grew in part from the literary skill of existentialist authors, who often wrote novels, but the philosophy was also popular because it affirmed the value of human action.

II. In contrast to the British linguistic philosophical concern with epistemology, Continental philosophy stressed the problems of being and consciousness.

A. These ontological issues had gained prominence in the writings of Husserl and Heidegger, both of whom analyzed the nature of existence.
1. Husserl had explored the ways that a conscious subject becomes aware of the objects and the world around it; Heidegger had said that people must act to define their own Being in the realm of time.
2. Similar issues emerged in the work of the German philosopher Karl Jaspers (1883–1969), who argued that people must act with free will.
3. Jaspers said that awareness of death creates anxiety, but it is out of this anxiety that people choose to pursue an active life.

B. French existentialists, especially Sartre, drew on these ideas to develop their own ideas about free human action.
1. They explored the phenomenological question of how one becomes conscious of "being" in the world; then they linked consciousness to free actions that would affirm the individual's existence.
2. German influences were crucial, both in the realm of thought and in the painful realm of war, repression, and military occupation.

III. Jean-Paul Sartre (1905–1980) was the key figure in French existential philosophy. He was born into a well-to-do, highly educated family, the son of a French naval officer.

    A. Sartre's father died when Jean-Paul was only 15 months old. He was raised by his mother and mother's parents, Protestants from Alsace. The family was the Schweitzers, which included the famous Dr. Albert Schweitzer.

        1. Sartre was a bookish but happy child—at least until his mother remarried when he was 11 (he detested his stepfather).

        2. He was educated at the École Normale Supérieure in Paris, where he studied philosophy, graduated first in his class, and met Simone de Beauvoir, the brilliant fellow student who became his life partner.

        3. Sartre and Beauvoir agreed to live a totally "transparent" relationship, to travel together, and to accept multiple sexual relations with others.

        4. This relationship endured to the end of their lives (with tensions); they never married and the friendship survived all their many affairs.

    B. After completing his studies, Sartre taught philosophy at a *lycée* in Le Havre. He began to write fiction and developed a plan to illustrate philosophical themes through literature, which was an unusual approach to philosophy.

        1. In 1933–1934, he had a fellowship to work at the French Institute in Berlin; he was in Germany during Hitler's first year in power.

        2. But Sartre was not interested in politics at this time; he studied the philosophy of Husserl and other German authors.

        3. His first published novel, *Nausea* (1938), showed a phenomenological quest for consciousness. The main character, Antoine Roquentin, explores both his physical and mental being, like an object to observe.

        4. The pain of this exploration (it induces feelings of nausea) became a literary example of the existential crisis that leads toward the self.

    C. Sartre had difficulty getting his work published and remained little known when France went to war with

Germany in 1939. He was conscripted into the French army, then captured with his unit in June 1940.

1. He spent nine months in a German prisoner of war camp before being released in March 1941; he remained in France during the occupation.

2. Before the war, he had shown little interest in public action of any kind, but the war and German occupation pushed him in a new direction; he joined (as a writer) in the Resistance and began to write about choices.

3. After the liberation, he made a four-month trip to America (1945), then became an extremely famous public intellectual in Paris—like Voltaire.

4. He wrote in many genres, including fiction, drama, philosophy, and essays; his famous essay "Existentialism Is a Humanism" (1945) was an example of his ability to popularize ideas for a broad public.

D. Sartre argued that the world has no intrinsic meaning because there is no God or higher reality to give meaning or truth to human beings.

1. Sartre was an atheistic existentialist (i.e., closer to Nietzsche than to Kierkegaard on this issue), and he stressed that individuals are both alone and alienated from one another.

2. There is no essence; there is only existence or, as Sartre puts it, "existence precedes essence," which means that there is no eternal soul.

3. Individuals must pass through an existential crisis in which they recognize the absurdities of existence: inevitable death, solitude, difficulty of communicating with others (Kierkegaard's theme).

E. Yet the painful confrontation with the absurd, meaningless human condition need not lead to complete despair; the individual can see that human consciousness exists in spite of the absurdity.

1. Human beings have the freedom to act, and the human mind and human acts can give meaning to individual lives and to the social world.

2. The meaning of individual life comes through actions that each person takes; there is no fixed essence, but there is human action.

3. In other words, you are what you do, and you define yourself by your acts. In Sartre's words, "Man is nothing else but what he makes of himself," and "full responsibility" for his existence rests on him.

F. Because human beings have no essence, they are always in a process of becoming; they have a radical freedom to become what they choose to be.

   1. But most people refuse to act with this freedom; they have "bad faith" because they let others define who they are.

   2. To be an authentic human being, Sartre said, you must use your freedom. You are not an artist unless you create or a political person unless you act politically—you cannot just talk in the café.

   3. Your actions will always define your existence; you must make choices—and even refusing to make choices is a choice.

   4. In the early postwar period, Sartre was critical of communism, but in the early 1950s, he tried to link Marxism and existentialism. This angered many of his friends and allies; it seemed to violate his themes.

G. Sartre became an advocate for anti-colonial revolutions; he stopped writing fiction and gradually lost influence in the later 1950s.

   1. Yet his account of how human beings must create meaning through free, decisive actions and choices retained cultural influence.

   2. He also had cultural influence through his journal, *Le Temps Modernes*.

IV. This emphasis on the need to take action in an otherwise absurd world appeared also in the work of Albert Camus (1913–1960), who nevertheless denied that he was an existentialist and eventually had a bitter falling out with Sartre.

A. Camus was born in Algeria; he had a Spanish mother and a French father, but his father was killed at the battle of the Marne in 1914.

   1. Like Sartre, he grew up close to his mother; she lived in poverty and supported herself by cleaning houses in Algiers.

2. Camus was an outstanding student who won scholarships and was able to attend the University of Algiers.

3. He married (1934), but the marriage dissolved within two years. He set off on travels and began to write; he later married again (to Francine Faure) and had two children.

B. He suffered from tuberculosis and did not serve in the military, but during the war and German occupation, he was an active journalist.

1. Camus wrote for Resistance publications and eventually became an editor of *Combat*, a newspaper that continued after the liberation.

2. In the midst of his journalism, however, he was also writing novels and drama. His first novel, *The Stranger* (1942), portrayed an alienated character, Meursault, who murders an Arab man.

3. Meursault never seems to find anything that is important to him; even his own mother's death evokes no feeling from him, and he goes to his own death with a strong sense of the absurdity of life.

C. Yet Camus moved on in his work to affirm that human choices could make a difference in the world, as he suggested in *The Plague* (1947).

1. This novel used the metaphor of a plague in a north African city to evoke the experience of World War II and the Occupation.

2. The main character, Dr. Rieux, struggles to act against forces he cannot control; he must work "to fight the plague."

D. Camus believed that "plagues" took many forms, but the greatest dangers emerged when human beings could not be free.

V. Despite their differences, Sartre and Camus came out of the Second World War with a shared belief that human freedom could make a difference in an absurd world. This idea of human action in a senseless world was appealing after 1945.

Essential Reading:

Jean-Paul Sartre, "Existentialism Is a Humanism," in *European Existentialism*, edited by Nina Langiulli, pp. 391–416.

Albert Camus, *The Plague*, part II, pp. 63–155.

Supplementary Reading:

Annie Cohen-Solal, *Sartre: A Life*, pp. 159–205, 247–269.

Herbert R. Lottman, *Albert Camus: A Biography*, pp. 425–438, 481–507.

Questions to Consider:

1. Do you agree with Sartre's claim that "you are what you do"?
2. Is existentialism ultimately an optimistic or pessimistic view of human life?

Lecture Eighteen—Transcript
Existential Philosophy

The ideas and themes of 20th-century philosophy can never be explained simply as a reflection of the era's terrible military and political events. And yet, as I was suggesting in the last lecture, the philosophers, like everyone else, were forced to respond to the world in which they were living. There was no way to ignore this context. And we've seen how German philosophers and social theorists had to make very difficult choices during the Nazi era. But their situation was by no means unique, because the Nazi army and occupation forces took control of many other European nations and forced intellectuals in France and elsewhere to choose sides. Wherever the occupying armies appeared, people had to decide what position they were going to take in this context. And if flight became impossible—if you couldn't leave, you couldn't go into exile—you had to decide. You had to decide between collaboration with the occupying force or resistance or the silence of what became internal exile. And the writers, like everyone else, had to make these decisions. Would you collaborate, resist, or simply fall silent and try to wait it out?

And this was the military and political context in which French existential philosophy emerged during the early 1940s. The existentialists stressed the absurdity of human existence. But they also stressed the human freedom to make choices no matter what the situation. And for various reasons, these ideas of existentialism seemed to fit very well in the post-war context. And the period after World War II became the sort of high point for modern existential philosophy.

The most important existential writers were the French authors—Jean-Paul Sartre, Albert Camus, and Simone de Beauvoir—all of whom in various ways responded to the German occupation of France. And all of them stressed the importance of taking personal action. They didn't all act in the same way, but they came out of this experience saying human beings must choose to act.

And so, in this lecture, I want to discuss existential thought with reference to this context—this context of the 1940s—and suggest why existentialism gained so much attention in the decade after 1945. And I think the broad cultural interest in existential philosophy far exceeded the public interest in the more technical, linguistic themes of England's logical positivism. We talked in an earlier lecture about the importance of linguistic philosophy in Britain, but the public really never took an interest in this. On the other hand, existentialism elicited enormous interest from people far beyond the university and far beyond academic circles. And I think the public response to existentialism grew in part from the literary skills of existentialist authors who often wrote novels to describe their ideas or to convey their ideas. And this is more appealing to people than the technical writing of academic philosophy.

But existential philosophy was also popular because it affirmed the value of human action. And so, for all of its pessimism in certain respects, it also had a rather optimistic claim that an individual human action could make some difference. At the very least, it could define a meaningful life. So, in contrast to the British linguistic philosophical concern with epistemology, the existentialists developed a new kind of concern with the problems of being and consciousness—what philosophers called the problem of ontology. Linguistic philosophers were concerned with epistemology—that's the question of how do we know what we know. But the existentialists focused on consciousness, on being, on the problem of reality and one's relation to it. And these ontological issues had already gained prominence in the 1920s and 1930s through the writings of philosophers such as Husserl and Heidegger, whom we discussed earlier, and both of who stressed the nature of existence. Heidegger and Husserl were very concerned with how one defines the meaning of human existence. Husserl had explored the ways in which a conscious subject becomes aware of the objects around it— the way in which consciousness reacts to the world around it. And Heidegger, for his part, had stressed that people must act to define their own being in the realm of time. And this concept of being would be important later for existentialist thought.

There are also other German philosophers who contributed to these ideas. One of who was the German philosopher, Karl Jaspers, who lived between 1883 and 1969. And Jaspers became famous for arguing that people must act with free will. He argued that human beings can act freely. And his thought also attracted wide attention. Jaspers said that it is the awareness of death that creates an anxiety in human beings. But it is also this anxiety about death that pushes people to pursue an active life. When you think about your own death, you feel a certain urgency to act in the world. And this is an interesting problem that the existentialists came back to again and again. How does the consciousness of your own death push you to take action? And the existentialists always put a lot of emphasis on that problem.

Well, the French existentialists, especially Sartre, drew on all of these ideas to develop their own conception of free human action. And they explored the phenomenological question of how one becomes conscious of being in the world. And then they try to link consciousness to free actions that could be used to confirm the individual's existence—a great deal of emphasis on existence and on actions.

So the German philosophical influences were crucial. The German thought of the early 20th century had an important impact on later existentialism. But the German occupation of France and the very painful experience of war, repression, and military occupation also contributed to the emergence and popularity of existentialism. So the Germans had both a philosophical and a material impact on the emergence of this movement.

I want to turn now to the specific work and ideas of Jean-Paul Sartre, because he is the key figure in French existential philosophy. Sartre was born in 1905. He would live until 1980. And he was born into a well-to-do, highly educated family. He was the son of a French naval officer, but his father died when young Jean-Paul was only about 15 months old. And so he was raised—the young Sartre—was raised by his mother and his mother's parents. His mother's family was originally from Alsace. They were a Protestant family, the Schweitzer family. This was the same family that included the famous Dr. Albert Schweitzer who went on later to win a Nobel Prize for his work—his medical work—in Africa. Sartre came from a family of well-educated and distinguished people.

As a child, Sartre was a bookish child. He loved books, but he seemed to have been quite happy. At least he was fairly happy until his mother remarried when he was 11 years old. I guess he had a kind of Oedipal dream life as a child. His father had died, and he had his mother to himself. And he always reported later that he detested his step-father, who appeared on the scene when he was 11 years old, and Sartre never reconciled with this step-father.

He went on to study at the École Normale Supérieur in Paris—that training ground for people who wanted to become philosophers and teach philosophy. And he graduated first in his class at the École Normale—was a top student and recognized from the beginning as an especially talented philosopher. He also at this time met Simone de Beauvoir, who was studying philosophy, although not at the École Normale. She was at the Sorbonne. She was a brilliant student. They became partners at this time, studying philosophy and preparing for their exams to become philosophy teachers. And Sartre and Beauvoir became in some way life partners. They agreed at this time that they would live a totally "transparent relation". That is to say that they would be totally honest with each other. They would confess all their personal thoughts and relationships. They would travel together, but they would also accept multiple sexual relationships with other people. This was to be a totally honest, transparent relationship. And it was a relationship that would endure to the end of their lives with some tensions, to be sure. But they remained intellectual partners throughout their lives. They never married, but their friendship survived all their many affairs. Neither of them were ever willing to marry anyone for various philosophical and personal reasons.

After completing his studies, Sartre went on to teach philosophy at a lycée in Le Havre, a port city in western France. And he began to write fiction. He began to develop a plan to illustrate his philosophical themes through literature. And this was quite unusual, because virtually no philosopher would think of illustrating his philosophical ideas through fiction, and yet this was one of Sartre's creative innovations. He would illustrate his ideas in literature.

In 1933 and '34, Sartre had a fellowship to work at the French Institute in Berlin, and so he spent a year in Germany. He was actually in Germany during the first year that Hitler was in power. But Sartre was not interested in politics at this time. He seemed what was more or less oblivious to what was going on in this very critical moment in German political and social history. He was studying the philosophy of German philosophers. He was reading the works of Husserl and other German authors. And when he went back to France, he set about to writing fiction that would somehow illustrate the phenomenological ideas that he had encountered in Germany. And his first published novel, which was called *Nausea*, was published in 1938. And it is, in many ways, an examination of this phenomenological exploration of consciousness.

The main character, a man named Antoine Roquentin—and Antoine passes life kind of traveling around to cafes and thinking about his own existence. And he explores both his physical and mental being—almost like an object to be observed. He will stare in the mirror, for example, becoming unconscious of himself as a physical object—just in the kind of phenomenological mode. And it is the pain of this self-exploration which induces feelings of nausea. Antoine becomes a kind of literary example of the existential crisis— a crisis of consciousness that leads finally towards itself—a consciousness of mortality, the consciousness of one's physical existence.

Sartre had difficulty getting his work published in the beginning, like most young authors. And even though he finally got the novel *Nausea* published in 1938, he remained very little known at the time France went to war with Germany in 1939. He was drafted into the French army, and then he was captured, taken prisoner with his military unit in June of 1940 during the catastrophic French military campaign when the Germans conquered France in June of 1940. And he spent the next nine months in a German prisoner of war camp, where he wrote extensively in journals and continued to develop his thought. He was finally released in March of 1941 under somewhat mysterious circumstances. It's never been known exactly how he got out of prison, but he then returned to France and remained in France during the occupation.

Now, before the war, Sartre had shown very little interest in public action of any kind. But the war and German occupation pushed him in a new direction. He joined, as a writer, into the campaign of the resistance—those people who were trying to resist the German occupation. He was not a particularly active member of the resistance. He was certainly not involved in any of the clandestine military activities and things like that. But he began to write plays about the necessity of making choices—about the problem of being free and how one resists forces outside the self. And in that sense, he made a kind of literary contribution to the evolving ideas and movement of the French resistance. And after the liberation in 1944, he went on to make a four-month trip to America. He was sent there in part of the American-French attempt to re-establish connections after the war. And he spent four months in early 1945 and then returned to Paris where he soon became an extremely famous public individual—much like Voltaire in the 18th century—an individual who published in all kinds of publications, who wrote in many genre, including fiction, drama, philosophy, political essays, and all kinds of commentaries on public affairs. He was the model of a kind of Enlightenment-style intellectual.

He also wrote for the general public, and one of his most famous essays was called *Existentialism Is a Humanism*, which he wrote in 1945. And this essay was an example of his ability to popularize philosophical ideas for a broad public. And in his work, Sartre argued that the world has no intrinsic meaning, because there is no God, there is no higher reality to give meaning or truth to human beings. So, we can say Sartre was an atheistic existentialist. In this respect, he was closer to the tradition of Nietzsche than to the Christian existentialism of someone like the 19th-century philosopher Søren Kierkegaard. Kierkegaard stressed many of the existential themes, but always insisted on the existence of God. But Sartre stressed that individuals are alone and alienated from each other. So there is no essence. There is only existence. Or, as Sartre puts it in a very famous phrase, "Existence precedes essence", which means there is no eternal soul. There is nothing that lives beyond the physical being of the individual.

Now, each individual as Sartre describes it, each individual must pass through an existential crisis in which he or she recognizes the absurdities of existence. What makes life absurd? Well, the inevitability of death—that issue of death again—you must die. Or the nature of solitude or the difficulty of communicating with other people—these are themes that Kierkegaard had already developed in the 18th century. That when you confront honestly the nature of your life, there is something deeply absurd about it, including your own death. And yet the painful confrontation with the absurd, meaningless, human condition does not have to lead to complete despair. Because even within this absurdity, the individual can see that human consciousness exists in spite of the absurdity. So above all, there is that consciousness—that thinking, conscious human being. And human beings have the freedom to act, drawing on that consciousness. So the human mind and human acts can give meaning to individual lives and to the social world. That's why there is not complete absurdity. There is meaning.

How does this meaning come about? The meaning of individual life comes about with the actions that each person takes. There is no fixed essence, but there is human actions. In other words, you are what you do. And you define yourself by your acts. And in Sartre words, "Man is nothing else but what he makes of himself. And full responsibility for his existence rests on him." You have to take full responsibility for your actions, but there is nothing else. You are what you do.

Since human beings have no essence, they are always in a process of becoming. They have a radical freedom to become what they choose to be. But Sartre insisted that most people refuse to act with this freedom. They have what he called bad faith, because they let others define who they are. And in order to be an authentic human being, Sartre said, you must use your freedom. If you don't use your freedom, you're abdicating your human ability to act in the world. So, for example, you may go around the world saying 'I am an artist'. But you are not an artist unless you actually create something. Or you may say 'I am very political. I'm involved in politics." But you are not a political person unless you act politically. You can't just sit in a café and talk about what you are. You are what you do. And your actions will always define your existence. In other words, you must make choices. And even refusing to make choices is a choice. And as Sartre points out, this is the choice that most people make, rather than taking a clear action—taking a strong action—they don't do anything. And yet in taking that non-action, people are in fact making a choice.

Now, in the early post-war period, Sartre was critical of communism. But in the early 1950s and throughout the 1950s, he worked increasingly to link existential with Marxism. And this was a philosophical and political move on Sartre's part that angered many of his friends and allies. It seemed to violate his main themes. It seemed to abdicate the individual to something beyond the individual. But Sartre became a strong advocate for several anti-colonial revolutions. He condemned the French policies in Algeria, and he stopped writing fiction and gradually lost much of his philosophical influence in the later 1950s and 1960s. And yet, his account of how human beings must create meaning through free action, through free and decisive actions and choices, retained a great deal of cultural influence. And he also had cultural influence through a journal that he had created with his friends and allies—a journal called *Le Temps Modernes, Modern Times,* which was a place that many of the most important writers of the period published their work. So Sartre was almost a cultural industry with his own publications and with his own journal.

Now, this emphasis on the need to take action in an otherwise absurd world appeared also in the work of Albert Camus. I want to say a few things about Camus. Camus lived from 1913 to 1960, and he regularly denied that he was an existentialist. And in fact he eventually had a bitter falling out with Sartre. But many of his themes resembled the key ideas of existential thought, and he has often been linked to existentialism despite his own protestations against certain aspects of existential philosophy.

Camus was born in Algeria. He had a Spanish mother and a French father. But his father was killed at the Battle of the Marne in 1914—another example of a family that was in some way shattered by the First World War. And so, like Sartre, young Camus grew up close to his mother and without a father. But Camus came from a much poorer family than Sartre did. His mother lived in poverty and supported herself by cleaning houses in Algiers. Camus had very little money. But he was an outstanding student that won scholarships, so he was able to attend the University of Algiers, where he studied philosophy. He married in 1934, but that marriage quickly dissolved within a couple of years. And then he later married again—a woman named Francine Faure. He had a couple of children. But he was mostly devoted to his writing and to his work.

He suffered from tuberculosis and health problems throughout his life, and he was unable to serve in the military, because of these health problems. But during the war and German occupation, he became a very active journalist. Camus wrote for various resistance publications, and eventually he became an editor of a newspaper called *Combat* that continued to publish after the Liberation. *Combat* was very well known as a center of resistance writing.

But in the midst of this journalism, he was also writing novels and drama. His first novel, *The Stranger*, appeared in 1942. And this work—one of those places where people often see the themes of existentialism—because it's a novel about an alienated character, a man named Meursault, who for no particular reason murders and Arab man on the beach in Algeria. Blinded by sun, he sort of absurdly just kills the man for no apparent reason. And Meursault never seems to find anything that is important or meaningful to him. So the world seems absurd. Even with his mother's death, he evokes no feeling from Meursault. And he goes to his own death—he's put to death for this murder—he goes to his own death with a strong sense of the absurdity of life. He's a stranger in the world in which he lives.

So there is in some of Camus' work a strong sense of the absurdity or purposelessness of life. And yet, Camus moved on in his post-war work to affirm that human choices can make a difference in the world, and this is suggested fairly clearly in his later novel, *The Plague*, which was published in 1947. This novel used the metaphor of a play in a North African city to evoke the experience of World War II and the occupation. It's sort of a metaphor of people who are trapped in a city. No one can go out or come in—much like during the occupation during the war. The main character is a doctor, a man named Dr. Rieux, who struggles to act against forces he simply can't control—the plague. It's something you're presented with. You can't control it. So the question is: how do you react to what you are given? And the narrator of the novel notes Rieux's belief suggests you have to take action. And this is a quote from the novel—"that a fight must be put up in this way or that and that there must be no bowing down." In other words, a doctor must try to save others. He must work to fight the plague, even though he didn't choose the plague, he can't control the plague. He has to fight against it.

And Camus believed that plagues took many forms. The plague could come in many ways, in many times. But the greatest danger emerged when human beings could not be free. That was the worst plague of all. And so, in contrast to Sartre, Camus condemned communist oppression in Eastern Europe. He also refused to support the Algerian Revolution. This was a great crisis in Camus' life, because he came from Algeria. He identified with the French settlers who had lived there for generations. He could never fully embrace the cause of the Algerian Revolution. And this kind of choice—both his critique of communism and his critique of the Algerian Revolution—separated Camus from Sartre and from many other French writers in the 1950s. But as Camus saw it, the imperatives of human freedom justified the political choices he made. He felt his side was the defense of freedom.

Well, as it happened, Camus himself died rather absurdly in a car accident at the age of forty-six. We don't know what else he would have done had he lived to a full lifespan, but he died at age 46 without reconciling with Sartre, who had been a friend during the Second World War and during the time they were writing the resistance publications. But despite their differences, Sartre and Camus came out of the Second World War with the shared belief that human freedom could make a difference in an absurd world—that human action gave purpose and meaning to what was otherwise a meaningless human existence.

Now, from the beginning, there were many critics of existentialism. And many of these critics said that the philosophy was flawed because it was too subjectivist—it placed too much emphasis in the hands of the individual actor or it assumed that individuals were free to do whatever they wanted to do. And the critics said that existentialism did not understand the social and cultural and psychological constraints on individual action. In fact, this critique of existentialism may explain Sartre's move towards Marxism. I think he wanted to show that existentialism could have a strong collective or social agenda. It could take a collective action.

There are other critics who saw in existentialism a kind of naïve optimism. An optimism that said even in the absurdity of this world, individuals are free. They can be whatever they want to be, they can do whatever they want to do. And many critics said that's not true. The constraints of social and historical condition are such that people are not really free.

And yet, I think that this idea that humans are free—that human action does make a difference in a senseless world was very appealing after 1945. And it was an idea that many other writers would pick up in their own ways in post-war literary work.

Lecture Nineteen
Literature and Memory in Postwar Culture

Scope:

The traumatic events of 20th-century European history provoked responses in every literary genre as writers struggled with the same problem: How could one make sense of brutal totalitarian regimes, modern warfare, and the Holocaust? This lecture looks at three authors who explored the modern European crisis from different cultural and personal perspectives: Primo Levi, George Orwell, and Günther Grass. All these writers sought to understand how lies and dehumanizing, irrational mass murder had shattered modern European civilization. Responding to what they had seen in their own lives, Levi, Orwell, and Grass wanted to remind readers of recent horrors and help prevent the recurrence of such deadly events in the future.

Outline

I. The violence and mass murder of the Second World War went far beyond anything that modern Europeans had ever seen, especially among civilians; some estimates place the total number of war-related deaths at 60 million (including deaths in Asia).

    A. The number of civilians killed in Europe alone can never be known, but at least six million died in the Holocaust and millions more died in bombed-out cities, forced labor camps, and brutal military reprisals.

        1. Postwar intellectuals faced painful, almost unanswerable questions about the sources of this mass violence and cruelty in modern history.

        2. Obviously, militarism, racism, and extremist ideologies had led to the war, but how could so many people cooperate in such policies?

    B. The attempt to describe and understand the scale of the tragedy became one of the most important themes in subsequent European cultural history.

1. The war, the Holocaust, and the terrible "banality of evil" (as Hannah Arendt described it) remain even now inescapable problems for anyone who tries to understand 20th-century European history.

2. The search for understanding can begin, among other places, in the writings of people who managed to survive the war's terrible events.

C. These literary responses to the war appear in the works of every postwar European culture, but I want to focus on three writers: Primo Levi, George Orwell, and Günther Grass.

1. These authors had very different experiences, yet all were determined to make their readers remember and analyze the meaning of the war.

2. They came from different societies (Italy, England, Germany), but their books attracted readers across all national boundaries.

3. They all show how writing was an essential tool for cultural memory.

II. The struggle to make sense of the recent violence was especially painful for those few people who actually survived imprisonment in a Nazi death camp.

A. This was the story of the Jewish Italian writer Primo Levi (1919–1987), who spent 10 months in the death camp at Auschwitz.

1. Levi grew up in a Jewish family in Turin, but he apparently felt little specific awareness of his Jewish identity as a young man.

2. He studied chemistry at the University of Turin and received a doctorate, though while he was there, the fascists banned Jewish students from future admissions to the university.

B. He began to work as a chemist, then joined an anti-fascist partisan group after the Germans occupied northern Italy to protect Mussolini.

1. Levi was soon arrested, however, and sent to a prison camp in Italy; he was held with more than 600 other Jewish prisoners who were deported to Auschwitz in February 1944.

    2. Levi was one of the very few deportees to survive Auschwitz. As a chemist, he was put to work in a laboratory that the chemical company I.G. Farben operated at Auschwitz.

C. Levi always described himself as a random survivor; he was in the infirmary as the Russian army approached (in January 1945) and the German guards fled.

    1. After his liberation from the camp, he wandered around Eastern Europe for almost 10 months before reaching Turin in October 1945.

    2. He soon began writing about his experiences and produced a book called *If This Is a Man* (1947); it was later republished and translated into English as *Survival in Auschwitz*.

    3. He also wrote an account of his long trip home (*The Reawakening* [1963]) and other important works in the 1970s and 1980s.

    4. He worked for more than 30 years as a chemist for a paint company and struggled with depression until committing suicide in 1987.

D. Levi's description of what he saw at Auschwitz is one of the most powerful memoirs ever written; he wrote in the dispassionate style of a scientist.

    1. He seems to have lived always with a sense of guilt about his own survival, but he was also determined to tell the story of Auschwitz to ensure that the dead would never be forgotten.

    2. He wrote about the humiliating treatment of prisoners, struggles to find food, the brutality of the guards, and prisoner betrayals.

    3. Levi described the dehumanizing, brutal processes of genocide as a complete breakdown of human rationality. Survival was a matter of blind fate, and prisoners were stripped of all human dignity.

    4. The images evoked the nightmares of Dante's Inferno— a place in which the damned must live without hope and without escape.

E. Reduced to nothing but a number (174517) that was tattooed on his arm, Levi felt that all human feeling, reason, and solidarity were taken from prisoners.

    1. "Here the struggle to survive is without respite," he wrote, "because everyone is desperately and ferociously alone."

    2. The horror of this experience emerged from Levi's remarkable book, yet he also wanted to show (by the act of writing) that memory and moral judgments could survive, so long as someone told the story.

    3. Levi's books, along with the memoirs of others, expressed the deep desire to pull human meaning and life from the ruins of the war.

III. Few writers could relate the horrific experiences of a death camp, but George Orwell found other themes and miseries to describe in his postwar novels.

    A. Orwell (1903–1950), whose real name was Eric Blair, grew up in southern England and attended the famous "public school" at Eton.

        1. He then went off to serve in the imperial police in Burma, avoiding the typical privileged education at Cambridge or Oxford.

        2. After five years in Asia, he decided to become a writer, returned to England, lived for a time in Paris, and began to worry about politics.

        3. He went to Spain during the Spanish Civil War and joined the anti-fascist troops in Catalonia; he was wounded in the throat in May 1937.

        4. Before leaving Spain, he witnessed a communist crackdown on other anti-fascist groups, including the socialists and anarchists.

    B. The encounter with communists in Spain provoked concerns about political ideologies that produce repression. Orwell himself was a firm democratic socialist.

        1. Orwell learned before World War II that he had tuberculosis and was unable to serve in the British army during the war; he wrote about the war for newspapers and found himself deeply involved in events.

2. He was in London during the massive bombing of the city. He and his wife (Eileen O'Shaughnessy) were even bombed out of their home.
3. In February 1945, he went to France as a war correspondent and pushed on to Germany. Meanwhile, his wife died after surgery in England.

C. Orwell emerged from the war with a deep sense of anxiety about the direction of modern society; he worried that totalitarianism would persist in new ways.
   1. His satirical novel *Animal Farm* (1945) warned about the dangers of communist dictatorships (he remained a democratic socialist).
   2. He wanted to make his warnings about totalitarianism even more pointed in his later novel, *1984* (1949), which gained a large audience.

D. Orwell wrote the book while he was, essentially, dying from tuberculosis; it has been criticized for its lack of artistic subtlety and nuance.
   1. Yet the book expressed a deep fear of totalitarianism that Orwell had drawn from his encounters with fascism and communism.
   2. The book portrays a society controlled by a single political party, the "Inner Party," whose leader is known as Big Brother. The party controls all definitions of truth and uses a kind of "doublethink."
   3. Thought Police keep track of everyone and promote such ideas as "War Is Peace," and "Ignorance Is Truth." Individuals have no autonomy.
   4. The main character, Winston Smith, learns that "Big Brother is watching" all the time and defending the "higher good."

E. The party also controls all information about the past so that "history" serves only the interest of the ruling group. For Orwell, this was the modern danger.
   1. Orwell's story differed from Levi's, but he, too, was worried about the loss of reason, judgment, memory, and individual dignity.

2. The end of World War II did not mean that the problem had gone away; Orwell's book soon joined the Cold War literary canon.

IV. The literary attempt to represent the experience and memory of totalitarianism and war could also be found in the postwar German writing of Günther Grass.

    A. Grass (1927–) grew up in a Catholic family in the German city of Danzig, which is now the city of Gdansk in Poland. He was five years old when Hitler came to power and his education was strongly affected by Nazism.

        1. Danzig became part of the Third Reich in September 1939, and young Grass soon enrolled in the Hitler Youth.

        2. He entered the German army in the last phase of the war and was wounded in late fighting; he ended up in an American POW camp.

    B. Out of this disorienting experience, he began to reevaluate all his earlier life; he learned about the death camps and heard stories that he disbelieved at first. But he later reported that his whole view of Germany was altered.

    C. He decided that he must keep the memory of what Germans had done (and not done) during the Nazi years in view of the German public.

        1. Grass became active in a new association of writers, the Group 47, which had been founded in 1947 to revive German literature after the war and to defend the traditions of Enlightenment tolerance.

        2. He settled in West Germany, married a Swiss woman (Anna Schwarz), and started to write a novel that would become *The Tin Drum* (1959).

    D. This novel told the story of a boy named Oskar who, at age three, stopped growing, but played a drum and watched his society during the rise of Nazism, World War II, and the postwar era.

        1. He is not exactly a hero, but unlike the adults, he refuses to join the frenzy for Nazism. His best friend is a Jewish toy merchant who kills himself because of Nazi anti-Semitism.

2. Oskar (and Grass) rejects dogmatic language and actions.
3. The novel shows the danger of conformity, simple clichés, and refusal to take responsible actions; the style is somewhat surreal.

E. Grass wrote other novels on these issues (*The Tin Drum* was part of a Danzig Trilogy), but he also threw himself into political action in the Socialist Party.

F. But Grass's postwar works are not about democratic socialism; they are, like the books of Levi and Orwell, part of the literary response to modern horrors.

G. Grass wanted Germans to remember what they had done and to defend reason, tolerance, and patient reformism in a world that must be rebuilt.

Essential Reading:

Primo Levi, *Survival in Auschwitz*, pp. 9–173.

George Orwell, *1984*, pp. 5–87.

Supplementary Reading:

Julian Preece, *The Life and Work of Günter Grass*, pp. 34–67.

Questions to Consider:

1. Were the events of the Holocaust unique in human history?
2. Does Orwell's *1984* portray dangers that exist only in totalitarian states?

Lecture Nineteen—Transcript
Literature and Memory in Postwar Culture

We've seen in the last several lectures about how European philosophers and writers were forced to respond to the events of World War II. And of course this war was an extraordinary event. It went beyond anything that Europeans had known before. The violence and mass murder of the Second World War went beyond even the horrors of World War I—and especially for civilians, because civilian deaths were very limited in the First World War. But in the Second World War, almost everyone in the countries that were at was affected by bombings and by military occupations.

Some estimates about the death toll of the Second World War placed the total number of war-related deaths as high as 60 million people, including deaths in Asia as well as in Europe. And that of course includes large numbers of deaths in China and Japan. But even in the Soviet Union alone, it has been estimated that between 20 and 25 million people died. We'll never know exactly how many civilians were killed in Europe or in other parts of the world, but we know that at least six million died in the Holocaust alone, and millions more died in bombed out cities and forced labor camps and brutal military reprisals in all the ebb and flow of the war, which millions of people had their lives shattered.

And so, post-war intellectuals faced a painful and almost unanswerable question trying to understand the sources of this mass violence and cruelty. How could such an explosion of mass violence and cruelty take place in what Europeans had always liked to think of as the most modern and civilized part of the globe. And yet, here was the center of the most barbarous actions that anyone could identify—certainly in modern times.

Now, it was obvious that various forms of militarism, racism, and extremist ideologies had led to this war, but the question always remained: how could so many people cooperate in these policies? How could so many educated, civilized people become part of this process? And so the attempt to describe and to understand the scale of this tragedy became one of the most important themes in subsequent European cultural history. Again and again, intellectuals have tried to understand the enormity of this event—the war, the Holocaust, the terrible banality of evil—as Hannah Arendt described it—all of this remained even now the inescapable problems of anyone who tries to understand 20th-century history. And there are many, many historians still at work trying to understand it. There are many writers and filmmakers and novelists who are still coming to terms with that moment in modern European history.

Well, I think that search for understanding this event can begin—among other places—in the writings of people who somehow manage to survive these terrible events. And these literary responses to the war can be found in every one of the post-war European cultures. You couldn't go anywhere without encountering writers who were trying to explain—to make sense—of what happened. But I want to concentrate on three writers to explore some of the ways in which the events of World War II were interpreted by creative thinkers. I want to focus on the works of Primo Levi, on George Orwell, and on Günther Grass. And these writers—although they had very different experiences—all tried to make their readers to remember and also to analyze the meaning of the way. And their work also reached wide audiences of readers.

They came from different societies—Levi from Italy, Orwell from England, and Grass from Germany. But their books also attracted readers from across national boundaries. So even now, you can find a great deal of these works that are not specifically limited to one national culture or experience. And above all, I think these writers show how writing was an essential tool for cultural memory—that writing has been one of the most important mechanisms for making sense of this experience and one of the ways of gaining some perspective for what seemed to be beyond sense—beyond any kind of normal analysis.

Now, the struggle to make sense of the recent violence—the violence of the war—was especially painful for those few persons who actually survived imprisonment in a Nazi death camp. And I want to begin by saying a few things about the work of the Italian Jewish writer, Primo Levi, who was one of these few survivors. His story is a remarkable story.

Levi was born in 1919. And he spent 10 months in a death camp—in Auschwitz. He came through the war. And Primo Levi was one of those people who was able to remember and write about it. In fact, he lived until 1987. His work has become one of the most important memoirs of this experience.

Levi grew up in a Jewish family in Turin. But apparently as a child and as a long man, he felt very little specific awareness of his Jewish identity. His family was highly assimilated into Italian culture. He was educated at the Italian schools and at the University of Turin. He studied chemistry at the University of Turin and received a doctorate in chemistry. Although while he was still at the university, the fascists banned Jewish students to future admissions to the university. This was one of the first moments when he began to be aware of the precarious situation of Jews in Italian society. But because he had already enrolled in the university, Levi was allowed to continue and complete his studies.

And after the university, he began to work as a chemist in Turin. But after the war had been going on for a while—the Second World War—he ended up joining an anti-fascist, partisan group. After the German army occupied northern Italy—this was to protect Mussolini. Germans actually sent their army into northern Italy, and this was the moment in which Primo Levi joined in the opposition— the resistance. But he was very quickly arrested and sent to a prison camp in Italy, where he was held with over 600 other Jewish prisoners who were then deported to Auschwitz in February of 1944. And Levi was one of the very few deportees to survive imprisonment in Auschwitz. Because he was a chemist, he was put to work in a laboratory that the chemical company I.G. Farben operated at Auschwitz—the big German chemical company was using some facilities at Auschwitz to pursue various forms of research. And Primo Levi had these unique skills as a chemist. But he always described himself as a random survivor. 'I'm a very lucky man,' he said, 'it could have happened in any other way.' But he survived. He happened to be in the infirmary. He had an illness—he had a lot of illnesses—but he was particularly ill at the moment when the Russian army approached in January of 1945. And at the very end, the German guards killed a number of the prisoners, but because he was away from the other prisoners, somehow he was missed, and the German guards fled as the Russian army arrived. And so he was liberated after roughly 10 months in the camp. And after his liberation, he wandered around Eastern Europe for almost 10 more months. He couldn't simply get on a train and go from Auschwitz back to Turin. He wandered into Russia, into various parts of Central

Europe, and finally returned home in October 1945—months after the war came to an end.

Well, this experience had, of course, completely transformed his understanding of himself and his place in the world, and he felt the need to begin writing about it. And so in the next two years, he wrote a book—a kind of memoir about his experience in Auschwitz. It was published in 1947—a very small press run—not too many copies published. The book was called, *If This Is a Man*. It was published and it soon kind of dropped out of sight. But then it was later republished and also translated into English under the title, *Survival in Auschwitz*, which is the most common title in English that one would encounter. If you look for the book, it's often called *Survival in Auschwitz*.

He later wrote also an account of that long, meandering trip home that took months after he fled the prison camp—after he fled Auschwitz. This book was called *The Reawakening*. It was published in 1963. And then he went on to publish other important works in the 1970s and 1980s, including works of fiction.

After he got back to Turin, he returned to his old work as a chemist. He worked for more than 30 years as a chemist in a paint company. But he always struggled with depression and anxiety and guilt— mainly, I think, because of his ambivalence about being a survivor. And in 1987, he seems to have committed suicide. It's a bit mysterious. He fell from his apartment on the fourth or fifth floor of an apartment building in Turin. And most people believe it was out of depression and despair and that he ultimately killed himself.

Now, Primo Levi's description of what he saw at Auschwitz is one of the most powerful memoirs ever written. He wrote in the dispassionate style of a scientist—he was, after all, a chemist. And he lays out this story with a kind of relentless, dispassionate, scientific style. And he seemed always to have lived after this experience with a deep sense of guilt. And it was, in part, this deep sense of guilt that made him so determined to tell this story. He wanted to tell the story of Auschwitz in order to ensure that the dead would never be forgotten.

And so he tried to describe the tedium, the banality, the terror of what it was like to be there, because all of these things were part of the experience. He wrote about the humiliating treatment of prisoners, what happened when they arrived at camp, how they went on to struggle to find food. He wrote about the brutality of the guards. He wrote about the betrayals of certain prisoners who tried to gain the favor of the guards. And above all, Levi described the dehumanizing, brutal process of genocide—a process that he saw as the complete breakdown of human decency and a process that destroyed human rationality among the prisoners themselves. It was a process in which people were reduced virtually to the level of animal survival. And survival was, in fact, the matter of blind fate—the whim of a guard or a prisoner's anger or simply being at the wrong place at the wrong time—being chosen to work for a while or being chosen to go right to the gas chambers. In other words, prisoners were stripped of all human dignity.

And the images that Levi develops in the book evokes some of the nightmares of *Dante's Inferno*, the great medieval Italian work that describes the entry into Hell. Because the entry into Auschwitz is like entering into a place of the damned—a place in which the damned have to live without hope and without any chance of escape.

And Primo Levi himself described the experience of being reduced to nothing else but a number. He remembered his number, because his number was tattooed on his arm. He had the number 174517. That's all he was. That's all these prisoners were. They each had a number. And Levi felt that all human feeling—all human reason and solidarity—were taken from the prisoners. As he explained in his memoirs, he said, "Here, the struggle to survive is without respite, because everyone is desperately and ferociously alone."—the endless struggle for survival, because everyone is desperately and ferociously alone. And the horror of this experience emerged from Levi's remarkable book. He tried to convey the meaning of this experience by the act of writing. He thought that by writing, he could show the meaning of this event and somehow the memory and also the possibility for moral judgment would survive so long as someone told the story.

And so, Levi's books along with the memoirs of others expressed this deep desire to pull human meaning and life from the ruins of the war. That even in this most desperate situation, humanity in some rare ways was able to continue. And Primo Levi himself was an example. He had survived. He had somehow shown a way to continue living.

Now, very few writers could describe the horrific experiences that Levi described in his death camp. But other writers wrote about other aspects of the experience of World War II. And I want to turn now to what George Orwell tried to do in the period following the war, because George Orwell found other themes and memories and miseries to describe in his post-war novels.

Orwell's real name was Eric Blair. He was born in 1903. He lived until 1950. He grew up in southern England and attended a famous public school in Eton. It was, of course, a private school, but the British say it was a public school at Eton. And then he went off to serve in the imperial police in Burma. He avoided the typical privileged education at Cambridge or Oxford and instead went off and became a policeman in Burma—a very unusual career path for someone coming out of Eton.

But after five years in Asia, he decided that he wanted to become a writer. So he returned to England. He began to write. He lived for some time in Paris—began to write there, wrote about his experiences in Paris. And he became increasingly concerned about politics in those years of the 1930s—those times when people had to choose their political position. In fact, George Orwell went on to Spain, because he was so concerned about the Spanish Civil War and the impending triumph of the fascist forces in Spain that Orwell joined the anti-fascist troops in Catalonia—the area around Barcelona. He fought in the Spanish Civil War. He was, in fact, wounded in the throat in May of 1937, and he eventually had to leave Spain because of his injuries.

But before he left Spain, he witnessed a communist crackdown on other anti-fascist groups, including the socialists and the anarchists. And this encounter with communist repression among the anti-fascist groups in Spain provoked a great deal of concern in Orwell about political ideologies that produced repression.

He was himself a confirmed democratic socialist. He wanted a democratic socialist system. But certainly after his time in Spain, he was very hostile to communism, and he wrote about this in a memorable book—a kind of autobiographical memoir called Homage to Catalonia, which is one of Orwell's best writings.

Well, Orwell learned just before World War II that he had tuberculosis. And so he was unable to serve in the British army during the Second World War. But he wanted to serve in some capacity, so he wrote about the war in newspapers. He became a kind of war journalist, and he found himself very deeply involved in the events of the period. In fact, he was in London during the period of the massive bombing of that city. And he was greatly affected by the bombing attacks. He and his wife, Eileen O'Shaughnessy, were even bombed out of their home. So it was not an abstract issue for him. It was something that he knew firsthand.

In February of 1945, as the English and America troops were making their way across Europe, Orwell went to France as a war correspondent, and he pushed on into Germany and was present in Germany during the last phases of the war. He had left his wife behind in England. She, in fact, died after surgery in England, so he never saw his wife again after this trip.

But he came out of the war with a deep sense of anxiety—and anxiety about the direction of modern society. And Orwell worried that totalitarianism would exist—would continue to operate—in new ways—that the end of the war did not mean the end of totalitarian systems, and he was particularly concerned about communism. But he was also worried about possible revival of other kinds of fascist and other forms of right-wing totalitarian movements.

He wrote a satirical novel called *Animal Farm*, which appeared in 1945. And this novel warned about the dangers of communist dictatorships. Remember, Orwell was always identifying with democratic socialism, and for him, in many ways, the communist dictatorship represented the greatest threat. So *Animal Farm* was a kind of satirical look at the way in which people operate in some kind of a dictatorship.

But he wanted to make his warnings about totalitarian regimes even more explicit. And so he went on to write the novel for which he is probably best known—a novel called, simply *1984*, which he wrote in 1948. He simply reversed 48 and it became 84. The book was published in 1949. It gained a very large audience—an international audience. And it became Orwell's most enduring work, in many ways.

He actually wrote this book while he was dying from tuberculosis. He was in very poor health. It was a great struggle to finish this book in the last two years of his life. And the book, *1984*, has often been criticized for its lack of artistic subtlety and nuance. And yet, this book expressed a deep fear of totalitarianism—a fear that Orwell had drawn from his encounters with fascism and communism. It portrays a society controlled by a single political party—the Inner Party, whose leader is known as Big Brother. And the party controls all definitions of truth, and the party employs a kind of double-think to keep the population propagandized. There's a thought police that keeps track of everyone. And this thought police promotes ideas that might seem absurd but are ideas of the society—ideas such as war is peach or ignorance is truth. In other words, what would seem to make sense is kind of turned upside down. It's a kind of strange reversal of terms. And we get an adjective from this—the Orwellian sense of bad language.

Well, in this world, Orwell shows that individuals have no autonomy. They are controlled by forces beyond their world. They have no way of staking out an independent position. The main character of the book, a man named Winston Smith, learns that Big Brother is watching all the time and defending what is called the higher good. The Party also controls all information about the past so that history only serves the interest of the ruling group. And this for Orwell was the great modern danger. Orwell's story differed from Levi's story. He was having a different concern—the problem of totalitarianism. However, much like Primo Levi, he was worried about the loss of reason—about the loss of judgment, about the collapse of memory, and about the decline of individual dignity. And for Orwell, the end of World War II did not mean that these problems did not go away. And, in fact, Orwell's book, *1984*, soon entered into the Cold War literary canon and became one of the most influential portraits of the problems of totalitarian societies.

The literary attempt to represent the experience and memory of totalitarianism and war also appeared in post-war German literature. And I want to turn now to the German writings of Günther Grass. Grass was born in 1927. And he grew up in a Catholic family in the German city of Danzig, which is now the city in Poland—Gdansk. It's right on the coast in northern Poland. Grass was only five years old when Hitler came to power, so his entire education was strongly affected by the Nazi ideology and by the Nazi system.

And Danzig itself became part of the Third Reich in September of 1939. He was aware of Nazism, there were agitators, there were people in Danzig who were promoting Nazism all along, but then it was officially part of the Third Reich from September of 1939 on. And young Günther Grass was enrolled in the Hitler Youth.

He later enrolled in the German army in the last days of the war, and he was wounded in fighting at the very end of the war. He actually ended up in an American POW camp, where he began to rethink the experience of the war. And out of this disorienting experience, he began to re-evaluate all of his earlier life. He began to re-evaluate what he had learned as a young man growing up. And he heard about the death camps and he heard stories that at first he disbelieved. He just couldn't imagine that all of these things could have happened. But later he reported that as he learned what had happened, his whole view of Germany was transformed. He wrote in one of his later writings, he said, "When I was 19, I began to have an inkling of the guilt our people had knowingly and unknowingly accumulated...of the burden and responsibility that my generation and the next would bear." And that became one of Günther Grass' main themes—the burden and responsibility that future German generations would have to bear.

Well, this dawning realization of German guild led Grass first toward withdrawal. He went to work on a farm—sort of pulled away from city life. And then he returned into an urban context. He began to study the arts. He studied graphic design. He studied sculpture. He became interested in jazz music. In fact, he began to play the drums in a jazz band. He began to write poetry and plays, and he felt that the arts—and particularly writing—offered a way to keep alive the memory of what Germans had done during the Second World War. He wanted Germans to remember not only what they had done but also what they had not done during the Nazi years. And he wanted to keep this period of Nazi history firmly in view of the German public.

Grass became active in a new association of writers—the so-called Group 47, which had been founded in 1947 to revive German literature after the Second World War. And this group also wanted to defend the traditions of Enlightenment and tolerance—those traditions that had been so completely rejected by the Nazi period in German history.

So Grass settled in West Germany. He married a Swiss woman—a woman named Anna Schwarz. And he started to write a novel that would become known as *The Tin Drum*. *The Tin Drum* was published in 1959 and immediately attracted enormous interest and international acclaim. This novel tells the story of a boy named Oskar, who at age three, somehow stops growing. Oskar is going to stay a child. But he plays a drum, and he goes around watching his society during the rise of Nazism, during the period of World War II, and also during the immediate post-war era. And little Oskar is not exactly a hero, but unlike the adults in his world, he refuses to join the frenzy for Nazism. He maintains some kind of critical distance. His best friend is a Jewish toy merchant who kills himself because of Nazi anti-Semitism. And it seems that Oskar rejects dogmatic intolerant language and actions. He looks at this with a kind of puzzled, bewildered look from the outside—a view that Grass himself seems to share—that he's looking at these events in the same way as Oskar.

And the novel shows again and again the danger of conformity, the danger of accepting simple clichés, the danger of refusing to take responsible actions. And the style of the novel is somewhat surreal. It's kind of unbelievable in some ways. And I think that what Grass is trying to do is to show how Germans had acted with what the existentialists would call bad faith. They refused to take responsible actions. They conformed to what the ruling powers told them to do.

Now, Grass went on to write other novels on these issues. *The Tin Drum* was simply part of what he called a Danzig Trilogy. But he also went on to throw himself into political action. He became active in the socialist party. He was a close ally of the democratic social chancellor, Willy Brandt. And his writing attracted wide recognition. In fact, he won a Nobel Prize for literature in 1999. But Grass's post-war works are not really about democratic socialism. They are part of the literary response to modern horrors and the Second World War. And in this respect, they can be compared to the works of Primo Levi and George Orwell, because Grass wanted Germans to remember what they had done and to defend reason and tolerance and patient reformism in a world that needed to be rebuilt. He wanted Germans to redefine themselves in a modern age.

And we can see this kind of theme emerging in other post-war work, including new feminist writers, who I want to discuss in the next lecture.

Lecture Twenty
Redefining Modern Feminism

Scope:

Intellectual and political interest in human freedom and personal choices contributed to a new wave of feminist thought that sought to describe and change traditional restrictions on the rights of women. As women gradually gained the right to vote, feminists developed a more general assessment of other social, cultural, and economic constraints that women faced in both their private and public lives. This lecture notes three "waves" of 20th-century feminist thought, giving particular attention to the ideas of Virginia Woolf and Simone de Beauvoir. European feminism drew many of its subsequent cultural themes from Beauvoir's influential book *The Second Sex* (1949), but her existential account of human identity also provoked criticisms from theorists who argued that language and the unconscious mind shape gender identities.

Outline

I. The struggle to define and defend human dignity and autonomy amid constraining or destructive modern social contexts extended also to movements for women's rights.

   A. Feminism became one of the most successful modern "isms" in that many of the traditional restrictions on women's voting rights, economic rights, education, and personal freedom disappeared in the 20th century.

      1. But changes in some spheres of political and economic life also created new awareness of the cultural limits that still shaped women's lives.

      2. The movement for women's rights evolved through what are often called three "waves" of modern feminist thought.

   B. The first wave was the (generally) successful campaign for voting rights; it was led by feminist activists, such as Emmeline Pankhurst (1858–1928).

      1. Pankhurst was one of the English suffragists who participated in a sometimes violent campaign for women's voting rights before World War I. English women got the right to vote at the end of that war.

2. Women also gained voting rights in Germany at that time, but they could not vote in France and Italy until the end of World War II.

C. The acquisition of voting rights did not end the debate about women's role in public life; it was a long time before they began to hold government offices.

    1. In the aftermath of the successful campaign for voting rights, however, some women started to develop a second wave of feminist writing that stressed the social, economic, and cultural constraints on women.

    2. This new phase of feminism developed in various national contexts, but it gained particular influence in England and France through the work of such writers as Virginia Woolf and Simone de Beauvoir.

    3. This lecture focuses on this second phase of 20th-century feminist thought and emphasizes the wide influence of Beauvoir's book *The Second Sex*.

    4. Both Woolf and Beauvoir urged women to pursue a new cultural liberation that would extend beyond the realm of political rights.

D. By the late 20th century, however, a third wave of feminist thought criticized Beauvoir for ignoring the deeper structures of language and unconscious thought that continued to impede women's liberation. This third wave of feminist thought has splintered in many directions, but it also builds on earlier feminist themes.

II. We have seen how Virginia Woolf (1882–1941) made important contributions to the literary style and themes of the modern English novel.

A. She tried to represent the complexity of women in her fictional works, but she developed her most notable commentary on women and society in her short book *A Room of One's Own* (1929).

    1. Published soon after women gained the right to vote, Woolf's book turned to the question of why women's cultural productions in art, literature, and scholarship had never matched the productions of men.

2. She said that women never had enough money to support artistic work, or enough time away from family obligations to write books.

3. The independent, creative woman needed "a room of one's own" and some financial autonomy; she also needed to resist the deep cultural message that said "women cannot create as well as men."

B. No wonder that women had not yet written plays like those of Shakespeare; if Shakespeare had had a sister, she could never have pursued literary work.

1. Women were blocked from the personal freedom (e.g., travel, love affairs, risk taking) and education that made creative work possible.

2. Woolf argued that this situation was changing in the modern era, though women should not write or create exactly like men.

3. Women must find their own cultural voices to represent their own experiences, friendships, and views of reality.

4. Women must also recover the history of women—a history that remained invisible in history books and official cultural memory.

III. Woolf's imaginative, concise description of the quest for a woman's voice and an independent "selfhood" offered a starting point for the work of Simone de Beauvoir.

A. Beauvoir (1908–1986) was an important existentialist philosopher in France whose early published works were mostly novels and short stories.

1. She grew up in a bourgeois Catholic family and went to Catholic schools until she entered the Sorbonne, where she studied philosophy.

2. Although few women at that time had ever taught philosophy, she decided to become a philosophy teacher. In studying for the qualifying exam, she met Jean-Paul Sartre.

3. They took the exam in the same year (1929); he placed first, and she placed second, but she was the youngest person ever to pass the exam.

B. The relationship with Sartre, as we've noted earlier, became an enduring, complex emotional component of Beauvoir's life. They struggled to have a completely "honest" relationship, but this carried emotional costs.

1. Beauvoir taught philosophy in provincial *lycées*, then settled in Paris during the Second World War.
2. She wrote novels (e.g., *She Came to Stay* [1943] and *The Blood of Others* [1945]) that explored relationships and personal choices.
3. Beauvoir used literature to portray her existential philosophical ideas; she also wrote philosophical essays.

C. After the war, she traveled in America, where she began a long affair with the American writer Nelson Algren, but she would not marry him, in large part because of her deep link with Sartre (who was involved with others).

1. In the late 1940s, Beauvoir became more interested in politics and social issues; this influenced her decision to write on gender relations.
2. She also became an activist who opposed the continued French occupation of Algeria.
3. Meanwhile, her writing moved from fiction and philosophy into a four-volume autobiographical work that also illustrated her ideas.
4. She was one of the editors of the journal *Les Temps Modernes*. This position was part of the relationship with Sartre, though she also lived for a number of years with another writer, Claude Lanzmann.

D. Beauvoir's life became as important as her writings for younger generations of women; she represented the woman who had created her own life as a writer and independent intellectual.

1. Later feminists often criticized her uncritical allegiance to and apparent emotional dependence on Sartre.
2. But her book *The Second Sex* (1949) remains one of the foundational works of modern feminist thought. Beauvoir did not call herself a feminist until the 1970s and kept her distance from women activists.
3. In later years, though, she was active in campaigns for abortion rights, contraception, and the defense of women who faced domestic violence.

IV. *The Second Sex* is a long book (over 700 pages in the English translation), and it ranges very widely in its description of patriarchal societies.

- **A.** The overall point of the book is to show how women have been defined and restricted by the history and myths that place them in an inferior position.
  - **1.** This long cultural history has prevented women from understanding and acting on their freedom, but women can begin to act freely when they reject the prevailing cultural myths and redefine themselves.
  - **2.** The argument built on the ideas of existential philosophy. It stressed that there is no "essence" or "woman's nature" that sets limits to what women might do; they can define themselves by their actions.

- **B.** Yet women cannot act freely because they allow men and cultural traditions to define who they are. Beauvoir rejects biological, psychological, and materialist arguments about the traits of women that are beyond cultural control.
  - **1.** The culture views women as the "other" of men, and women take this perception into their own identities. Men are active; women are passive.
  - **2.** As Beauvoir described it, "One is not born, but rather becomes, a woman." From earliest childhood, girls are given their cultural roles.
  - **3.** Men are better able to act on their freedom ("the male is called upon for action"), but a woman is enclosed "within the circle of herself."

- **C.** Given these cultural structures, Beauvoir argues that women have no chance for freedom or equality in the reigning structures of marriage, motherhood, and male-female relationships; the structures deny her freedom.
  - **1.** But Beauvoir remained an optimist; she assumed that women could find the means to liberate themselves.

2. They could challenge the cultural myths; they would find ways to gain more economic autonomy (the point Woolf had also developed) and could overcome their sense of inferiority in the arts and literature.

3. Most important, they could insist on equality in relations with men—an equal relation between two independent consciousnesses.

4. "On the day when it will be possible for woman to love not in her weakness but in her strength," she wrote, "…love will become for her, as for man, a source of life and not of mortal danger."

V. Beauvoir's vision of women's identity and modern social position built on a classical Enlightenment-style definition of the self.

A. The free woman (like the free man) could recognize her social position, define her opposition to oppressive forces outside herself, and claim her freedom as she rejected the ways in which others described her.

1. These assumptions led to the criticisms of a third wave of feminists.

2. In France, this critique emerged in writers such as Luce Irigaray (1932–), Hélène Cixous (1937–), and Julia Kristeva (1941–).

B. These writers placed more emphasis on the distinctiveness of the female body, suggesting that people like Beauvoir still wanted women to be like men. Beauvoir had not gone far enough in analyzing masculine language. She had not seen how language limits freedom.

C. Other critics claimed that Beauvoir did not grasp the complexity of motherhood; she devalued women's distinctive experiences.

D. Amid these critiques, other feminists praised Beauvoir for showing how woman's social position is culturally constructed rather than natural.

E. This emphasis on the redefinition of the self offered alternatives to other theories about cultural structures that limit and define everyone.

Essential Reading:

Virginia Woolf, *A Room of One's Own*.

Simone de Beauvoir, *The Second Sex*, pp. xix–xxxvi, 139–198, 679–732.

Supplementary Reading:

Toril Moi, *Simone de Beauvoir: The Making of an Intellectual Woman*, pp. 1–72, 179–213.

Questions to Consider:

1. Do the experiences of women and men differ in ways that require different literary voices?

2. Was Beauvoir naïve when she argued that women could reject traditional cultural definitions of womanhood?

Lecture Twenty—Transcript
Redefining Modern Feminism

We've seen how writers attempted to defend human dignity and freedom against the dehumanizing effects of totalitarianism and war. And we've stressed the importance of the Second World War in pushing these processes forward. But the struggle to define and defend human dignity and autonomy amid various constraints extended also to movements for women's rights, and there was a great deal of interest in the period after World War II in rethinking the position of women in modern society. In fact, feminism became one of the most successful modern isms in that many of the traditional restrictions on women's voting rights, women's economic rights, women's education, women's personal freedom. Many of these restrictions disappeared in the 20th century. In fact, if one were to do a cultural history of 20th-century European life, I think the change in the position of women would be one of the most dynamic historical changes that we could talk about. It's truly a dramatic change from, say, 1900 to the year 2000.

But these changes in various spheres of political and economic life also created a new awareness of the cultural limits that still shaped women's lives. And so, the movement for women's rights evolved through what are often called the three waves of modern feminist thought—that feminism took different forms, and each of these forms was a kind of wave of critical thinking.

The first wave was the generally successful campaign for voting rights. This was a campaign that had begun in the 19th century, and it was led by political activists, such as Emmeline Pankhurst, who was British. Pankhurst lived from 1858 to 1928, and she was one of the English suffragists—they called theme suffragettes, or suffragist advocate—who participated in a sometimes violent campaign for voting rights before World War I. But this campaign ultimately succeeded in that women got the right to vote at the end of the First World War. And women also gained voting rights in Germany at that time—and also in the United States at that time. But they could not yet vote in France or Italy. In fact, women did not get the right to vote in France or Italy until the end of World War II.

And yet, there had been a political change, and that first wave of feminism had brought it about. But the acquisition of voting rights did not end the debate about the role of women in public life. Because, in part, it was a long time before women began to hold government offices, and it was very difficult for women to actually maintain a prominent role in public life. That came quite a bit after they actually got the vote.

But in the aftermath of the successful campaign for voting rights, some women began to develop a second wave of feminist writing. And this second wave of 20th-century feminism stressed the social, economic, and, especially, the cultural constraints on modern women. And this new phase of feminism developed in a number of national contexts, including contexts in North America and in various parts of Europe. But it gained particular influence in England and in France on the European side in the works of writers such as Virginia Woolf and Simone de Beauvoir. And in this lecture, I want to focus on this second phase of 20th-century feminist thought—this second wave of feminism. And I particularly want to emphasize the wide influence of Beauvoir's book, *The Second Sex.*

Both Woolf and Beauvoir urged women to pursue a new cultural liberation that would extend beyond the realm of political rights. But by the late 20th century, there was yet a new wave of feminist thought, which is often called the third wave of feminism. And the third wave feminists criticized Beauvoir for ignoring the deeper structures of language and unconscious thought that continued to impede women's liberation. And this third wave of feminist thought has splintered in recent decades in many different directions. But I think it's important to note how this third wave of feminism built on earlier feminist themes and feminist critiques of modern culture. And I want to come back to that third wave at the end of this lecture.

But to understand where feminism came from and how it evolved in the 20th century, I want to go back to that earlier period and look at a few of the ideas of Virginia Woolf. We've seen how Virginia Woolf made important contributions to the literary style and themes of the modern English novel. She was truly one of the early innovators in early 20th-century writing. And in her literary works—in her novels—she tried to represent the complexity of women and women's experiences. But she went on to develop a more systematic commentary on the position of women in her short book, *A Room of One's Own*—a very important commentary on women in modern society. *A Room of One's Own* was published in 1929. It gained a lot of attention at the time, but I think it has gained even m ore attention in recent decades. It was published soon after women gained the right to vote. So, Woolf was starting from the assumption that women could vote. So she turned to the question of why women's cultural production in art, in literature, in scholarship, philosophy had never matched the production of men. Why had most of the important literary and artistic works always been the product of male work?

And Woolf said that there were explanations for this—there were cultural explanations for this and economic explanations. She said that women never had enough money to support artistic work. How could they be artists if they didn't have the money to be artists or writers? And they didn't have enough time to be writers. They didn't have enough time away from their family obligations. To write books requires a lot of time. And women were always caught up in the processes of taking care of the houses, of taking care of children, of taking care of their husbands. And in fact, she said, the independent, creative woman needed "a room of one's own", by which she meant a woman needs some sort of financial autonomy. A woman needs some space. A woman needs a place where she can develop freely her own cultural aspirations.

And also, and this was equally important, a woman needed to be able to resist the deep, cultural message that said, "women cannot create as well as men." I think that this is something that Virginia Woolf heard in her own life. It was a refrain in her work. And so, as she thought about this problem, Woolf said, it's no wonder that women had not yet written plays like Shakespeare, because they face cultural constraints that men never had to deal with. She said if Shakespeare had a sister, this sister could never pursue literary work. There couldn't have been a female Shakespeare in the 16th century, because women were blocked. They were blocked from the personal freedom and the education that made creative work possible. She said that men had always been free to travel, men had always been free to pursue love affairs, men had always been free to take risks, and these are the kinds of experiences—travel, risk taking, multiple love affairs, complex education—these are the kinds of experiences that creative work grows out of. How could a woman do these things if she had no space of her own—no freedom to pursue these types of activities?

But Woolf argued that this situation was now changing in the modern era—that in the 20th century, women could pursue more of the activities that men had pursued—the activities that made possible creative work. But she insisted that as women pursued these activities, they should not write or create exactly like men. Women must find their own cultural voices. Women must find their own voice to represent their own experiences, their own friendships, and their own views of reality. And she suggested that these experiences are somewhat different from what men experience—not that men and women are totally different. There are some things male in the female experience. There is something female in the male experience. She insisted on that. But she also said that there is something different. And it is the difference and the similarity that women must explore in their writing.

And she also said that women must recovery the history of women. They must find a history that makes women visible in the historical record, because the history of the human race had always been told in terms of what men did, and women remained invisible in history books and in official cultural memory.

Well, Woolf's imaginative and concise description of a quest for a women's voice and an independent selfhood provided an important starting point for many later feminist writers. And it was Woolf's work that provided the starting point for the work of Simone de Beauvoir. And now I want to turn to say a few things about Simone de Beauvoir.

Beauvoir was born in 1908, and she would live until 1986. And she was an important existentialist philosopher. She lived in France virtually all of her life, although she traveled a lot. And she worked in a number of different literary genres, much like other existentialist writers. She wrote novels, she wrote short stories, she wrote memoirs, and she wrote philosophical essays and works.

Beauvoir grew up in a bourgeois Catholic family. She went to Catholic schools throughout her childhood, so she was very rooted in the Catholic Church. She remained in the Catholic schools until she went to the Sorbonne to study philosophy. Although very few women at that time had ever taught philosophy, she decided to become a philosophy teacher. And it was in studying for the qualifying exams that one had to take to become a philosophy teacher that she met Jean-Paul Sartre.

They took the exam in the same year—in 1929. And the story of this exam is a famous story. He placed first in the exam, and she placed second among all of the people who took it that year. But she was the youngest person ever to pass the exam. No one had ever been as young as Beauvoir was when she took the exam. She was only 21 years old.

This relationship with Sartre, as we noted earlier, became an enduring, complex, emotional component of Beauvoir's life. I talked about the complexity of this relationship when we were discussing the life and career of Sartre. Both of these writers struggled to have a completely honest relationship. This was very difficult. It carried a lot of emotional cost for both of them. And I think that many of the biographers that study Beauvoir suggest that this struggle to have a completely honest relationship was a difficult emotional process for Beauvoir. Her relationship with Sartre was complex.

In any case, she went on to teach philosophy in a provincial lycée. She taught at several lycées before the Second World War. And then during the Second World War, Beauvoir settled in Paris, where she lived the rest of her life.

She began writing novels. Her early work was in the form of fiction. She wrote a novel called *She Came to Stay*, published in 1943. And another novel called *The Blood of Others*. *The Blood of Others* was published in 1945. And these were novels in which Beauvoir explored the meaning of personal relationships and personal choices. Like other existentialists, she was trying to explore the meaning of identity and existence through literature. And she used literature to promote various existential philosophical ideas. She also wrote some essays that were more explicitly philosophical.

After the war, Beauvoir traveled in America. She spent quite a bit of time going around the United States. She also met the American writer, Nelson Algren. Algren lived in Chicago, and she became acquainted with him there. And this relationship went on for several years. In fact, Algren wanted her to marry him, but she would not do this in large part because of her deep link with Sartre and that commitment to maintain that relationship, although as I noted before, Sartre was often involved with other people. They were both involved with other people. So she never married.

In the late 1940s, Beauvoir became much more interested in politics and in social issues. And I think that this growing political interest influenced her decision to write about gender and about the experience of women. During the 1950s, she also became an activist who opposed the continued French occupation of Algeria. She wrote about the Algerian war, she became active in the anti-Algerian war movement in France.

And meanwhile, her writing moved steadily away from fiction and philosophy into a four-volume autobiographical work. She wrote the memoirs of her own life, which she thought could be used to illustrate her main ideas—the idea of a human being coming into consciousness, recognizing her freedom, and acting on that freedom in the world. And Beauvoir was also one of the editors of the journal, *Le Temps Moderne—Modern Times*—that journal that she had helped to found along with Jean-Paul Sartre and other existentialists. So she was in a whole range of intellectual communities and groups. It was also in these later years that she lived with a writer, Claude Lanzmann, who was another part of the intellectual circles in which she and Sartre moved. So she had a number of other relationships, but she always held onto that link with Sartre.

Well, Beauvoir's life became as important as her writings for many younger women. And she came to represent the woman who created her own life as a writer and independent intellectual. It was Beauvoir's life as well as her work that became symbolically important to a whole generation of women that came of age in the 1950s, '60s, and '70s. Many of the later feminists criticized Beauvoir. They said she had an uncritical allegiance to Sartre, that she had too much emotional dependence on this man, that she ignored Sartre's own sexism and his own blind spots about women. So there were often criticisms of Beauvoir. And yet even the critics would concede that her work had redefined the meaning of modern feminism. It had created a foundation for the modern women's movement.

Her book, *The Second Sex*, which was published in 1949, remains one of the main foundational works for modern feminist thought. Even though Beauvoir herself didn't define herself as a feminist until the 1970s. In fact, she often kept her distance from women activists. But in later years, she became more active in campaigns—campaigns for abortion rights, for rights of contraception, and especially also the defense of women who face domestic violence. She became active in all of these campaigns in France—especially in the 1970s.

Well, I want to say a few things now about the themes of *The Second Sex*, because this book is truly a critical work in the emergence of the modern women's movement. *The Second Sex* is a very long book. It's over 700 pages in the English translation, and the English translation excludes large sections of the original French text. And the book ranges very widely in its description of what Beauvoir called the history of patriarchal societies. She deals with relationships between men and women going back all the way to the beginning of human history. She deals also with the modern period—the 18th, the 19th, and the 20th century. And she deals with a very wide range of themes.

The overall point of the book is to show how women have been defined and have been restricted by the history and myths that place them in an inferior position. She stressed that women had never been free to develop their own lives. And this cultural history of women's position—this long history—has prevented women from understanding and acting upon their freedom. And, of course, for an existentialist like Beauvoir, the existence of your freedom is essential. You have to be able to act on that freedom. So, by denying women their freedom, societies have prevented women from achieving their own full consciousness and their own full identity.

But she also argued that women could begin to act freely when they rejected the prevailing cultural myths and when they set about redefining themselves. And so her argument built upon the core ideas of existential philosophy. In many ways, it's a fusion of themes from feminism and existentialism. She stressed, like the existentialists, that there is no essence or no essential women's nature. This had long been one of the ways in which women's rights had been denied—the claim that women have a certain essence or nature that prevents them from acting, for example, in public life or in politics. And this nature sets limits to what women can do. She said, no, there is no essence, there is no nature—that women can define themselves by their actions, just like men. And yet, women have not been able to act freely, because women have allowed men and cultural traditions to define who they are. So, Beauvoir set out to reject all kinds of biological or psychological or materialist arguments that tried to give women and essential identity. She said, no, there is no essential identity. There are no traits of women that are beyond cultural control. The problem is to redefine modern culture, and this will enable women to act freely in the world.

She said that human cultures view women as 'the other' of men—that men represent the active agent in culture and in history. And women accept this definition—a definition developed by men—and they internalize this perception into their own identity. They allow men to tell them who they are. And above all, they allow men to tell them men are active and women are passive. As Beauvoir described it in one of the famous passages of this book, she said, "One is not born but rather becomes a woman." That is the key idea—that you're not simply born as a woman. You learn to be a woman. And from earliest childhood, young girls are given their cultural role. They are told who they should be, and they are unable, then, to get beyond that definition by others.

Men, on the other hand, are better able to act upon their freedom. As she said, "The male is called upon for action, but a woman is enclosed within the circle of herself." This is the meaning of modern history—that women, even when they get voting right, even when they make progress in that sphere—they remain caught within these cultural structures. So she says women must have the chance for freedom and equality, but they have no chance for freedom or equality within the reigning structures of marriage, motherhood, and male/female relationships. These structures deny woman her freedom.

And yet, Beauvoir remained an optimist. She assumed that women could find the means to liberate themselves—that women could find the means to define their own freedom. They could challenge the cultural myths. They could find ways to gain more economic autonomy—the same point that Woolf had been developing earlier in her work. And Beauvoir said that women could overcome their sense of inferiority in the arts and in literature. Most important, if women defined their own identities and if women insisted on equality in their relations with men, it would be possible to have new relations between the sexes—that male-female relations would be seen as an equal relation between two, independent consciousnesses. Remember again, the existentialists on consciousness—you have two equally autonomous, free consciousnesses. And when this interaction takes place, then you can have equal relationships. As she said in *The*

Second Sex—this is a quote about the meaning of love, "On the day when it will be possible for women to love not in her weakness but in her strength, love will become for her as for man a source of life and not of mortal danger." That women—when they enter into relations of equality—then love itself is transformed into a relation of equality rather than a relation of danger.

Now, Beauvoir's vision of woman's identity and modern social position built upon a classical, Enlightenment-style definition of the self, because she assumed that the free woman—like the free man—could recognize her social position, define her position against oppressive forces outside herself, and then claim her freedom as she rejected the ways in which others described her. And it's this assumption of the autonomous woman that led to the critique of the third wave of feminists in the later 20th century. And I want to refer briefly to this third wave by giving some examples of themes in French feminism in the period about after 1970.

You can see this new wave—this new wave—in a series of French writers, including a woman called Luce Irigaray, Hélène Cixous, and Julia Kristeva. These were all women who were writing in the 1970s, the '80s, and into the 1990s. And this third wave of feminists placed much more emphasis on the distinctiveness of the female body. They suggested that people like Beauvoir still wanted women to be like men. They said that Beauvoir had not gone far enough in analyzing the constraints of masculine language and the constraints of the male model of the independent subject—the independent acting person.

This new wave of feminist thought argued that language itself shapes the limits of freedom, and it defines and limits what women can do much more acutely than what Beauvoir had understood. This new wave of feminists argued that language itself creates limits to consciousness. And so, it was necessary to question Beauvoir's confidence that language could be redefined—her confidence in the knowing free subject. They said that Beauvoir—her ideas rested on that old Enlightenment ideal—that sort of old, classical liberal ideal of the autonomous individual. But feminists in the 1970s and 1980s argued that there is no single self. There cannot be a fully autonomous self—that there are always multiple selves and that these selves—these multiple selves—are expressed in the body, in multiple languages, and even in the unconscious mind. And Beauvoir did not talk about the unconscious mind and the constraints of language.

Other critics claimed that Beauvoir did not understand the complexity or the creativity of motherhood. And they complained, in fact, that Beauvoir devalued women's distinctive experiences as mothers. In short, many of these third-wave feminists claimed that Beauvoir did not understand the value or meaning of difference—and this would be a key theme of third-wave feminists—that women's difference from men must be analyzed and explained and kept in view. And the problem with Beauvoir and her kind of feminism and perspective is that it remained male identified—that it used the male model of the autonomous subject as the model of the independent person and that Beauvoir herself remained to close to Sartre and to this notion of the male subject.

But even amid these critiques, many feminists continued to praise Beauvoir as someone who had shown how women's social position is culturally constructed rather than natural. And it is this emphasis on the historical and cultural construction of women—a construction that takes place through myths, through families, and through education—that made Beauvoir's existential feminism and enduring force in later cultural debates. Perhaps she had not fully freed herself from some of the myths that she questioned, and yet she pointed toward a new selfhood for women. And this existential emphasis on the redefinition of the self offered alternatives to other kinds of theories that stressed women's embeddedness in structures that couldn't be changed. And so, at the very time Beauvoir was advocating the autonomy of women, other theorists in anthropology and history were increasingly stressing the limits of deep cultural structures. And I want to turn to those structuralist theories in the next lecture.

Lecture Twenty-One
History, Anthropology, and Structuralism

Scope:

Although the existential account of human freedom attracted wide interest among postwar intellectuals, the social sciences tended to stress the controlling power of historical systems and cultural traditions that limit the individual's ideas and actions. This lecture examines the emphasis on social "structures" and cultural "systems" that reshaped historical studies and anthropology after the Second World War. It discusses the so-called "*Annales* School" of historians in France, noting the role of its early leaders, Lucien Febvre, Marc Bloch, and Fernand Braudel. Meanwhile, anthropology also took a "structural" turn in the work of Claude Lévi-Strauss, who developed influential theories about the deep structures and rituals that give cultural meaning to all forms of social life.

Outline

I. Descriptions of the "human condition" in the 20th century often moved in contrasting directions.

   A. Some intellectuals, including the existentialists, stressed the autonomy of individual consciousness and action and emphasized the reality of human freedom.

   B. Many others, however, stressed that individuals inevitably live in social and cultural structures that limit their thought and actions.

   C. This emphasis on the structures that define what people can think or do became a common theme in the social sciences, including history, sociology, and anthropology. It drew on earlier thinkers, such as Durkheim.

      1. Among the "limiting structures" of human thought, the social scientists noted the importance of cultural traditions, language, and religion.

      2. People learn how to think and act within these structures; therefore, as many theorists argued, most individuals are only "free" within narrow limits.

   D. These themes became especially influential in structural anthropology, which emerged most notably in works by the French theorist Claude Lévi-Strauss.

1. Similar structural themes had appeared earlier in the new social history of writers such as Lucien Febvre and Marc Bloch.
2. Febvre and Bloch founded a famous historical journal in the late 1920s; their approach to history led to the work of Fernand Braudel.
3. In this lecture, we'll look at the new social history in France, then note how its themes also evolved into structural anthropology.
4. The themes in all this work challenged the existential belief in free individual consciousness and shaped a powerful critique of traditional (liberal) ideas about the autonomy of the individual subject.

E. Such ideas gained wide influence in postwar European intellectual life, especially among intellectuals who worked in the universities.

II. The new attempt to understand the constraining social and cultural components of human action and thought showed up in the study of history during the 1930s.

A. Modern professional historical studies had developed in Germany during the 19th century in the works of historians such as Leopold von Ranke.
1. Ranke (1795–1886) and his followers generally saw state institutions or leaders as the decisive actors in human history; they used government documents as the key sources for historical narratives.
2. These research methods gave political elites and government policies the greatest significance in the whole narrative of human history.

B. By the 1930s, however, there was a growing dissatisfaction with historical work that focused mainly on government leaders or political events.
1. Younger historians, who were influenced by sociology, preferred to emphasize social processes and the cultural aspects of human history.
2. Individuals were seen as the products of long-term social forces that they do not control and often do not fully recognize.

3. This conception of historical experience became important in the work of the so-called "*Annales*" historians in France.

C. The key figures in this historical "school" were Lucien Febvre (1878–1956) and Marc Bloch (1886–1944); they were co-founders of the *Annales d'histoire économique et sociale*, which began publication in 1929.

    1. Both Febvre and Bloch studied sociology and geography at the École Normale Supérieure before World War I; they served throughout that war in the French army.

    2. They met in 1920 in Strasbourg, where they were both appointed to teach history at the University of Strasbourg.

D. Febvre worked on 16th-century French history and Bloch studied the Middle Ages. They were close friends, but their lives differed in important ways.

    1. Febvre was from a French Catholic family, he was older than Bloch, and he moved up the academic hierarchy more quickly, becoming a professor at the Collège de France in 1933.

    2. Bloch was from an Alsatian Jewish family; he lagged behind Febvre in academic appointments, finally reaching Paris in 1936 with a position at the Sorbonne. Bloch joined the French army again in 1939; after the Germans occupied France, he could not resume his academic work.

E. Bloch tried to go to America with his wife and six children, but he was unable to get visas for his family; he later joined the French Resistance.

    1. In 1944, Bloch was arrested by the Gestapo and, after several months in jail, was executed near Lyon (June 1944).

    2. His life story, as well as his work, made him one of the most important historians in 20th-century France.

III. The main objective of the *Annales* historians was to analyze the enduring structures of social life and thought across long periods of time.

  A. Febvre wrote, for example, about the structures of religious thought in 16th-century culture, showing how it was then impossible for one to be an atheist.

  B. Bloch wrote about the social relations and ideas in medieval feudal society; he described the layout of fields, conceptions of time, and social relations.

   1. Bloch's most famous book, *Feudal Society* (1939–1940), examined the "collective consciousness" of people in that culture.

   2. He did not write about the kings fighting heroic battles; he discussed the social experience of everyday life in villages or fields.

   3. He showed social and cultural structures that defined what a person could do or think in the "mentality" of the medieval world.

  C. This approach to history emphasized that social processes evolve slowly over time and suggested that the natural and social world limit human action.

   1. Bloch himself (as we've seen) tried to act within the limiting structures of his world, but his emphasis on structures influenced later historians.

   2. The books of Fernand Braudel became the most well known examples of later works in the *Annales* tradition.

  D. Braudel (1902–1985) became an editor of the *Annales* journal after World War II and a professor at the Collège de France. He lived in Algeria and Brazil before the war and spent most of World War II in a German POW camp.

   1. Isolated in that camp, Braudel wrote a first draft of his famous book *The Mediterranean and the Mediterranean World in the Age of Philip II* (1949). He drew only on his memory of his prewar research.

   2. Perhaps influenced by the sense that events were beyond his control, Braudel portrayed history on three levels: geographic time, social time, and the time of events— and the events are the least significant.

E. Braudel devoted most of his book to descriptions of natural environments and impersonal social structures; these seem to be the decisive historical forces.

    1. He described specific historical events as "surface disturbances, crests of foam that the tides of history carry on their strong backs."

    2. The individual is like foam on the waters of a vast sea, tossed about by great waves of history that a person can never control.

    3. Following this perspective, the new social history in France set out to describe enduring structures rather than specific persons or events.

IV. A similar interest in the deep, shaping structures of human culture appeared also in the new structural anthropology of Claude Lévi-Strauss (1908–).

    A. Lévi-Strauss came from a family of artists. He was born in Belgium but grew up in France and attended the Sorbonne, where he studied philosophy.

        1. Simone de Beauvoir was one of his classmates at the university.

        2. His interests shifted to anthropology, however, when he moved to Brazil in 1934. He taught at the University of São Paulo (1934–1939).

        3. During these years, he traveled into the interior of Brazil and met remote Indian tribes; these people lived entirely pre-modern lives.

        4. He studied ethnology and went back to France to pursue this subject.

    B. He served in the French army in 1940, but after the Germans occupied France, he escaped to America (Lévi-Strauss was Jewish and at great risk).

        1. He made his way to New York, where he lived among exiles, worked at the New School for Social Research, and studied linguistics.

        2. He became a good friend of the Czech linguist Roman Jakobson; this connection led him to a new linguistic understanding of culture.

3. Lévi-Strauss remained in the United States until 1947; he taught at Barnard College and served after 1945 as a French cultural attaché.

4. But his intellectual roots were in France, and he returned there to publish numerous anthropological works. He later became a professor of social anthropology at the Collège de France (1960–1982).

C. Lévi-Strauss was influenced by Durkheim's influential successor, Marcel Mauss, and wrote a long introduction to an edition of Mauss's writings. He also described his Brazilian experiences in a famous book called *Tristes Tropiques* (1955) and later published *Structural Anthropology* (1961) and *The Raw and the Cooked* (1964).

D. Lévi-Strauss understood culture in terms he borrowed from structural linguistics. He said that cultures are like languages in that they are built on underlying structures, which are invariable and create meaning.

1. Structural linguistics had been developed earlier in the century by Ferdinand de Saussure, who emphasized the unchanging deep structure or grammar of language.

2. He noted that individual words can be arranged into an infinite combination of specific sentences, but all these sentences (to make sense) will use a common underlying grammar.

E. Lévi-Strauss drew on this idea to argue that a primitive Brazilian society and an advanced urban society share various underlying structures.

F. The meaning of these structures, according to Lévi-Strauss, depends on dichotomies, or binary oppositions. These oppositions include such categories as nature and culture, raw and cooked, spoken and written, male and female, and so on.

G. Lévi-Strauss's structuralist theory thus carried a strong relativist element. It said that cultures are not good or bad; they simply differ in their rituals. The theory also carried a strong sympathy for pre-modern cultures; they were seen as less alienated from nature.

H. Lévi-Strauss's emphasis on the value of pre-modern cultures and the influence of cultural structures had wide influence in the 1960s.

I. Like most social historians, structuralists assumed that individuals cannot free themselves from deep cultural systems.

Essential Reading:

Marc Bloch, *The Historian's Craft*, pp. 3–47.

Claude Lévi-Strauss, *Tristes Tropiques*, pp. 42–53, 275–358.

Supplementary Reading:

Peter Burke, *The French Historical Revolution: The Annales School, 1929–89*, pp. 12–53.

Questions to Consider:

1. Do cultures, languages and historical contexts define the limits of what any individual can think, say, or do?

2. Do all cultures have the same deep structures and rituals?

Lecture Twenty-One—Transcript
History, Anthropology, and Structuralism

In the last lecture, we discussed how various European women writers and feminists in the 20th century began to argue for the expansion of women's rights and the personal autonomy of women in new writings that stressed the importance of individual rights and individual freedoms as they might apply to women. But this emphasis on individual rights was by no means the only important theme in 20th-century thought. And, in fact, the descriptions of the human condition in the 20th century often moved in contrasting directions between an emphasis on individual autonomy and a contrasting emphasis on the way that individuals are embedded in social and cultural systems.

The existentialists, for example, always stressed the autonomy of individual consciousness and action. And they emphasized the deep reality of human freedom. But many other intellectuals stressed that individuals are inevitably living within social and cultural structures that limit their thought and actions. And this particular approach—this emphasis on the structures of cultural life—defined the human being as somewhat of a product of a cultural system. It was an approach that stressed the limits on what individuals can think or do. And this theme—this theme on the limits of structure—became a common theme in the social sciences during the 20th century. And we can see it in many places in 20th-century thought, including history, sociology, and anthropology. And this kind of thought drew to an extent from earlier thinkers like Émile Durkheim. And it was this emphasis on structures that gradually replaced existentialism as a dominant form of thought—or as an influential form of thought. You might say existentialism gave way to structuralism as a dominant paradigm for understanding human actions in modern cultural life.

Now, among the limiting structures of human thought, the social scientists especially noted the importance of cultural traditions, of language, and of religion. They put a lot of emphasis on all of these structures. And the new social scientists stressed that people learn how to act and to think within these structures. And so, as these theorists explained it, most individuals are only free within fairly narrow limits. You're always limited in what you can actually do, think, or say, because you're operating within a cultural system. And these themes became especially influential in structural anthropology, which emerged most notably in works by French theorists, Claude Lévi-Strauss. And I'm going to talk some about his ideas in this lecture.

But similar structural themes had already appeared in the earlier social history of a group of writers who had become some of the most influential historians in France. And these historians included Lucien Febvre and Marc Bloch. And Febvre and Bloch founded a famous historical journal in the late 1920s, and their approach to history—their social approach to history—led to a whole school of new historians in France, which in some ways culminated in the work of another historian named Fernand Braudel.

And in this lecture, I want to talk about this new social history—how this new form of social history developed in France. And then I want to suggest how the themes of this new social history were related to the themes of cultural anthropology. And the themes in all of this work—the new social history, the new structural anthropology—the themes in all this work challenged the existential belief in free individual consciousness. This kind of structural thought became a kind of powerful critique of traditional liberal ideas about the autonomy of the individual subject. And I think it's fair to say that this new kind of structural thought gained very wide influence in the period of the 1950s and particularly in the 1960s in European intellectual life—especially among intellectuals who worked in the universities.

So, we have here a kind of important transformation taking place in which there's a whole new attention to the constraining social and cultural components of human action.

Well, these patterns began to show very clearly in the 1930s—a period when people gave a lot of attention to social life. And we can see them as essentially in the new history. The history of the 1930s marked a departure from the kind of historical work that had evolved in the 19th century. Modern professional historical studies actually developed in Germany during the 19th century. And the key figure in that process was the historian Leopold von Ranke. Rank was a German historian who lived between 1795 and 1886. And Ranke and his followers essentially developed the principles of modern historical scholarship, emphasizing the importance of careful archival research, primary documents, and careful, empirical analysis of information from the past.

But Ranke and his followers generally saw state institutions and state leaders or political leaders as the decisive actors in human history. And they always used government documents for the most important sources of historical narratives. And so, this kind of research method gave political elites and government policies the greatest significance in the whole narrative of human history so that the classical professional model of historical studies tended to look at governments and at the state.

But by the 1930s, there was a widespread and growing dissatisfaction with this kind of historical work. There was a feeling that the historical studies that focused mainly on government leaders or political events left out a huge amount of human history and in fact distorted the nature of human history. And so, a new generation of younger historians—who were very much influenced by sociology—wanted to emphasize social processes and especially the cultural aspects of human history. And in this view of history, individuals were seen as the products of long-term social forces— long-term, long-developing social forces that individuals do not control and in fact forces that individuals do not recognize in their own lives—that human beings are caught up in vast processes that are very difficult to understand.

Well, this conception of historical experience—social components of historical experience—became important in the work of the so-called Annales historians in France. The *Annales* was the name of a journal, and this became the name of this group of historians. And the key figures in this historical school were Lucien Febvre and Marc Bloch. Febvre lived from 1878 to 1956, and Marc Bloch was born in 1886 and died in 1944.

They were the co-founders of the journal the *Annales d'histoire économique et sociale*, which might be translated roughly as the *Journal of Economic and Social History*. And this journal began publication in 1929. Both Febvre and Bloch studied sociology and geography at the École Normale Supérieur in Paris before World War I. And they both served throughout the First World War in the French army. But they met after the war in 1920 in the city of Strasbourg, where they were both appointed to teach history at the University of Strasbourg in Alsace. And this was a very dynamic moment at the University of Strasbourg, because Strasbourg had just been transferred back to French control at the end of the First World War, and the university was being reorganized—a lot of new people were coming in. So it was an opportunity to for creative, intellectual work. So, Febvre and Bloch became acquainted as colleagues at the University of Strasbourg, and they became good friends.

Febvre worked on 16th-century French history, and Bloch studied the Middle Ages. And they were always close friends as well as intellectual allies. But their lives also differed in some important ways. Febvre was from an old French Catholic family. He was older than Bloch, and he also moved up the academic hierarchy more quickly. He was in certain ways more professionally successful. He became a professor at the College de France—the epitome of French academic life—and he was appointed to this position in 1933, leaving Strasbourg at that point.

Bloch, on the other hand, was from an Alsatian Jewish family. He lagged behind Febvre in the academic appointments game, so to speak. He was not able to get a position in Paris for several years after Febvre left Strasbourg. Bloch finally got to Paris in 1936 with a position at the Sorbonne, rather than at the College de France. And during the Second World War, Bloch went once again into the French army—1939. And after the Germans occupied France, he was unable to resume his academic work, whereas Febvre continued in an academic position. In fact, Bloch tried to emigrate to America with his wife and six children, but he was unable to get visas for his family.

He later joined the French resistance. And in 1944, Bloch was arrested by the Gestapo, and after several months in prison, he was executed near Lyons in June of 1944, just after the D-Day Invasion—one of the tragic stories of the war. And his life story—Bloch's life story—as well as his work, made him one of the most important historians in 20th-century France—a greatly admired historian and human being, because of what he did.

Well, the main objective of the Annales historians was to analyze the enduring structures of social life and social thought across long periods of time—what would come to be called the Long Durée—the long scope or span of time. Febvre, for example, wrote a great deal about the structures of religious thought in the 16th century, and he showed how it was impossible for someone in the 16th century to be an atheist, because it was impossible to think in that kind of language—in those terms. If you lived in the 16th century, the structures of thought and language precluded the conceptualization of atheism as an intellectual position. This was part of Febvre's argument, and it showed how the structures of thought determine the parameters or the limits of what a human being can think.

And in this same period that Febvre was writing about the 16th century, Bloch was writing about the social relations and ideas in medieval feudal society. He described the layout of the fields, the conceptions of time, the nature of social relationships, and a whole network of interlocking social and cultural relationships. Bloch's most famous book was called *Feudal Society*. It was published just at the beginning of the Second World War in 1939–1940. And this book examined what he called the collective consciousness of people in that culture—in the medieval period. Bloch did not write about the kings fighting heroic battles or about the great political events of the middle ages. Instead, he discussed the social experience of everyday life in villages or in the fields where people work. And above all, Bloch showed how social and cultural structures defined what a person could do or think within the mentality of the medieval world. This idea of a mentality became very important in the development of the Annales approach to history. And this approach to history always emphasized that social processes always evolved slowly over time. And it was a view of history that suggested that the natural and social world inevitably limit human action. There are limits to what any human being can do, and these limits are set not only by the social world but by nature itself.

Now, Bloch himself, as we've seen, tried to act as a free individual in certain ways. He tried to act within the limiting structures of his world—particularly faced with the limiting experience of the German occupation. But his emphasis on historical structures influenced a whole approach to history that always stressed the limits to what a human being can do. And we can see the later development of this approach in the work of Fernand Braudel.

Braudel became later the best-known example of this evolving Annales tradition of historiography. Braudel, who lived from 1902 to 1985 later became an editor of the Annales journal, after World War

II and after Bloch's death during that war. And Braudel also rose to the exalted position of professor at the College de France.

He had lived in Algeria and in Brazil before the war. He traveled widely around the Mediterranean world. And then in the war, he went in the army, and he was captured, and he spent most of World War II in a German POW camp as a prison of war. And while he was isolated in that camp, Braudel wrote a first draft of his famous book, *The Mediterranean and the Mediterranean World in the Age of Philip II*. He wrote this book drawing only upon his memory of the notes he had collected before the war—an amazing intellectual enterprise of reconstituting a research project in the isolation of a prison camp. And then this book was published after the war in 1949.

And I think that Braudel was perhaps influenced by this experience of being in a prison camp to argue that events are beyond the control of individual human beings. Braudel always portrayed history on three levels: the level of geographic time—the evolving natural world; the level of social time—the vast network of social relations; and then the timing of event—specific events. And he said that events are always the least significant. And in fact, in his own book, Braudel devoted most of the book to descriptions of natural environment and impersonal social structures. He said that these are the decisive historical forces, and he once described specific historical events as "surface disturbances or crests of foam that the tides of history carry on their strong backs." The individual is like foam on the waters of a vast sea—tossed about, bouncing up and down on the great waves of history, but the individual cannot control these waves. A person cannot ever control these vast processes.

And following this kind of perspective, the new social history in France set out to describe the enduring structures of history rather than specific persons and events. And this model of historical research spread through much of Europe and, in fact, into North America and around the world so that many 20th-century historians wrote history about structures rather than about people or events. This is a pattern that has continued even down to the present.

Well, a similar interest in the deep, shaping structures of human culture appeared in the new structural anthropology of Claude Lévi-Strauss. Lévi-Strauss came from a family of artists. He was born in

1908 in Belgium, but he grew up in France and attended the Sorbonne, where as a young man he studied philosophy. In fact, Simone de Beauvoir was one of his classmates at the university, and he and Beauvoir knew each other for many years after that. Although their work moved in different directions after that, they were friends and acquaintances.

But Lévi-Strauss' work gradually shifted away from philosophy and into anthropology. And this happened after he moved to Brazil in 1934 where he taught at the University of São Paulo from 1934 to 1939. And during these years, Lévi-Strauss traveled into the interior of Brazil. He traveled widely into the back country, and he met remote Indian tribes in the back country. And he found people who were living entirely pre-modern lives—people whose lives had been barely touched in any way by modern culture and modern civilization, and he became fascinated by this encounter—by the lives of these people.

And so he began to study ethnology. He became interested in anthropology, and he eventually went back to France to pursue this subject and to turn away from philosophy. He had to go into the French army in World War II, but after the Germans occupied France, he escaped to America. Lévi-Strauss was from a Jewish family, and he was at great risk. And he managed to get out. He made his way, eventually, to New York where he lived among a group of French exiles who were living in New York, and he worked at the New School for Social Research and began to study linguistics and other forms of modern thought while in New York.

Also, while he was in New York, Lévi-Strauss became a good friend of the Czech linguist, Roman Jakobson, who was also working at the New School and was also living in New York. And this connection with linguistics gave Lévi-Strauss a new linguistic understanding of culture, which would be very important in his work.

Lévi-Strauss went on to work in the United States until 1947. He taught for a while at Barnard College in New York. And he served also after 1945 as a French cultural attaché. But his intellectual roots were in France, and he returned there to publish numerous anthropological works. He became a very prolific author, and he later became a professor of social anthropology at the College de France—another one of these people who makes it to the pinnacle of the academic establishment. He was a professor at the College de France from 1960 to 1982.

Now, Lévi-Strauss was very much influenced by Durkheim's influential successor and nephew, Marcel Mauss, whom we discussed in an earlier lecture. Mauss had written an important essay about the gift and trying to understand how the gift functioned in social relationships. And Lévi-Strauss was very interested in Mauss' work. He, in fact, wrote a long introduction to an edition of Mauss' writings.

And then he went on to write a number of other books. Lévi-Strauss describes his Brazilian experiences in a famous book called *Tristes Tropiques*, which was published in 1955. And he later published a number of other books, including a work called *Structural Anthropology*, which appeared in 1961, and *The Raw and the Cooked*, which appeared in 1964. These expanded on things he had written about in his work on Marcel Mauss. Lévi-Strauss thought that Mauss had pointed the way to a new way of understanding anthropology.

Now, Lévi-Strauss always understood culture from terms he borrowed from structural linguistics. This takes us back to the influence of Jakobson and the linguists. He said that cultures are like languages in that they are built on underlying structures, and these structures are invariable—they create meaning. And they have to be there for a culture to exist. And in this respect, a culture is very much like language. And in developing these theories, Lévi-Strauss was drawing on structural linguistics as this kind of work had been developed earlier in the century by a linguist called Ferdinand de Saussure. And Saussure had emphasized the unchanging, deep structure of grammar and of language. He had argued that you can arrange individual words in many different combinations. In fact, there is almost an infinite number of sentences—there is an infinite number of sentences—that can be constructed using different words. But all of these sentences—no matter how diverse they might be— will have to use a common underlying grammar to make sense. You have to have a subject and a verb; you have to have an object or an indirect object. You have structures that are always there, even though you can express an enormous range of ideas and thoughts with specific words. And this was the key idea of structural linguistics that Lévi-Strauss used as he began to write about the

Brazilian tribes—Brazilian societies—that he had encountered in South America.

He argued that a primitive Brazilian society and an advanced, European society in fact shared various underlying structures. And these cultural structures give meaning to all specific activities. So, for example, all cultures—no matter how advanced or primitive they might seem to be—they're all held together by myths, by certain kinds of rituals, which all give some kind of structure to human life. And the specific content of these myths and rituals will, of course, vary enormously. But the social significance or meaning is roughly the same—that is, these rituals, these myths, and structures enable people to live together in a society. And he said that all cultures, for example, must have structures to regulate relations between the sexes, to create systems of marriage, to pass on knowledge, to organize political power, to share food, to provide shelter, to manage economic relationships and production. In short, you cannot have a social and cultural life without these deep structures.

And equally important, according to Lévi-Strauss, the meaning of these structures always depends on dichotomies or what he called binary oppositions. There are structures that are always in relation to each other, and they are always in opposition. So, for example, we have a whole set of structuring oppositions that give meaning to cultural life. We have categories such as nature and culture, which stand in opposition to each other. Or in relation to food, we have a category like raw versus cooked. But when we talk about language, we have a category spoken versus written, or we have the category male versus female, and so forth and so on. We can imagine a whole range of binary oppositions which provide the organizing structure of social and cultural life. And according to Lévi-Strauss, all people learn to think and organize their experiences within these shaping cultural categories. So in this respect, the rituals that surround, say, the president of France, will resemble the rituals that also surround a Brazilian chief. There will be certain kinds of rituals to suggest this person has power. There will be certain forms of ritual deference. There will be certain kinds of ritual service, and so forth. And these rituals are necessary to define relations of power and authority and deference. You're going to have to have these kinds of structuring rituals no matter how advanced or undeveloped a culture might be.

So, Lévi-Strauss' structuralist theory carried a strong relativist element. It said that cultures are not good or bad—they simply differ in their rituals. But who is to say that this culture is a horrible culture and this one is a wonderful culture. They're going to have deep similarities if you just look at the level of structure.

In general, though, Lévi-Strauss' theory carried also a strong sympathy for pre-modern cultures. He believed that these cultures in general were less alienated from nature. And Lévi-Strauss was, in fact, a great admirer of Rousseau, the old Rousseauian idea of a natural life. So Lévi-Strauss' emphasis on the value of pre-modern cultures and on the pervasive influence of cultural structures began to have a very wide influence in French and European culture by the early 1960s. And it also contributed in part to a new fascination with pre-modern cultures almost in some ways as a romanticization of pre-modern cultures.

There were also many critics of Lévi-Strauss' work. The critics said that his theory was too static—that it didn't explain history; that it didn't explain how these structures change across time—it was simply in place the way he described it. There were other critics who rejected his binary oppositions as being too rigid. And this was particularly a theme of the post-structuralist critics, who complained that he opposed the same structures and the same binary oppositions on all cultures.

But like most of the social historians and the structural anthropologists and the post-structuralist thinkers, Lévi-Strauss assumed that individuals cannot free themselves from deep, cultural systems. And this is a theme that would reappear in a whole series of later thinkers, including the post-structuralist theorists that we will discuss in the next lecture.

Lecture Twenty-Two
Poststructuralist Thought—Foucault and Derrida

Scope:

In the 1960s, a new generation of French social and cultural theorists developed an important critique of both the existential philosophical tradition and the structuralist ideas that had become important in cultural anthropology. This new critical movement became known as poststructuralism—a term that suggests the attempt to move beyond structuralist ideas. This lecture examines the lives and poststructuralist theories of Michel Foucault and Jacques Derrida, both of whom had wide international influence. Foucault was especially concerned with the relation between power and knowledge. Derrida was more concerned with the metaphysical philosophical traditions that remain embedded in all forms of language. This lecture summarizes the main themes of these complex authors and notes their international influence.

Outline

I. The key ideas of post-World War II social history and structural anthropology portrayed individuals as embodiments of cultural discourses that they could neither transform nor escape; these themes rejected the belief in radical existential freedom.

   A. Structuralist views of language and culture also challenged the idea that an artist or author expresses a distinctive personal vision.
       1. There was, instead, a tendency to describe the "death of the author" or the "death of the subject"; everyone simply expresses a cultural system.
       2. Such views seemed to suggest that social or cultural change would be unlikely; at the very least, such change would be very slow because the structures of language, culture, and social life endure for long periods of time.

   B. Critics began to complain, however, that this view would foster a passivity or an abandonment of social critique; structures would simply be accepted.

1. Meanwhile, there was a growing disillusionment with Marxism, in part because of Stalinism and in part because economic analysis alone did not seem to account for the realities of social and cultural life.
2. Both Marxism and structuralism suggested rigid views of social life; they defined social relations in terms of binary oppositions.

C. In this cultural and political context, a new group of poststructuralists began to challenge the "binary" thinking of structuralism, Marxism, and philosophy.
    1. The poststructuralists remained interested in deep structures of thought, but they saw these structures as complex, overlapping forms of language, power, and discourse that went beyond binary oppositions.
    2. This critique of structuralist thought and (more generally) of the whole modern structure of knowledge emerged most notably in the works of Michel Foucault and Jacques Derrida.

D. Foucault examined the relation between power and knowledge, while Derrida was more concerned with the relation between truth claims and language.
    1. They shared a critique of traditional conceptions of truth, however, and their critique gained wide international influence.
    2. To understand the complexity of the poststructuralist critique, we need to look more closely at the ideas of Foucault and Derrida.
    3. They sought alternatives to the dominant "discourses" of modernity to sustain post-Marxist, poststructuralist forms of cultural critique.

II. Foucault (1926–1984) was from the French city of Poitiers, where his father was a prominent surgeon; he wanted his son Michel to be a surgeon, too.

A. The young Foucault attended Catholic schools, then moved away from the idea of studying medicine. He entered the École Normale Supérieure in Paris and studied philosophy; he became skeptical of Sartre's existentialism.

1. He turned from philosophy to the history of medicine, psychiatry, and hospitals and worked in a psychiatric hospital.
2. He later taught French for six years in Sweden, Poland, and Germany. He then became a professor of philosophy at the University of Clermont-Ferrand (1960), though his research dealt with medicine.
3. He began to publish widely acclaimed books in the 1960s, but he still worked abroad often (he taught in Tunisia between 1966 and 1968).
4. His writings on medicine and on the nature of scientific knowledge attracted public attention. He was appointed professor of the "History of Systems of Thought" at the Collège de France in 1970.

B. Foucault also became a public intellectual; he was active in campaigns for prison reform and a critic of various government health care policies.
1. His lectures at the Collège de France drew large crowds. He had a dramatic personal appearance; he was bald, wore glasses, and spoke in complex and even lyrical language.
2. He was an unconventional philosopher, historian, and literary critic.
3. He was also a homosexual who was drawn to gay culture in San Francisco. He lived in California at various times in the 1970s and 1980s while lecturing at Berkeley; he died of AIDS.
4. Some historians have stressed these personal and contextual aspects of Foucault's life. This experience may have intensified his concern with repression, cultural discourses, and the language of scientific experts.

C. Foucault's work is difficult to categorize, but in most general terms, he repeatedly emphasized the relation between power and knowledge.
1. This theme appears in his major books, including *Madness and Civilization* (1961), *The Birth of the Clinic* (1963), *The Order of Things* (1966), and *Discipline and Punish* (1975).

2. Similar issues emerge in a three-volume history of sexuality, which was his last major work.

3. In these books, Foucault argued that modern society relies on structures of dominance, control, and surveillance.

4. Power is diffused throughout society through institutions of social control, such as schools, prisons, hospitals, and armies. What Foucault called the "discourse" of control expressed the authority of experts.

D. The knowledge of scientists, doctors, and teachers is, thus, linked to power; therefore, knowledge is neither neutral nor benign—it is a method of social management.

1. Foucault said that this connection between power and knowledge has shaped modern rationalizing societies since the Enlightenment.

2. His work examined historical issues, such as modern reforms in asylums, prisons, and schools—the culture of rational humanitarians.

3. He argued that the late Enlightenment created "man" as an object of analysis, much as an earlier era had created "nature."

4. His book *Madness and Civilization*, for example, claimed that modern experts created "madness" as a category of knowledge, then took control of the "mad" by placing them in asylums.

E. In other books, such as *Discipline and Punish* and *The History of Sexuality*, Foucault stressed that experts transformed individuals into objects whose behavior could be categorized and brought under the gaze of science.

1. He took the example for this from Jeremy Bentham's dream of a perfect prison that would have a system of constant surveillance.

2. Guards watch the prisoners from a tower (a "panopticon"), but the prisoners can't see the guards; this is Foucault's image of modernity.

3. We are all being watched and categorized, and we internalize these categories into the ways we describe ourselves. We discipline ourselves with the language our culture gives us.

F. For Foucault, power does not come from an economic class or from specific government officials, as Marxists or political historians argue.

1. Instead, power is diffuse and internalized. Power "doesn't only weigh on us as a force that says no," he argues; "...it induces pleasure, forms knowledge, produces discourse."

2. Foucault's ideas on such subjects were influenced by Nietzsche, who had argued that thought is linked to the will to power.

3. Nietzsche had also described truth as a cultural construction and as a concept that is linked to relations of power.

4. Nietzsche's claim that healthy instincts and drives were condemned and distorted by civilization was also important to Foucault.

G. Foucault's response to the historical patterns he described also drew on Nietzsche's precedent. He wanted to "think outside the tradition," to explore transgressions, challenge values, and move beyond limits.

1. He also argued that it was impossible ever to achieve a complete escape from traditions, though he wrote in unconventional ways.

2. Foucault offered a new critique of the Enlightenment, and he may have offered theoretical justification for spontaneous acts of rebellion.

3. Yet his thought also contributed to a more general pessimism about what individuals can actually do in modern societies.

H. Like Lévi-Strauss and many other theorists, he suggested that the constraints of culture are everywhere; the autonomous "self" seems to be a myth. The "self" is a construction of multiple discourses.

III. A similar emphasis on the multiplicity of language and the cultural construction of the "self" appears in the poststructuralist theories of Jacques Derrida (1930–).

A. Derrida was born in Algeria and lived there until he went to Paris to study philosophy at the École Normale Supérieure in the early 1950s.

    1. He came to French culture from the margins, a position that was intensified because his family was Jewish.

    2. Perhaps this influenced his interest in questions about the relation between the center and margins of culture, thought, and language.

B. Derrida eventually became a philosophy professor at the École Normale (1964–1984) and at the École des Hautes Études en Sciences Sociales. He often visited American universities and especially influenced literary criticism.

    1. His important early books included *Of Grammatology* (1967) and *Writing and Difference* (1967); he developed ideas of "deconstruction."

    2. Derrida's principal theoretical objective was to challenge the Western philosophical belief in the clarity and rational distinctions that constitute conceptions of truth.

    3. According to Derrida, we can't have ideas or categories that are pure and distinct from other ideas or categories; we can't get to what philosophers used to call the "Thing Itself."

    4. He argued that our accounts of reality depend on metaphors, and our binary oppositions can never be pure dichotomies.

C. Every idea requires supplements, or otherness, to establish meaning. For example, it's impossible to think of nature without culture or day without night. These ideas are never simply binary oppositions. Every idea or concept is already carried by the other, by a supplement that is part of the idea; the other is always in the self.

D. What does this mean? There can never be a fully coherent, autonomous identity or idea that has full presence or meaning in and of itself.

1. Language shows this because no claim about reality or truth can simply stand alone; truth claims are always relational.
2. This becomes the theme of postmodernism. Derrida argues that everything we encounter in the world—material objects, as well as ideas—is always already embedded in language and thought.
3. There is no way to get outside of language to some deeper reality; in other words, "there is nothing outside the text."

IV. Derrida's themes led him more often to philosophers and literary figures than to the social "experts" whom Foucault describes.

   A. Yet their "poststructuralist" project shared a critical interrogation of the metaphysical conception of stable truths and the transparency of language.

   B. This emphasis on the multiple levels and power of language shaped a new analysis of how cultural systems define truth and social order and fostered a postmodern interest in fragmentation and difference.

Essential Reading:

Michel Foucault, *The History of Sexuality*, vol. 1.

Jacques Derrida, *Of Grammatology*, pp. 6–26, 101–164.

Supplementary Reading:

Didier Eribon, *Michel Foucault*, pp. 212–332.

Questions to Consider:

1. Does the language or "discourse" of experts define people's identities in the modern world?

2. Do you think all ideas need "supplements" to acquire meaning?

Lecture Twenty-Two—Transcript
Poststructuralist Thought—Foucault and Derrida

In the last lecture, we discussed some of the ways in which post-World War II history and social anthropology portrayed individuals as embodiments of cultural discourses—discourses which individuals could neither transform nor escape. And I suggested that these themes rejected the belief in radical existential freedom—the kind of ideas that had been promoted by writers like Jean-Paul Sartre after the Second World War. The structuralist views of language and culture also challenged ideas about art and literature and even the idea of the author, because the structuralists tended to argue that the artist or the author doesn't really express a distinctive personal vision. Instead, there was a tendency in this kind of analysis to describe what is called the death of the author, or the death of the subject by which these kinds of theorists argue that every writer simply expresses a cultural system. It is very difficult ever to achieve a truly individual point of view, and of course this conception of literature challenged and rejected the key assumptions of existentialism.

Now, these kinds of structuralist assumptions seemed to suggest that social or cultural change would be unlikely. At the very least, these ideas suggested that it would be very difficult to change the ideas of language or culture or social life, because these deep structures endure for a very long period of time. They're structures that simply cannot be transformed in a short period of history.

But there were critics who began to complain that this view—this view of structures—would foster a passivity or an abandonment of social critique, because structures would simply be accepted as inevitable, or structures would be viewed as beyond human influence. And at the same time that people were beginning to have doubts about this structuralist interest on long-term structural systems, there was a growing disillusionment with Marxism—in part, because of Stalinism and in part because the economic argument of economic theory did not seem to account adequately for the realities of social and cultural life. And we've seen in earlier lectures how Marxist thinkers in places like the Frankfurt School had begun to rethink the relation between culture and economics. And so all of these patterns continued to develop in the 1960s and 1970s and evolve into a critique of certain forms of structuralism and Marxism.

And what both structuralism and Marxism shared, according to their critics, was a somewhat rigid view of social life. They defined social relations in terms of binary oppositions—rigid categories—in the Marxist case, rigid class categories, binary oppositions: worker and bourgeoisie or worker and capitalist. Or in the case of the structuralist, there were rigid binary oppositions such as for example, nature versus culture.

And so in this cultural and political context of the 1960s and 1970s, a new group of writers and critics began to develop a new movement that was called post-structuralism. That is, the post-structuralists began to challenge the binary thinking of structuralism, of Marxism, and more generally the binary thinking of Western philosophy, which was based on a system of logic that was always rooted in binary oppositions.

Now, the post-structuralists remained interested in deep structures of thought, but they saw these structures as complex, overlapping forms of language—also, overlapping forms of power, overlapping forms of discourse. The post-structuralists always emphasized the intricate inter-relationship between categories of thought rather than simple binary oppositions. And this post-structuralist critique of structuralism and structuralist thought moved toward a new conception of knowledge. It was a new conception of knowledge that stressed the ambiguity of analytical categories, and it also stressed the way knowledge had been merged with power in Western culture.

And we can see these themes coming out most notably in the work of the French writers, Michel Foucault and Jacques Derrida. Foucault examined the relation between power and knowledge and stressed that these two categories—power and knowledge—are always connected in some way in social life. Derrida, on the other hand, was somewhat more concerned with the relation between truth and language or the way in which the metaphysical philosophical tradition continues to influence the use of language even in modern science, modern positivism, all forms of religion, and so forth. He was more concerned with the philosophical dimensions of language usage.

But Foucault and Derrida shared a critique of traditional conceptions of truth, and their critique of these traditions gained very wide international influence in the 1970s and 1980s. And in order to understand the complexity of this post-structuralist critique, we need to look more closely at the ideas of both Foucault and Derrida. Their writings are notoriously challenging and difficult to read, but they've also had a remarkable influence, including among many intellectuals in North America.

Now, both Foucault and Derrida sought alternatives to the dominant discourses of modernity. They were criticizing the way modern thought had evolved. And in this respect, they are drawing on a kind of Nietzschian tradition—the idea that we somehow have to get beyond the metaphysical Western forms of thought to something new. And in their case, what they wanted to get beyond was also Marxism and structuralism. They wanted to create what came to be called a post-Marxist or post-structuralist form of cultural critique. So I want to turn now to Foucault, and I'll turn to Derrida later in this lecture.

Foucault was born in 1926 in the French city of Poitiers, and he would live until 1984. His father was a prominent surgeon, and he wanted his son, Michel, to be a surgeon also. He wanted him to go into medicine. The young Foucault attended Catholic schools, but then he gradually moved away from the idea of studying medicine. He became interested in philosophy. And he was accepted into the École Normale Supérieur in Paris—that breeding ground for many French intellectuals. He went there and studied philosophy. This was in the period of Sartre's great influence and the existential philosophy in the post-war period.

But after he began his philosophical studies, he became skeptical of Sartre's existentialism, and he turned from philosophy to the history of medicine, psychiatry, the history of hospitals and medical practice. And he also worked at a psychiatric hospital. He went to work at a medical clinic.

So, in a way, he kind of returned to where his father wanted him to be, but in a very different way. He was not a physician, but he was a historian of medicine. He later taught French for about six years in various countries around Europe. He taught in Sweden, he taught French in Poland. He lived in Germany and taught there. But he eventually became a professor of philosophy at the University of Clermont-Ferrand in France in 1960, although his research dealt primarily with medicine.

And he began to publish widely in the 1960s. And he published books that were widely praised for new departures in the history of medicine. But he was always drawn abroad at the same time. It was an interesting pattern in Foucault's life. So, for example, even after he had this position at Clermont-Ferrand, he headed to Tunisia in 1966 and taught between 1966 and 1968 in Tunisia. He was actually out of France during the great upheaval in May of 1968.

His writings on medicine and on the nature of scientific knowledge attracted wide public attention. And remarkably enough, he was appointed professor of the history of systems of thought at the College de France in 1970—still a relatively young man in his early 40s, and he's suddenly given this highly prominent position. And Foucault also became a public intellectual. Although he had an academic position, he was active in campaigns for prison reform. He was a critic of various government healthcare policies, and he was a public figure. In fact, his lectures at the College de France drew very large crowds. And I can say at this point that your humble teacher enters into intellectual history, because I remember going to hear Foucault at the College de France in the early '80s. He had a dramatic personal appearance. He came onto the stage. He was completely bald. He wore glasses, and he spoke in a complex and even lyrical language. And there were hundreds of people there, hanging on every word. Or maybe they simply couldn't understand every word, but there they were. It was an event. And Foucault was one of those figures whose work reached far beyond the academy—beyond the university.

He was also an unconventional philosopher, historian, and literary critic. He worked in many different genres of intellectual work. And Foucault was also a homosexual who was drawn to the new gay culture in San Francisco. He lived several times in California in the 1970s and 1980s, because he had visiting physicians as a lecturer at Berkeley—the University of California. And ultimately, Foucault died of AIDS—one of the early victims of that epidemic. And so he had a very complex personal and public life—both inside and outside the university.

Some historians have stressed that his personal and contextual experiences had a very important influence on his thought. That is, his encounter with gay culture, for example in California, gave him an increasing interest and concern with problems of repressions or the problems of cultural discourse or the language of scientific experts—how do experts categorize people? How do they define them? These are all issues that were important to Foucault in both his personal and his intellectual life.

But Foucault's work is difficult to categorize. But in most general terms, he repeatedly emphasized this complex relation between power and knowledge. And we can see this theme running through his major books, beginning with the book *Madness and Civilization*, which was published in 1961 and then in later books like *The Birth of the Clinic*, *The Order of Things*, and then later *Discipline and Punish*, which was published around 1975. So in a period from the early '60s to the late '70s, he published a series of books on the relation between the new forms of knowledge and new modern social institutions. He often focused particularly on the period of the 18th century and the 19th century—the emergence of modernity.

And this interest in the relation between power and experts and knowledge appeared also in his last work, a major three-volume history of sexuality, which was his last major work in which he tried to explain how the scientific and psychological study of sexuality and sexual behavior had transformed the meaning of these forms of human life.

But in all of these books, Foucault argued that modern society relies on structures of dominance and control and surveillance. He said that power is diffused throughout society, and it's diffused through institutions of social control—institutions like schools and prisons and hospitals and armies and many other institutions which individuals encounter in their daily lives. And he called these systems of control a kind of discourse of control, because in all of these institutions, there are experts who describe the people who fall under their surveillance, under their control—people are always being categories, placed in a file, given an identity by experts. And this happens from the day you begin school until your last illness in the hospital. You are put into categories by experts.

And so the knowledge of scientists and doctors and teachers is always linked to power. Knowledge is neither neutral nor benign. It is a method of social management. And Foucault said that this connection between power and knowledge has shaped modern rationalizing societies since the Enlightenment. This is why he was so interested in that period beginning in the late 17th and early 19th century down to the mid 19th century. This was the critical moment in which modernity is created.

So his historical work examined historical issues, such as the emergence of reform movements that created modern asylums, the creation of modern prisons, the development of modern school systems, the creation of modern rational humanitarian policies in modern social life. And he argued that the late Enlightenment had created man as an object of analysis—that man, human beings, must be studied and analyzed and categorized much as an earlier era had created nature as an object of analysis and study. So what he was really interested in was the sciences of man, as he put it—the human sciences in that classical period of the late Enlightenment.

So, for example, his book, *Madness and Civilization*—his first important publication—claimed that modern experts had created madness as a category of knowledge, and then these experts took control of the mad—the people defined as mad—by placing them into asylums. You create a new institution—the modern insane asylum, the modern hospital for the insane—where the experts used knowledge to categorize and control people. This kind of hospital is a point where knowledge and power come together.

And in other books such as *Discipline and Punish* or the history of sexuality, Foucault stressed that experts transformed individuals into objects whose behavior could always be categorized and brought under the gaze of science. As one of his great examples, he took the ideas of Jeremy Bentham, the early 19th-century British utilitarian theorist and philosopher who had an idea about how to create a perfect prison. Bentham wanted a system where the prisoners would be under constant surveillance. And this, to Foucault, was almost a metaphor of the whole modern project. In Bentham's model, the guards would watch the prisoners from a tower—a panopticon—but the prisoners could never see the guards. The guards were on a tower, they were above the prisoners, they were looking down on the prisoners who were in a lighted space, but they couldn't see the guards. And this is Foucault's image of modernity. He says that we are all being watched. We are all being categories. We are all being in some sense under surveillance all of the time. This is how we understand ourselves. But we internalize these categories into the ways we describe ourselves. We discipline ourselves with the language our culture and our experts give us. So if our teachers tell us we're a certain kind of person, that's how we come to understand ourselves. Or if our psychiatrist tells us you have this problem, you say 'ah, that's who I am.' We internalize the discourse of experts.

So power, for Foucault, power which is everywhere, doesn't come a specific economic class or specific government officials, as the Marxists would say or as the political historians have traditionally argued. Instead, for Foucault, power is diffuse, and it is internalized. Power, as he says, "doesn't always weigh on us as a force that says no…it induces pleasure. It forms knowledge. It produces discourse." It is something that enters into us, and we in a way become accomplices of the power system. We don't have to be watched all the time just to feel that we have an identity that has been given to us by our guards, just as the guards in a prison don't have to watch all the time. It's just the thought that they might be watching that keeps you in line.

So Foucault's ideas on these subjects were very much influenced by Nietzsche, because Nietzsche had argued that thought is always linked to the will to power. And in some sense, this is what Foucault is doing. He is arguing that knowledge is always linked to power. And also, Nietzsche had described truth as a cultural construction— as a concept that is always linked to relations of power. So, Nietzsche's claim that healthy instincts and drives were condemned or distorted by civilization was also an important idea for Foucault— that the human being is somehow distorted, redefined by the whole process of modern knowledge and power.

And Foucault responded to these historical patterns much like Nietzsche had responded by saying that he wanted to think outside the tradition. He wanted to explore transgressions. He wanted to challenge values. He wanted to move beyond limits. But at the same time, he suggested that it was more or less impossible to achieve a complete escape from traditions. He wanted to write in unconventional ways, he wanted to live his life in unconventional ways, but he also suggested that it's almost impossible to ever get really outside of this system. It is impossible.

So Foucault offered a new critique of the Enlightenment. He criticized the Enlightenment and the conceptions of the Enlightenment reason. And some theorists thought he provided a theoretical model for spontaneous acts of rebellion or resistance to the modern system of power and knowledge. And yet, I think more generally there's a kind of pessimism here, because in Foucault's account, it's almost impossible to imagine how individuals could ever move outside of this power-knowledge system. There's a kind of pessimism about the limits of human autonomy.

And like Lévi-Strauss and many other theorists, he suggested that the constraints of culture are everywhere—that the autonomous self is a myth. The self is always a construction of multiple discourses and a multiple set of relationships of power and knowledge. There is no fully autonomous self.

Well, a similar emphasis on the multiplicity of language and the cultural construction of the self appears also in the post-structuralist theories of Jacques Derrida. I want to discuss now some of Derrida's ideas.

Derrida was born in Algeria in 1930, and he lived there until he went to Paris to study philosophy once again at the École Normale Supérieur in the early 1950s. And so Derrida came to French culture from the margins, in some sense. He came from the margins in Algeria. But he also came from a marginal position in that he was from a Jewish family in Algeria. So he was, in a sense, doubly marginalized in relation to French society. And perhaps this coming from the margins influenced Derrida's interest and questions about the relation between the center and the margins of culture, thought, and language. He was always in some sense trying to de-center the center of Western thought and Western culture—to think critically about what that center means.

In his own work, Derrida de-emphasized the cultural significance of biography. And he always looked at writing and at ideas in terms of cultural traditions. And yet, I think his own history helped him to question the philosophical tradition. You can see certain elements in his own biography that enable you to see how he developed this critical position toward the main traditions of Western metaphysical thought. Derrida eventually became a philosophy professor at the École Normale in the period between 1964 and 1984. He taught seminars there. He later was at the École des Hautes Études en Sciences Sociales—the social science institute in Paris. And he often visited American universities. Derrida had an enormous influence on

American literary criticism beginning in the 1970s and especially in the 1980s.

And his important early books developed the ideas of deconstruction. His important early books included a book called *Of Grammatology*, which was published in 1967, and another book called *Writing and Difference*, which was also published in 1967. And herein these works, he developed the idea that critical thinkers needed to deconstruct—to take apart aspects of the Western philosophical tradition and think critically about its founding assumptions. Someone like Heidegger had said that in order to think, you have to understand the foundation of being—what is the meaning of being. Derrida said in order to think, you have to understand the metaphysical philosophical assumptions that underlie modern Western thought.

And so Derrida's principle theoretical objective was to challenge the Western philosophical belief in the clarity and rational distinctions that constitute conceptions of truth. He wanted to question those clear and distinct oppositions between categories that are based on logic. And this was similar in some ways to Nietzsche's project—the idea, for example, that there is a clear distinction between nature and culture as Lévi-Strauss had argued.

According to Derrida, we cannot have ideas or categories that are pure and distinct from other ideas or categories. We can't get to what philosophers used to call the thing itself. There's no object, there's no idea that stands unrelated to other ideas. And therefore, the idea of a full presence in some concept—a full presence in some being—is always problematic. He argued that our accounts of reality and our ideas always depend upon metaphors. We always have to use language to approach an object. And our use of binary oppositions can never be pure dichotomies. This is the assumption of the philosophical tradition. You have A and B. And A cannot be B. A and B—category A and category B—stand in clear opposition to each other. But Derrida says no, that's not true, because every idea requires supplements of some kind of otherness to establish its meaning so that A and B are not in complete opposition. They are related to each other.

For example, it's impossible to think of nature without culture. The very meaning of the category of nature carries with it the supplement of the other idea of culture. Culture and nature are inseparable. Or we cannot think of the idea of day without the category of night—or the meaning of male is already always linked to the idea of female. These ideas are never simply binary opposition. Every idea or concept is always already carried by the other—by a supplement that is part of the idea. And the other is always in the self. You might think of it as those yin-yang models where you have a little dot in the other. That's a supplement. The meaning is related to its other.

Now, what does this mean in philosophical and cultural terms? It means that there can never be a fully coherent, autonomous idea or identity—an idea which has full presence or meaning in and of itself. Even the most transcendent idea—say, the idea of God—requires the existence of something that is not God to have its meaning. You can never get to something that is pure and completely enclosed within itself. Every idea requires some other in order to have its meaning or its coherence even as an idea.

And language shows how these relationships work. Derrida stressed that there can be no claim about reality or truth or knowledge that does not depend on language. And these linguistic claims are always relational. And this becomes the theme of post-modernism—a claim that Derrida also develops in his work; a claim that we can never get to a material object that is beyond symbolic meaning—that is beyond language. All objects, all ideas, are always already embedded in language.

As he said in one of his most famous lines, "there is nothing outside the text." That is, you can never reach something that is not somehow mediated or described by language. Reality cannot escape language or writing. But at the same time, the meaning of language always exceeds or escapes what we intend for it to mean. We simply cannot control language, because in some sense, language contests what we want it to do.

Well, Derrida's themes led him more often to philosophers and literary figures than to the kind of social experts whom Foucault described. The work of Derrida and Foucault appeals to somewhat different readers and critics. And yet their post-structuralist projects shared a critical interrogation of the metaphysical conception of stable truth and the transparency of language. And this emphasis on the multiple levels and the power of language shaped a whole new system of thought—a new analysis of how cultural systems define truth and social order. And it also fostered a post-modern interest in fragmentation and difference, which we will continue to discuss in the next lecture on post-modernism.

Lecture Twenty-Three
European Postmodernism

Scope:

"Postmodernism" is difficult to define, but it has deeply affected contemporary art, literature, architecture, and social theory. This lecture notes how postmodern thinkers describe the fragmentation and contingency of social life and personal experience. Postmodernism questions universalisms and the belief in "objective reality," thus developing a new critique of Enlightenment traditions. This lecture discusses three authors who have contributed to postmodernist thought: Jean Baudrillard, Jacques Lacan, and Julia Kristeva. These French theorists—especially Lacan—revised Freud's psychoanalytic theory and claimed that it is impossible to achieve a fully coherent or unified identity.

Outline

I. A wide range of influential tendencies in European intellectual life over the last 30 or 40 years are often lumped together under the general term "postmodernism."

   A. The term is vague and people disagree about both its meaning and significance. It has been important in the arts, advertising, and the study of cultures.

   1. The term suggests that we have moved beyond modernity, which is usually linked to the legacy of the Enlightenment and the Scientific Revolution; this tradition assumed the existence of an objective reality.

   2. The modern Enlightenment tradition also assumed that we can know this reality through the use of science and reason.

   B. We've seen how modernism in literature and the arts reacted against these Enlightenment ideas. "Modernist" literature appeared most notably in the works of writers such as Proust, Joyce, and Woolf.

   1. Modernism questioned and rejected the idea that there is simply a reality "out there" that can be known and described.

   2. Yet modernist artists and writers often stressed the specific vision or insights of creative persons; the artist has a unique vision.

3. Modernism tended to emphasize the unique language, memory, and internal life of the individual artist (an old Romantic theme).

C. Postmodernism has moved beyond both Enlightenment modernity and literary modernism. It claims that objects are never simply "there" as the Enlightenment assumed; objects are "constructed" by cultural discourses.
   1. Foucault's accounts of sexuality or madness, for example, showed how these "realities" were created by modern scientific experts.
   2. Postmodernism also challenges the belief in a distinctive vision of authors or artists; it sees authors as exemplars of cultural discourses.

D. In place of the Enlightenment's unified, coherent world and modernist art's autonomous creative work, postmodernism stresses fragmentation.
   1. Postmodernist culture is said to lack unity or coherence; it's a world of constant movement, change, contingency, and flux.
   2. One analyst of postmodernism, David Harvey, says, "Post-modernism swims, even wallows, in the fragmentary and the chaotic currents of change, as if that is all there is."
   3. This view assumes there are no stable identities or truths, only shifting cultural constructions that evolve through the dialogic interaction of different languages, cultures, and discourses.

E. Postmodernism rejects the desire for a systematic master narrative or universalizing theory, such as Enlightenment rationalism, Marxism, or religion.
   1. Unlike Enlightenment thinkers (e.g., Voltaire), the postmodern writer cannot claim to defend social or legal reforms in the name of reason.
   2. The postmodern writer can only interpret cultures or discourses in relation to other cultures because there are no fully coherent cultures or persons.
   3. This theory accepts and promotes the idea of fragmentation as an alternative to the hierarchies and unities of inherited cultural truths.

F. Postmodernist themes can be found in the works of the French theorists Jean Baudrillard, Jacques Lacan, and Julia Kristeva.

    1. Each of these authors pointed to the contingency of ideas, the fluidity of identities, and the relational nature of truth.

    2. But their ideas, like the work of all other theorists, has evolved out of a particular historical and cultural context; what is this context?

II. Baudrillard (1929–) described the contemporary world as a fragmented cultural and economic system that produces what Durkheim had described as anomie.

  A. Baudrillard studied German philosophy and literature in the 1950s and began his career as a sociology teacher, but even his earliest works showed a deep interest in the characteristics of modern consumer culture.

    1. Like many late 20th-century European intellectuals, he spent time in America, lectured in American universities, and interpreted American culture as the advanced example of a postmodern social world.

    2. He discussed American culture in such works as *Simulacra and Simulation* (1981) and *America* (1986).

    3. America represents the culmination of a social process in which consumerism, anonymity, and visual images define social experience.

  B. For Baudrillard, the postmodern world is a "simulation" of reality; it is constructed in television images or imitations of reality (e.g., Disneyland).

    1. It is also a world of "virtual reality" or what Baudrillard calls "hyperreality," in which the simulation becomes what we know best.

    2. This is a world of public and personal fragmentation into subcultures. The freeways of big cities are examples of this world of vast movement in all directions by anonymous people in cars.

    3. Economic life is dominated by consumer culture and massive advertising. In this world, you are what you buy.

4. Consumption rather than production is the theme of postmodern economies. Television and visual culture are the media for our time; people consume images with little interest in deeper complexities.

C. In this kind of world, we can have no faith in master narratives of political progress or political action; people watch TV and shop until they drop.

1. Baudrillard's themes build on the assumption that there is no unified or coherent self; the person (like other realities) is fragmented.

2. This idea was also one of the key themes of Jacques Lacan.

III. Lacan (1901–1981) was born into a prosperous family of vinegar merchants in Paris. He attended a Jesuit school and lived virtually his entire life in Parisian culture.

A. He renounced Catholicism, studied medicine, and became a practicing psychiatrist with a special interest in criminality and paranoia.

1. He was active in various Freudian psychoanalytic groups, but he was eventually expelled from all orthodox psychoanalytic associations.

2. He became closely connected to surrealism (André Breton was a good friend) and studied the linguistic theories of Saussure.

3. He was always something of a "rebel," but he also married twice and had four children. He wanted intellectual acclaim.

4. In his later years, he taught famous seminars in such places as the École des Hautes Études and the École Normale Supérieure.

5. He hesitated to publish his ideas (fearing misinterpretation), and his writings were often almost impossible to understand.

B. Lacan's most well known book was a collection of essays called simply *Ecrits* (*Writings*, 1966), but his seminar lectures were also transcribed and published.

1. Lacan gained great influence by developing several key themes; he especially wanted to bring together linguistics and psychoanalysis.

2. He sought to revise psychoanalysis by stressing the role of language in the unconscious ("the unconscious is structured like a language").

3. He also sought to revise linguistics by stressing the role of desire, the body, sexuality, and pleasure in the workings of all language.

C. Lacan also argued that both the language and the unconscious prevent people from achieving a fully coherent self; everyone has multiple selves.

1. People often deny this multiplicity, however, and pathologies emerge when people fail to understand the multiple levels of the ego or the self.

2. The problem evolves from what Lacan called "The Mirror Stage of Development" that each child goes through between the ages of six and 18 months, when people begin seeing themselves as coherent beings.

D. This discovery of the self occurs literally when we see ourselves reflected in a mirror, but more generally, this mirror experience occurs for all people in our relations with other people.

1. Parents and others respond to the child and confirm his or her identity as an autonomous being.

2. But Lacan argued that this sense of coherence cannot last as we grow older because we learn through symbolic languages and interactions that we are really many different people; we have no single self.

3. Each of us is a set of multiple selves, depending on contexts, relations, and interactions with others. Lacan called this process the "splitting of the ego" and said that you must see your multiple selves in order to mature.

E. If you go on believing in or yearning for that sense of full unity or presence that you had at the mirror stage of development, you will be unhappy.

1. This unity cannot be achieved; yet the desire for this complete unity can lead to anger or violence if people demand full recognition of their unity or coherence.

2. People need to learn symbolic languages that enable them to see themselves and others as people with multiple identities.

F. For the child, the strongest desire for unity comes in the desire to be united with the mother, but the healthy person learns to see the mother as "other."

    1. This identity—this separation from the mother—is described with language that comes from the father because that is also his relation to the child's mother: She is "other" to him.

    2. The language of identity is, therefore, "gendered" male. Woman is the other of language and identity, and language is "phallocentric."

G. Lacan's work has two crucial themes: People must give up the desire for full unity or coherence, and they should recognize the connection between (phallocentric) language and the body.

IV. Lacan's arguments had a wide influence on postmodernist thought, which has stressed the importance of language and the fragmentation of identities.

    A. These themes were picked up and revised by Julia Kristeva (1941–), who came from Bulgaria to study in France in 1966.

    B. She was interested in the relations between margins and the "center" of language and culture; this issue was part of her own experience as a Bulgarian and a woman in French society (she married the writer Philippe Sollers).

        1. Kristeva accepted Lacan's idea that the self comes to identity through reflections of others. She agreed that the language people use to define their identities comes from fathers (for whom women are "others").

        2. Unlike Lacan, Kristeva thought that one did not have to go on repeating the language of the father. It is possible to find the voice of the mother and move beyond gendered male language.

    C. Kristeva argued that pure identities cannot exist; the mother and father are already interdependent, and identities are "dialogic."

    D. French theorists led the cultural challenge to (French) Enlightenment conceptions of identity and knowledge; they influenced postmodern thought everywhere by showing the fluid interrelations of all identities and ideas.

Essential Reading:

Jean Baudrillard, *America*.

Julia Kristéva, "Women's Time," in Toril Moi, editor, *The Kristeva Reader*, pp. 188–211.

Supplementary Reading:

Elisabeth Roudinesco, *Jacques Lacan*, pp. 260–290, 319–348.

Questions to Consider:

1. Do you think that "virtual reality," images, and simulations have become the dominant shaping forces in contemporary social and cultural life?

2. Do you agree with Lacan's claim that all people have multiple selves?

Lecture Twenty-Three—Transcript
European Postmodernism

The themes of post-structuralist theory, which I discussed in the last lecture, became part of what is often called postmodernism. And a very wide range of influential tendencies in European intellectual life over the last 30 or 40 years have often been lumped together under this term of postmodernism. It's a term that is vague, and people disagree about both its meaning and its significance. But generally, I think we can say postmodernism has been important in the arts, it has been important in advertising, it has been important in the study of culture, it's been important in a whole range of academic and intellectual endeavors as well as certain aspects of popular culture.

And in general, this term suggests that we have moved beyond modernity. And in this sense, modernity is usually linked to the legacy of the Enlightenment and the scientific revolution. And in this tradition—the tradition of modernity—it was assumed that there was an objective reality—there is a world out there that science and systematic analysis can explain and describe.

This modernist Enlightenment tradition assumed that we can know this reality through the use of science and reason. So, one of the ways to think about modernity is to see it as a form of thought that believes we can know the world objectively through science. But we've also seen how modernism in literature and the arts acted against these Enlightenment ideas so that there was a modernist literature that appeared in writers such as Proust or James Joyce or Virginia Woolf—a modernist literature which, in some ways, called into question the Enlightenment tradition and Enlightenment assumption of a coherent, stable reality.

So, modernism questioned and rejected the idea that there is simply a reality out there which can be known and described. And yet, the modernist artist and writers often stressed the specific vision or insights of creative persons. In other words, they assumed the artist has a unique vision—a unique understanding of the world. And so, modernism tended to emphasize the unique language, memory, and internal life of the individual artist. In this respect, modernism might be compared to certain older themes in romanticism.

Now, postmodernism has moved beyond both Enlightenment modernity and literary modernism. And postmodernism claims that objects are never simply there, as the Enlightenment assumes or as scientific language had assumed. Postmodernism stresses that objects are constructed by cultural discourses. So, for example, as we saw in the case of Michel Foucault, Foucault describes sexuality or madness to show how these realities—these apparent realities—were created by the language and the discourse of modern scientific experts—that something called madness came into existence as the language constructed this reality.

Well, postmodernism challenges that Enlightenment conception of something simply being there. But postmodernism also challenges the belief in a distinctive vision of authors or artists, and it sees authors as exemplars or as expressions of broad cultural discourses. So it also breaks with the idea of literary modernism, the distinctive artistic vision.

So, in place of the Enlightenment's unified, coherent world and the modernist arts' conception of the autonomous creative work, postmodernism stresses fragmentation, and that might be one way to think what this term means. Postmodernist culture is generally said to lack unity or coherence. It is a world of constant movement, change, contingency, and flux. Everything in this world is in a process of change. There is no stability—no stable center.

One of the important analysts of postmodernism, a man named David Harvey, has written that "postmodernism swims—even wallows—in the fragmentary and the chaotic currents of change as if that is all there is." That's a nice way, I think, of describing it—a notion of swimming, even wallowing, in the fragmentary and the chaotic. And this view—this postmodernist view—assumes that there are no stable identities or truths—only shifting cultural constructions that evolve through dialogues or through dialogic interactions of different languages, cultures, and discourses—that what we understand as truth is simply a set of competing languages—competing symbolic systems—in which different speakers try to define reality in their own terms and in their own set of cultural references.

And so postmodernism tends to reject all desire for a systematic, master narrative. Postmodernism rejects the universalizing theory such as Enlightenment rationalism or Marxism or religion. It claims there are no universals in this respect—certainly no cultural universals.

And unlike Enlightenment thinkers, for example, Voltaire or some of the other great writers of the 18th century, the postmodern writer does not claim to defend social or legal reform in the name of reason, because there is no position beyond culture where one can stake out a claim for a universal reason. This is the basic assumption of postmodernism. The postmodern writer can only interpret writers or discourses to other discourses, because there are no coherent cultures—no fully coherent cultures—or persons, no universal positions from which truth can be confidently asserted.

And so, this theory accepts and promotes the idea of fragmentation as an alternative to the hierarchies and unities of inherited cultural truths. And this emphasis on fragmentation is one of the reasons the theory has often been criticized—it seems to lack any conception of unity.

Well, in order to understand how this postmodernist theory has evolved, we could look at a number of recent writers, but I want to look at the example of three French theorists who have had an important influence on postmodernist thought. I want to refer to Jean Baudrillard, Jacques Lacan, and to Julia Kristeva. And I want to suggest that all of these authors—for all of their differences—emphasize the contingency of ideas and the fluidity of identities and the relational nature of truth—something that we already saw in the example of Derrida—the idea that there is no stable position of truth. Truth is in a set of relationships. And this is also true of identities. The human identity is always multi-dimensional and always embedded in a set of relationships. There is no simple self that can be identified as a fully coherent entity.

But the ideas of the postmodernists, for all of their radical critique of various traditions, the ideas of the postmodernists also have evolved out of a particular historical and cultural context. And so, as cultural and intellectual historians, we can attempt to situate them in place and time. So what is the context in which the postmodernists have developed their ideas?

I think a place to start here is the work of Baudrillard. Baudrillard was born in 1929, and he has written a number of works describing the contemporary world as a fragmented cultural and economic system—a fragmented system that produces what Durkheim described at the beginning of the 20th century as an experience of anomie—a separation, a disconnectedness. And I think that this is the contextual theme that Baudrillard and others draw from the world in which they live.

Baudrillard studied German philosophy and literature as a student in the 1950s. And then he began his career as a sociology teacher. But even in his earliest work, Baudrillard showed a deep interest in the characteristics of modern, consumer culture. And like many 20th-century European intellectuals, Baudrillard spent time in America. He lectured in American universities, he interpreted American culture, he wrote about America as the most advanced example of what he would call the postmodern social world.

And he discussed American culture in various works, such as *Simulacra and Simulation* in 1981 or another book simply called *America*, published in 1986. These are books in which Baudrillard tries to explain how America somehow represents the culmination of a social process that has carried us beyond the modern world to something that we can call the postmodern world. And in the postmodern world, we see a society dominated by consumerism and by anonymity and especially by visual images. In this postmodern world, our understanding of reality is given to us by images that define social experience. So, when someone has an experience, they might say it was something like in a movie or it was like something you might see on TV. In other words, the image of the world that we see in film or television gives us our understanding of reality itself.

So, for Baudrillard, the postmodern world is a simulation of reality. It is always constructed in television images or in imitations of reality. So, for example, Disneyland is the ultimate kind of postmodern place for Baudrillard. It's a place that's not a real place. It's a virtual reality, created to look like something that it really isn't. It isn't really a turn-of-the-century small town in America. It is a simulation of something else. This is what Baudrillard calls virtual reality, or sometime he calls it hyper-reality in which the simulation becomes what we actually know. There is no there. There is only a simulation of something else.

And this is the world of public and personal fragmentation in which we all live in a relationship with our television sets rather than with something is part of our daily lives. So he says that so much of the modern world is mediated by these images. For example, even warfare for modern people at the end of the 20th century is something you see on TV. It's something like a video game that you watch on TV rather than some experience like people experienced war in the 18th century, or some other period in time.

And he also says that the sort of metaphor for this postmodern world is the freeway of a big city. Imagine yourself driving down the freeway in Los Angeles where you don't know another person. Everyone is scattered in their own car. This is the world of vast movement in which people are moving in all directions, but you don't know who they are. You have no idea of where anyone is going. That is the postmodern world—isolated selves floating around in cars and watching the world go by on television.

And this is also a world in which economic life is dominated by consumer culture and mass advertising so that in this postmodern world, consumption is more important than production. You are what you buy. You want to know who you are? You show yourself by what you wear and what products you buy. And this is the theme of the postmodern economy—consumption rather than production. And so the television, the visual culture, the media of our time—these are the things that are giving people their identity and their reality. And people consume images with little interest in deeper complexities.

And in this kind of world, all of the traditional ways that we understand life are mediated through these images. So politics also, for example, is something we see on TV, and it's something that is presented to us in a series of images or sound bites rather than in the classic debate of a post-Enlightenment public sphere.

So, in this kind of world, we can have no faith in a master narrative—a progress. We can only assume that there can be isolated actions, and we may even watch politics like we watch other things. We watch TV and basically people shop until they drop. That's the modern experience.

Now, Baudrillard's themes build on the assumption that there is no unified or coherent self. And this is that crucial postmodern idea. The person, like other realities, is fragmented. There is no fully coherent identity. And this is the idea also that is one of the key themes of Jacques Lacan, the theorist I want to turn to now, and one of the most influential theorists in the development of certain forms of postmodernist thought.

Lacan was born in 1901 in Paris and lived until 1981—lived about 80 years. He was born into a prosperous family of vinegar merchants in Paris—an interesting background for a postmodernist theorist—he came from a vinegar merchant family. He attended Jesuit schools and lived virtually his entire life in Parisian culture.

But as he reached his maturity, he renounced Catholicism. He turned to the study of medicine and became a practicing psychiatrist with a particular interest in criminality and paranoia—studying people who were suffering from various forms of paranoia. And he was active in various Freudian psychoanalytical groups in France.

But he was eventually expelled from all orthodox psychoanalytic associations. Whenever he tried to be part of these groups, they found his ideas so disconcerting or alien to the main themes of their association, that he was pushed out. He formed his own groups, and some of these also went out of existence.

Now, Lacan was a psychoanalyst or a psychiatrist who was closely connected to Surrealism. And André Breton was one of his good friends in the interwar period—the late '20s and 1930s. And he also studied the linguistic theories of Saussure. Lacan was very interested in structural linguistics. And he was in his personal life and in his intellectual life always something of a rebel. He liked to think of himself as an outside. There were also some conventional things about Lacan. He was married twice, he had four children, he had some family life. He was not totally on the Bohemian edge.

And he also wanted intellectual acclaim in Paris. He had that very conventional intellectual ambition. In his later years, he taught a series of famous seminars in places like the École des Hautes Études in Paris and at the École Noramle Supérieur—these special elite schools in Paris. And one of the interesting things about Lacan is that he hesitated to publish his ideas. For years, he published very little. He was always afraid that his ideas would be misinterpreted and that people would misappropriate his ideas. And that's easy to understand why he would worry about that, because his writings are virtually impossible to understand. Reading Lacan is one of the most difficult intellectual experiences one could have. He stymies every attempt for a nice, logical discourse, and he always explores things in a sort of labyrinth puzzle of meaning.

His best-known book was a collection of essays that was called simply Ecrits, which means writings. This was the title of the book, and there was this whole collection of his writings that appeared in 1966. But his seminar lectures were also transcribed and published. He became—Lacan became—almost like a cult figure where people would go year after year to his seminars and write down what he said and work with him and eventually many of these seminar presentations were published.

And Lacan gained great influence by developing several themes in these seminars. He especially wanted to bring together linguistics and psychoanalysis. That's the distinctive intellectual project of Lacan. He wanted to revise psychoanalysis by stressing the role of language in the unconscious. As he said in some of his seminars, "The unconscious is structured like a language." So just as Lévi-Strauss was trying to understand how culture is structured like a language, Lacan was saying the unconscious mind is like a language. It has certain categories that are organized in the way we organize language. And the access to the unconscious is, of course, always mediated through language.

But he also wanted to revise linguistics. He wanted to revise psychoanalysis by stressing the importance of linguistics. And he wanted to revise linguistics by stressing the role of unconscious, the role of desire, the role of the body, the role of sexuality, the role of pleasure in the workings of language. He wanted to give a physical dimension to linguistic meaning. So he argued that both the language and the unconscious prevent people from achieving a fully coherent self—that language always distorts or alters what we might think of as a fully coherent self. But also, the unconscious deifies any attempt for simple categorization.

So everyone has multiple selves. And this is Lacan's other critically important idea. There is no single self. And yet, he said that people often deny this multiplicity. And because they refuse to see that they have these multiple selves, they have pathologies. They develop problems like paranoia or criminal behaviors, because they fail to understand the multiple levels of the ego or of the self. Now, why does this problem develop? Where does this problem come from?

According to Lacan, this problem—the problem of not realizing the multiplicity of the self—this problem evolves from what Lacan calls the mirror stage of development. The mirror stage of development is something that each child goes through between the ages of six and 18 months—when people begin to see themselves as coherent beings. This is when you begin to have a coherent sense of self. And discovery of the self occurs literally when we see ourselves reflected in a mirror. You say, 'oh, there I am.' And you begin to realize that you are something separate from others—that you have a self.

So there's literally an encounter with a mirror. But more generally, this mirror experience occurs for all people in our relations with other people. Other people in a sense are like a mirror to ourselves. We see ourselves mirrored in others. So as a child grows up, the parents and others respond to the child and confirm his or her identity as an autonomous being. The self is always constructed in these mirror relationships with other people.

But Lacan argued that this sense of coherence cannot last as we grow older, because we learn through symbolic languages and actions that we are really many different people. We have no single self. Each of us is a set of multiple selves depending on the context and the relations and interactions with other people. And this you can note from your own experience—for example, the sort of person you are with your parents is different from the kind of person you are with your friends or your professional colleagues or your children. Every set of relations brings out a slightly different self. And this is the sign of a healthy person as being able to recognize, according to Lacan, the multiplicity of the self. And Lacan called this process the splitting of the ego. You must see your multiple selves in order to mature. But if you go on believing in or yearning for that full sense of unity or a completely coherent self that you had at the mirror stage of development, you will always be unhappy, because you can't get back to that. This unity—this mirrored unity of the self—cannot be achieved. And yet, some people continue to yearn for it. And it is this desire for complete unity—for a wholly unified self that can lead to anger or even violence. If people demand full recognition of their unity or coherence from other people, and they don't get it, they become angry. They can become violent, because they don't feel that they are getting what they really need to have themselves affirmed. But if the self is understood to be multiple, then there's less tension—less demand—for a fully coherent identity.

So, according to Lacan, people need to learn symbolic languages that enable them to see themselves and others as people with multiple identities. And for the child, the strongest desire for unity comes from the desire to be united with the mother. But the healthy person learns to see the mother—as something outside the self—as separate from the self. And this is how an identity comes about—it's through separation from the mother.

But according to Lacan, this separation comes from language that comes from the father, because that is always his relationship to the child's mother. That is, in order for the child to learn a language about the mother as someone other, this has to come from the father, because the mother is also other to the father. It's a kind of complicated idea, but it's essential to Lacan's notion of language, because it means that the language of identity is gendered male—that woman is the other of language and identity. And language is always, in some sense, phallo-centric, which means that it comes from the phallic position of the male. He uses that term—the phallo-centric language.

So there are two crucial, complex themes in Lacan's work. The first stresses that people must give up their desire for full unity or coherence. And the second stresses that they should recognize the connection between a phallo-centric language and the body—that language is rooted in the male and female bodies.

Well, Lacan's argument had a very wide influence on postmodernist thought, despite its difficulty. And it has had an influence in that it stresses the importance of language and fragmentation of identities—something that is picked up again and again in postmodernist thought. And we can see these ideas also appearing in the work of Julia Kristeva.

Kristeva, who was born in 1941 in Bulgaria, and moved from Bulgaria to study in France in 1966. She attended Lacan's seminar—became very familiar with his work. But Kristeva also worked closely with Roland Barthes, who was another influential theorist in Parisian academic circles. And she made a very rapid advance in the intellectual culture of Paris. In fact, Kristeva eventually became a professor of linguistics in Paris.

But she was also interested, like Lacan, in this link between language and psychoanalysis. And she was also interested in the relations between the margins and the center of language and culture—much like Derrida. And I think this issue was important for Kristeva, in part, also because of her experience as a Bulgarian and a woman in French society. She felt herself both inside and outside that society. She eventually married a French writer, Philippe Sollers, and made her permanent home in French life.

Kristeva accepted Lacan's idea that the self comes to identity through the reflections of other people—through the interactions with others. And she agreed with Lacan that the language that people use to find their identities comes from fathers, for whom the women are always other. But unlike Lacan, Kristeva thought that one did not have to go on simply repeating the language of the father. It's possible, she said, to find the voice of the mother or the voice of the woman and move on beyond this gendered male language—this language that she also would call the phallo-centric language of the cultural tradition.

Now, Kristeva denied that there could be an essential feminine language or an essential male language. She wanted a mediation between the two—what she called a kind of dialogic relationship or an endless dialogue between the similarities and the difference between women and men. So Kristeva argued that pure identities or pure languages cannot exist. The mother and the father are always already interdependent. And identities are already dialogic. They are interrelated. And so, as the child grows up, as the human being reaches a mature identity, this human being has to recognize a male-female dialogic relation within the self—between various forms of language.

And so, in this emphasis on the internal dialogue of the self, Kristeva shared the postmodern emphasis on flux, on movement, and on dialogic exchanges rather than this concept of a classical, stable identity. She said that gendered identities, like all other identities, are not stable. And so, in this respect, she resembled Lacan in stressing the multiple layers of the self but stressing that this self could be female and male—that the language, the discourse—could be multiple in its linguistic and gendered meaning.

So, the French theorists led a cultural challenge to the French Enlightenment. It was the French theorists of the 1970s and 1980s that challenged the Enlightenment concepts of identity and knowledge. And they influence postmodern thought everywhere by showing the fluid interrelations of all identities and all ideas. And yet, as postmodernism gained wide support, there were a number of other theorists who began to criticize postmodernisms rejection of the Enlightenment. And in the final lecture, I want to turn to the critique of postmodernism that emerged in the late 20th century.

Lecture Twenty-Four
Changes and Traditions at Century's End

Scope:

European societies were deeply affected by late 20th-century events, including the Cold War, the "Americanization" of cultural life, the arrival of large immigrant populations, the demise of communist regimes, and the expansion of the new global economy. Although Europe was uniting in a new "European Union," no single European intellectual culture existed at the end of the 20th century. Yet there was a renewed interest in Enlightenment conceptions of reason and the critically engaged intellectual, and elements of classical liberalism reappeared in new intellectual support for "neo-liberal" ideas. This lecture summarizes these cultural patterns, with specific reference to the German thinker Jürgen Habermas and the Czech writer Václav Havel. It also notes that European intellectual life remained a center of lively debate at the end of the 20th century.

Outline

I. We are coming to the end of a survey of 20th-century European intellectual history, but there is no simple way to summarize European thought in the late 20th century.

   A. The fragmentation of European cultural life in the modern era precludes the possibility of final synthesis; there is rarely a closure to historical processes.

   D. There were, however, a number of important changes in the late 20th-century historical context, and this changing context (as always) affected intellectuals.

   C. During more than four decades (1947–1989), Europe was deeply affected by the Cold War and the growing influence of the United States in European economic, political, and cultural life.

      1. The American economic and cultural influence appeared in fashion, films, television, music, politics, and even universities.

      2. European intellectuals often expressed concern about the impact of "Americanization" on Europe's cultural traditions and social life.

D. At the same time, those traditions seemed to be changing as millions of new immigrants streamed into Europe from Africa, Asia, and the Middle East.

    1. A new debate about "multiculturalism" emerged in all the major European nations. How would the languages, religions, and cultural values of non-European peoples be assimilated into European life?

    2. Such questions redefined the meaning of European nations; the creation of the European Union was also redefining nation-states.

E. Finally, the end of the Cold War, the collapse of communist regimes in central Europe, and the new global economy all changed the context for intellectual debate in Europe, as in all other parts of the world.

    1. Such changes surely contributed to the popularity of postmodernism, the emphasis on fragmented identities, and the decline of Marxism.

    2. Marxism seemed an inadequate social theory in this context, as did the nationalist belief in coherent, unique national identities.

    3. As we've seen, modern capitalist advertising, consumerism, entertainment, and travel all suggested a breakdown of older traditions.

F. Late 20th-century European intellectual life did not, however, turn entirely to postmodernism. In fact, postmodernist critiques of the autonomous "subject" and liberal definitions of reason provoked new defenses of the Enlightenment.

    1. This lecture concludes our survey of 20th-century thought with a discussion of what might be called the challenges to postmodernism.

    2. These challenges include a new affirmation of two key Enlightenment ideas: the critical importance of reason in public life and the critical role of intellectuals in political and cultural debates.

    3. These trends can be seen in two representative intellectual figures, the German social theorist Jürgen Habermas and the Czech writer Václav Havel; both of these intellectuals have reaffirmed Enlightenment ideas.

G. Critics have attacked postmodernist thought for promoting an excessive emphasis on the shaping power of language. Habermas and Havel recognize the importance of language, but they argue that language is not just arbitrary.

    1. They come back to the Enlightenment belief that language can convey general and even universal truths that can be defended in public life.

    2. They also argue (like most Enlightenment intellectuals) that personal freedom requires an engagement with public life and public issues.

II. The challenge to poststructuralism and postmodernism has been particularly notable in Germany; this is perhaps ironic because postmodernist thought in France and elsewhere drew on German thinkers, such as Nietzsche, Husserl, and Heidegger.

    A. Many intellectuals in post-Nazi Germany, however, wanted to recover the positive aspects of the Enlightenment and worried about the nonrational themes of Romanticism and anti-Enlightenment thought.

        1. A skeptical view of Romanticism was particularly evident in the work of Jürgen Habermas (1929–). Habermas grew up near Cologne in western Germany; his father directed a local chamber of commerce.

        2. Habermas was too young to be in the German army during World War II, but he was much affected by postwar revelations of Nazi atrocities.

        3. He studied philosophy and sociology and became affiliated with the reorganized Frankfurt School of critical theory in the 1950s.

        4. He spent most of his later career as a professor in Frankfurt but also participated widely in public debates; he wrote often in newspapers.

    B. Habermas was disturbed by the failure of German intellectuals and political leaders to come to terms with the Nazi past.

        1. He believed that intellectuals in Germany had wrongly turned away from reason and Enlightenment ideals of public debate. (Heidegger was, for Habermas, a prominent example of this error.)

2. Habermas sought to revise aspects of Kantian philosophy, to warn against the dangers of Romanticism; he favored democratic socialism.

C. He developed many of his major themes in his first book, *The Structural Transformation of the Public Sphere* (1962).
   1. This book argued that the Enlightenment had created a model for a public sphere in which debates flourished on the basis of reason.
   2. He admired the Enlightenment but argued that the Enlightenment ideal of a rational public sphere had declined in the modern world.

D. Habermas argued that intellectuals and everyone else who cared about democratic public life should defend the use of reason and rational criticism.
   1. This defense of Enlightenment reason led to his strong critique of such thinkers as Foucault and Derrida, whom he saw as too hostile to the values of reason.
   2. He laid out his critique of postmodern theories in *The Philosophical Discourse of Modernity* (1985) and other works.
   3. Habermas argued repeatedly that it was impossible to fight the residue of Nazism or the distortions of radical ethnic, national, and religious movements by using philosophies that challenge rationalism.
   4. He said that various forms of "instrumental" reason were dangerous or insufficiently critical, but "communicative" reason offered essential tools for critical judgment, analysis, and debate.

E. He criticized the philosophical legacy of Nietzsche and insisted that postmodernism had abandoned the all-important belief in rational criticism.
   1. Habermas resembled Kant in arguing that the critical use of reason could bring about cross-cultural agreements on truth and public actions.
   2. His own goal was to develop a democratic public life in which communication could take place without coercion or domination.

      3. Arguments would develop through clear speech, and rational debaters would reach agreement on reasonable, just forms of action.

    F. Habermas shared the common modern concern with language but rejected the postmodern emphasis on the indeterminacy of linguistic meaning.

    G. His critique of postmodernism has been influential in historical studies, philosophy, and political theory; it also promotes Enlightenment ideas about the public role of intellectual work.

III. Habermas defended aspects of the Marxist intellectual tradition in his work on the flaws of the modern "public sphere." Other intellectuals shared his sympathy for the Enlightenment but moved much further away from Marxist ideas.

    A. This other pattern of the non-Marxist public intellectual can be seen in the life and career of Václav Havel (1936–).

        1. Havel was born in Prague; his father was an architect and building contractor. Young Václav grew up during the Nazi occupation and was later excluded from a university education during the communist era.

        2. His family was deemed too bourgeois, so Havel made his own way on the margins of Czech cultural and intellectual life.

        3. He became a writer and, by the early 1960s, was producing absurdist plays for theaters in Prague.

    B. Havel became much more concerned with political issues after the Soviet invasion of Czechoslovakia in 1968.

        1. He wrote a series of dissenting political commentaries, including a famous essay called "The Power of the Powerless" (1978).

        2. He also became a founding leader of a humans rights group called Charter 77, which demanded protection for democratic civil rights.

        3. In his writings, Havel argued that the people could reshape public life, even if they appeared to be "powerless" under dictatorial regimes.

C. Havel argued that "people power" could, in effect, overcome the dead hand of authoritarianism. Intellectuals had a crucial role to play in this process. Havel was arrested and imprisoned for his writings; he spent four years in prison (1979–1983) but did not turn away from his ideas.

D. When the nonviolent, "velvet revolution" overthrew the communist regime in Czechoslovakia (1989), it seemed that Havel's ideas had been confirmed. He was, in fact, chosen to be president of the new Czech government and went on to a prominent, sometimes controversial political career.

IV. Did European thought at the end of the 20th century come back to the point where modern intellectual life began: the rationalist themes of the Enlightenment?

A. Many intellectuals clearly expressed a renewed appreciation for classical Enlightenment beliefs in tolerance, reason, and human rights. The horrors of 20th-century history pushed many writers to reaffirm the important 18th-century roots of modern cultural life.

B. These same events also made it impossible to return to any simple faith in the absolute virtues of science, rationality, progress, or technology.

C. Yet the dialogue with the Enlightenment will surely continue, and modern European art, literature, social theory, philosophy, and intellectuals will continue to influence people around the world.

Essential Reading:

Jürgen Habermas, *The Structural Transformation of the Public Sphere*, pp. 1–88, 141–180.

Václav Havel, "The Power of the Powerless," and "A Word about Words," in Havel, *Open Letters: Selected Writings, 1965–1990*, pp. 127–214, 377–389.

Supplementary Reading:

Craig Calhoun, "Introduction: Habermas and the Public Sphere," and Jürgen Habermas, "Further Reflections on the Public Sphere," both in Calhoun, editor, *Habermas and the Public Sphere*, pp. 1–42, 421–457.

Questions to Consider:

1. Does the "public sphere" in contemporary democratic nations consist of rational public debate or manipulation by powerful private interests?

2. Are the ideas of the European Enlightenment the best foundation for cultural and political life in an age of multicultural and global exchanges?

Lecture Twenty-Four—Transcript
Changes and Traditions at Century's End

We're coming to the end of a survey of 20th-century European intellectual history, but there is no simple way to summarize European thought in the late 20th century. The postmodern emphasis on fragmentation, which I discussed in the last lecture suggests that the problems we face are pretty enormous when you try to think of bringing it all together. Because, in fact, what we're facing here is a story of fragmentation.

The fragmentation of European cultural life in the modern era obviously precludes the possibility of any final synthesis. It's not like the Middle Ages or the medieval synthesis. What we find is that there's no closure—no synthesis—at the end of the 20th century. In fact, there's very rarely ever any kind of closure to historical processes. There's always something else—the dialectic of change goes on.

And yet, there are certain important changes that we can identify in the late 20th-century European historical context. We can see that things were changing, and this changing context, as always, affected intellectuals. And in this final lecture, I want to allude to some of the changes that were taking place at the end of the 20th century, and then I also want to note some ways in which European intellectual traditions were being reaffirmed and reasserted at the end of the 20th century.

So first a couple of things about the changing context of European intellectual life. During more than four decades—a period from roughly 1947 to 1989—Europe was very deeply affected by the Cold War and by the growing influence of the United States in European economic and political and cultural life. And this American influence can be seen in many ways. There was a strong American economic and cultural influence in fashion, in films, in television, in music, in politics, and even in universities you could see the growing influence of certain patterns of American thought that were showing up also in Europe.

So one of the important patterns of European life during the period of the Cold War and since the Cold War was a growing pattern of Americanization that elicited concern from European intellectuals. Intellectuals in Europe often expressed concern about the impact of

Americanization on Europe's cultural traditions and social life. Was Americanization coming at a serious price in European culture? So that was one of the changing contexts—the growing influence of America.

A second important change in the late 20th century was the enormous influx of new immigrants into European society. And these immigrants came mostly from Africa, from Asia, and the Middle East. And many Europeans worried that their traditions—their cultural ideas—were unfamiliar to the immigrants and that these traditions were being threatened by the arrival of new populations. So just as intellectuals worried about the impact of Americanization, there were people who worried about the impact of immigration from other parts of the world—particularly from Europe's former colonies.

And so, in European cultural life, there was a wide debate about what we call multiculturalism in contemporary American language. In all the major European nations, this debate about multiculturalism has become an important intellectual theme. How would the languages, religions, and cultural values of non-European peoples be assimilated into European life? What would this mean for the traditional concerns of European education, economic life, and so forth?

So this multicultural debate in European cultures redefined the meaning of European nations. There was a growing sense of multiplicity within the nation rather than a fully coherent national culture. And also, the nation was being transformed in Europe by the emergence of the European Union, which also redefined the nation-state. So, on the one hand, there was the internationalization of the nation-state, and within the nation, there was distinctive multiculturalism. So immigration was a second major effective changing force in late 20th century Europe.

And finally, the end of the Cold War and the collapse of communist regimes in Central Europe and the development of a new global economy all changed the context for intellectual debate in Europe as in fact these changes affected the context throughout the world. And these changes—including the demise of the communist regimes in Central Europe—these changes surely contributed to the popularity of postmodernism, the emphasis on fragmented identities, and the decline of Marxism as an important theoretical position within

European intellectual life. Marxism, by the end of the 20th century, seemed to many intellectuals to be an inadequate social theory in this new context just as the old nationalist belief in coherent, unique national identities also began to seem inadequate to people at the end of the 20th century.

Meanwhile, within all of these changing contextual factors, we can see that the growth of the modern capitalist advertising system, modern consumerism, entertainment, the spread of travel—all of which suggested a breakdown of older traditions. And many of these changes were seen as threatening by European intellectuals who, after all, worried that the book was becoming less important or that writing was being displaced by visual images. So there was a lot of anxiety among European intellectuals in the late 20th century.

But late 20th-century European intellectual life did not turn entirely to postmodernism, despite these changes and fragmentations that I've been describing, there were a number of critiques of postmodernism. And in fact, there was a strong critique of the postmodernist conception of a de-centric subject. There was an attempt to revive the notion of an autonomous subject—the liberal idea of a human being which had been a part of Enlightenment tradition in Europe. And there was a new defense of reason as a response to the postmodernist critique of the Enlightenment.

So, in this lecture, I want to conclude our survey of 20th-century European thought with a discussion of what might be called the challenges to postmodernism. And I think these challenges include a new affirmation of two key Enlightenment ideas or traditions—two important traditions that had been part of European intellectual life since at least the 18th century. One of these traditions was the insistence on the critical importance of reason in public life. And the other of these traditions was the insistence on the critical role of intellectuals in political and cultural debates. And both of these ideas can be traced back to the Enlightenment and to people like Voltaire and the great intellectuals of the 18th century.

Now, these trends, which I might call generally a recovery of the Enlightenment, these trends can be seen in two representative intellectual figures—the German social theorist and philosopher, Jürgen Habermas and the Czech writer and political leader, Václav Havel. Both of these intellectuals reaffirmed Enlightenment ideas, reconfirmed certain conceptions of Enlightenment reason and human rights, and insisted on the important public role of the intellectual. And in this respect, they went far beyond the university. And this debate that I referred to throughout this course—the debate between intellectual life within the university and outside the university— well, this debate can be seen again in the example of Havel and Habermas who take a critical position on public issues and go far beyond the university itself.

Well, let's look at some of the ways in which these critics have attacked postmodernist thought. The essential point for many of these critics is that postmodernism puts too much emphasis on the shaping power of language—the shaping power of symbols and abstract discourse. And although Habermas and Havel both recognize the importance of language—in fact, they both insist on it—they also argue that language is not just arbitrary. They come back to the Enlightenment belief that language can convey general and even universal truths, which can be defended in public life. And they also argue—like most Enlightenment intellectuals—that personal freedom requires an engagement with public life and public issues—that one cannot be fully free simply by pursuing personal happiness and personal goals—that intellectuals and, in fact, all people have a stake in public issues. That's one of the traditional Enlightenment issues that both Habermas and Havel insist on.

Well, this challenge to post-structuralism and postmodernism has been particularly notable in Germany, and I think that perhaps this is ironic, because postmodernist thought in France and elsewhere drew on German thinkers such as Nietzsche and Husserl and Heidegger. So there's a curious way in which the French use the Germans to challenge the Enlightenment and then many intellectuals in post-Nazi Germany went back to the French Enlightenment to recover a tradition with which they could attack what had happened in Germany and also to attack postmodernism—so that kind of recovery of the Enlightenment outside of France.

And in fact many German intellectuals felt that Germany had gone off track—it had made its great mistake—by embracing the non-rational themes of romanticism and anti-Enlightenment thought. And so, there was a strong skepticism about romanticism, about many post-Nazi, many post-1945 German intellectuals. And I think we can see this pattern particularly in the work of Jürgen Habermas.

Habermas was born in 1929—he was born near Cologne in western Germany. He grew up in that part of Germany. His father directed a local chamber of commerce and was active in local business and community activities. Habermas was too young to be in the German army in World War II, but he was very much affected by post-war revelations of Nazi atrocities. And he went on to the university to study. He studied philosophy and sociology. And then he became affiliated with the re-organized Frankfurt School of Critical Theory in the 1950s—that Frankfurt School which included important writers and theorists, such as Theodor Adorno and Max Horkheimer. These were the people who came back to Germany after the war and re-established the Frankfurt School.

And Habermas went on to spend most of his later career as a professor in Frankfurt. But he also participated widely in public debates. He wrote often in the newspapers and played an active role in intellectual debates, beginning in the 1950s and all the way through the 1990s.

Habermas was deeply disturbed by what he saw as the failure of German intellectuals and political leaders to come to terms with the Nazi past. He believed that intellectuals had never fully faced what had happened in Germany. And he believed that the problem in Germany emerged because intellectuals had wrongly turned away from the Enlightenment, from the ideals of reason, from the Enlightenment idea of public debate, and they embraced an irrational philosophy. And for Habermas, Heidegger was a prominent example of this error—that Heidegger represented exactly what went wrong in German intellectual life.

So Habermas sought to revise aspects of Kantian philosophy. He wanted to go back to that 18th position that stressed the value of reason. He warned against the dangers of romanticism. Habermas himself favored a kind of democratic socialism of a kind that was quite popular among many intellectuals in Germany who were also active in the socialist party—a democratic socialist. But the emphasis also, I would stress, on democratic debate grounded in reason.

Habermas developed many of his major themes in his first book—his first important book, which was called *The Structural Transformation of the Public Sphere*, which was originally published in Germany in 1962. And in this book, Habermas argued that the

Enlightenment of the 18th century had created a model for a public sphere in which debate flourished on the basis of reason. This was the ideal of the Enlightenment writers, Enlightenment political figures. And he had a great admiration for the Enlightenment—Habermas did. But he also argued that the Enlightenment ideal of a rational public sphere had declined in the modern world—that public life by the 1950s and 1960s when he was writing this book—that public life had become dominated by advertising, that the old model of rational debaters coming to a rational decision—this was being displaced by the modern economic system, modern commercial system, and the modern political system that basically turned to the selling candidates, for example, rather than rational debate.

So Habermas argued that intellectuals and anyone else who cared about democratic public life should defend the use of reason and rational criticism. And this defense of Enlightenment reason would remain part of Habermas' work throughout his later publications. And this defense of the Enlightenment also led to his strong critique of postmodernist or post-structuralist thinkers—people like Foucault and Derrida, whom Habermas saw as too hostile to the values of reason.

Habermas laid out his critique of postmodernism in an important book called *The Philosophical Discourse of Modernity*, which was published in 1985. But he also developed these themes in a whole series of other publications. And Habermas argued repeatedly that it was impossible to fight the residue of Nazism or the distortions of radical ethnic and national and religious movements by using philosophies that challenged rationalism. He said this is what postmodern intellectuals have gone right off track. He said the only way to challenge this kind of behavior is by a defense of the Enlightenment tradition of reason.

But he did concede that there are different forms of reason. Habermas said that there was a kind of instrumental reason, which could be dangerous, because it was insufficiently critical. This is the kind of reason that we see in a kind of rationalizing bureaucracy that just looks at how we're going to get a certain policy implemented, that's going to make the trains run on time—that's instrumental reason. That's the kind of instrumental reason that produced something like genocide in Europe. So he sees there is a danger in reason.

But he says there's another kind of reason, which he called communicative reason, and this is the essential kind of reason. Communicative reason offers the central tools for critical judgment, for critical analysis, for critical debate. And so, Habermas criticized the philosophical legacy of Friedrich Nietzsche and other sort of neo-romantic writers. And he claimed that this Nietzschian legacy had pushed postmodernism in the wrong direction. He insisted that postmodernism had abandoned the all-important belief in rational criticism.

And so, Habermas resembled Kant—Emmanuel Kant—the 18th-century German philosopher—he resembled Kant in arguing that the critical use of reason could bring about cross-cultural agreement on truth and public actions. Even people who come from different cultural backgrounds, by using reason, they can come to an agreement. And this is what he said had to happen in modern democratic societies. His own goal was to develop a democratic public life in which communication could take place without coercion or domination. And these arguments in the public sphere would develop through the use of clear speech and by the use of clear arguments so that rational debaters would finally reach an agreement on reasonable and just forms of action.

So Habermas shared the common modern concern of language. In fact, he wrote a lot about language—about problems of communication. But he strongly rejected the postmodern emphasis on the indeterminacy of linguistic meaning. He said we can actually use language to understand the world and to reach agreement.

And I think that Habermas' critique of postmodernism has had a great deal of influence among thinkers and theorists who are looking for an alternative to the postmodern critique of modernity. Habermas' ideas became important in historical studies, in philosophy, and in political theory. And in all of these areas, the Habermasian model promotes Enlightenment ideas about the public role of intellectual work.

Now, Habermas defended also various aspects of the Marxist intellectual traditions in his works on the problems of the modern public sphere. For example, he thought that capitalism distorted what happened in the public sphere. He wanted free speech. He worried about the impact of money, for example, in public life, public debates. So he retained certain Marxist themes. But other intellectuals who shared his sympathy for the Enlightenment moved much further away from the Marxist intellectual tradition. And I think we can see this other pattern of the non-Marxist public intellectual in the life and career of Václav Havel. I want to say a few things about Havel at this point.

Havel was born in 1936 in Prague. His father was an architect and a building contractor in Prague, and young Václav grew up during the Nazi occupation and was very much affected by that experience. Then, after the Nazi occupation, when he wanted to go to the university—later—he was barred from the university, because his father was deemed to be a bourgeois figure—part of the bourgeois class—and he was not allowed to go to the university.

So Havel made his own way into Czech cultural and intellectual life from the margins—from outside the university—from outside the official centers of Czech culture during the communist period. He became a writer, and by the early 1960s, he was producing a series of plays for the Prague theater. He particularly wrote absurdist plays, which were very much the model of drama for many people in the late 1950s and 1960s.

But then, beginning in the late 1960s, Havel became much more concerned with political issues—especially after the Soviet invasion of Czechoslovakia in 1968. This political event—military event— changed the context for Havel and pushed him in a much more political direction. And he wrote a series of dissenting political commentaries, including a famous essay called *The Power of the Powerless*, which he wrote in 1978. This became a very influential essay among people who were critics of the communist regime in Czechoslovakia.

He also became a founding leader of a human rights group called Charter 77, which demanded the protection of democratic civil rights. And so, in his writings, Havel argued that the people—the people of society—could re-shape public life, even if they appeared to be powerless under dictatorial regimes. The powerless have a certain power. He said that people could stand for what he called life—they could stand for life. And this conception of life—and this is a quote—he said, this conception of life "moves toward plurality, diversity, and fulfillment of its own freedom." This is his conception of what the people represent—the life of the people. Whereas, in contrast to the life of the people, you could front a repressive government that demands uniformity and discipline. The people promote plurality and diversity. The government—the authoritarian government—promotes uniformity and discipline.

But Havel argued that people power could, in effect, overcome the dead hand of authoritarianism. And in this process, the intellectuals had a crucial role to play - that intellectuals had a public responsibility to participate in the public political process.

As he wrote in one of his essays, "We have always believed in the power of words to change history." In other words, language can speak truth against power. Language can transform the social and political system. And in making that kind of claim, Havel was, in a sense, reaffirming the Enlightenment idea of the intellectual as a critic in the republic of letters and that this republic of letters can play a role in transforming the social and political world.

Well, Havel was arrested and imprisoned because of his writings. And he spent four years in prison—from 1979 to 1983. But he did not turn away from his ideas. And finally, his release from prison, and then in 1989, there was a non-violent revolution in Prague—the so-called Velvet Revolution—which overthrew the communist regime. And in a way, it seemed that this Velvet Revolution confirmed Havel's ideas—the claim that people power could ultimately overcome the dead hand of authoritarian regimes.

And because of his prominence in this movement, in his writings, Havel, in fact, was chosen to be president of the new Czech government. And he went on to a prominent and sometimes controversial political career throughout the rest of the 20th century.

So, Havel's life and writings defended the importance of a rational, critical, intellectual project. He defended key Enlightenment traditions and ideas, including human rights and the use of reason and public intervention on the part of intellectuals. And this defense of human rights and the free-market economy led Havel—as well as many other European intellectuals—back to many of the themes of classic liberalism, which was seen as an alternative to the totalitarian state. So, in Havel, we see the example of the intellectual engaged in public life.

So we come to a final question: Did European thought at the end of the 20th century come back to the point where modern intellectual life began?—the point of the Enlightenment? Do we see at the end of the 20th century a return to the rationalist themes of the Enlightenment?

While I think that many intellectuals clearly did express a renewed appreciation for classical Enlightenment beliefs—Enlightenment beliefs and tolerance and reason and in human right—and these rights seemed essential for the continued survival of free, multi-cultural democratic societies at the end of the 20th century. In fact, the horrors of the 20th century—the horrors of 20th-century European history—ultimately pushed many writers to reaffirm the important 18th-century roots of modern cultural life. And so, in one respect, I think that we can say that the end of the 20th century witnessed a reaffirmation of the Enlightenment tradition.

But these same 20th-century events—these same horrors of the 20th century—also made it impossible to return to any simple faith in the absolute virtues of science, of rationality, of progress, or technology, because clearly these phenomena—these kinds of progress and technology were also very dangerous. They could have negative as well as positive implications. And there were clearly some political dangers in these ideas, and these dangers had to be measured against the many important benefits of the Enlightenment tradition. Reason, for example, can be used to repress people as well as to free them. And generally, I think the preoccupation with language and the interest in the cultural construction of truth had undermined much of the Enlightenment confidence in pure knowledge and in universal truths. And European had to live in a new world—a multi-cultural world, a world of fragmentation, world of difference, a world that was not simply created by the ideas of postmodernism. These were ideas—these were realities—that were being created by the changing context.

And so, even as European intellectuals might reaffirm important aspects of the Enlightenment tradition, they also seem to realize that we can't simply return to the days of Descartes or the ideas of Voltaire. And yet, I think that this dialogue with the Enlightenment will surely continue as we move into the 21st century. And modern European art, literature, social theory, philosophy, all of these intellectual traditions of the 20th century will continue to influence people around the world—even in this global age.

Europe is not simply a museum of the past. Europe remains one of the most dynamic centers for contemporary intellectual debates— debates about truth, about democracy, about the use of reason, and about the construction of modern, multi-cultural societies. So Europe's 20th-century conflicts, ideas, and anxieties are still with us as we move into an unpredictable and always unknown future.

Timeline

1876 ....Stéphane Mallarmé writes "*L'Après-Midi d'un Faune*," which exemplifies the emerging themes of symbolist poetry.

1879 ....Émile Zola publishes "The Experimental Novel," calling for a new "naturalist" fiction.

1899 ....Joseph Conrad's novel *Heart of Darkness* portrays the brutal consequences of European imperialism in Africa.

1903 ....Henri Bergson summarizes his intuitionist philosophy in *An Introduction to Metaphysics*.

1905 ....Albert Einstein publishes a paper on the "Special Theory of Relativity."

1905 ....Max Weber publishes *The Protestant Ethic and the Spirit of Capitalism*.

1905 ....Sigmund Freud publishes *Three Essays on Sexuality*.

1907 ....Pablo Picasso paints *Les Demoiselles d'Avignon*, an early work of Cubist art.

1907 ....Edmund Husserl summarizes his conception of consciousness in *The Idea of Phenomenology*.

1908 ....Henri Matisse argues in "Notes of a Painter" that modern artists should not paint literal representations of reality.

1912 ....Wassily Kandinsky's publishes *Concerning the Spiritual in Art*.

1912	Émile Durkheim's publishes *Elementary Forms of Religious Life.*
1913	The first volume of Marcel Proust's novel *Remembrance of Things Past* appears in France.
1914–1918	World War I kills 10 million people; causes the collapse of imperial governments in Germany, Austria-Hungary, and Russia; and leads to the Communist Revolution in Russia.
1918	Oswald Spengler publishes *Decline of the West*, an account of European decay and cultural crisis.
1922	T.S. Eliot publishes *The Waste Land*
1922	The first complete edition of James Joyce's modernist novel *Ulysses* is published in Paris.
1922	Ludwig Wittgenstein publishes his philosophical study of the limits of human language, *Tractatus Logico-Philosophicus.*
1922	Benito Mussolini seizes power in Italy.
1924	André Breton writes the first "Surrealist Manifesto."
1924	Thomas Mann publishes *The Magic Mountain.*
1925	The posthumous publication of Franz Kafka's nightmarish novel *The Trial.*

1927	Werner Heisenberg's "Uncertainty Principle" shows the limits of knowledge about electrons, thus suggesting that science cannot produce a total knowledge of nature.
1927	Martin Heidegger publishes *Being and Time*.
1929	Virginia Woolf describes the social and cultural constraints on women in *A Room of One's Own*.
1929	Lucien Febvre and Marc Bloch found the historical journal *Annales d'histoire économique et sociale*.
1930	Sigmund Freud publishes *Civilization and Its Discontents*.
1930–1937	Antonio Gramsci writes his *Prison Notebooks* in Italian jails.
1933	Adolf Hitler and the Nazi Party gain power in Germany and establish the Third Reich.
1936	John Maynard Keynes publishes *The General Theory of Employment, Interest and Money*, which argues for an active state role in modern economies.
1938	Jean-Paul Sartre summarizes the early themes of his existential philosophy in his novel *Nausea*.
1939–1945	The Second World War causes roughly 60 million deaths around the world, including the Nazi regime's systematic genocidal murder of 6 million Jews.
1944	Friedrich Hayek condemns government interventions in

economic life in his book *The Road to Serfdom*.

1945 ....The Nazis execute the theologian Dietrich Bonhoeffer for his involvement in a resistance group.

1947 ....Albert Camus publishes *The Plague*, which portrays the human need to take action during times of crisis.

1947 ....Primo Levi describes his experiences as a prisoner in a Nazi death camp, in *Survival in Auschwitz*.

1949 ....George Orwell provides a fictional representation of a totalitarian state and political party in his novel *1984*.

1949 ....Simone de Beauvoir's *The Second Sex* contributes influential historical and theoretical arguments to the postwar campaign for women's rights.

1951 ....Hannah Arendt publishes her influential study of authoritarian regimes, *The Origins of Totalitarianism*.

1959 ....A novel by Günther Grass, *The Tin Drum*, challenges Germans to confront the memory of Nazism.

1961 ....Claude Lévi-Strauss publishes *Structural Anthropology*.

1962 ....Jürgen Habermas publishes *The Structural Transformation of the Public Sphere*.

1966 ....Jacques Lacan describes his unconventional psychoanalytical and linguistic theories in a collection of essays called *Ecrits*.

1967 ....Jacques Derrida develops his poststructuralist method of literary deconstruction in *Of Grammatology*.

1975 ....Michel Foucault's analysis of power and knowledge appears in his historical study of modern institutions, *Discipline and Punish*.

1985 ....Jürgen Habermas publishes *The Philosophical Discourse of Modernity*.

1986 ....Jean Baudrillard publishes his account of a postmodern society in a work called *America*.

1989 ....Communist regimes in Eastern European nations collapse in a "velvet revolution."

1992–1999 ....The European Union reshapes the context of intellectual life by promoting the political, economic, and cultural integration of European nations.

Glossary

Abstract expressionism: A form of early 20th-century art that used color rather than recognizable forms to convey personal visions of the artist. Wasily Kandinsky and others argued that the colors of nonrepresentational art could express spiritual and emotional truths.

Analytical psychology: The term used by Carl Jung to separate his psychological work from the psychoanalytical theories of Sigmund Freud. Breaking with Freud's emphasis on sexual drives and the Freudian views of religion, Jung stressed the importance of adult experiences and a "collective unconscious."

***Annales* historians**: A group of French historians associated with the journal *Annales d'histoire économique et sociale* (founded in 1929). Under the early leadership of Lucien Febvre and Marc Bloch, the *Annales* historians emphasized long-term social processes, collective mentalities, and deep structures rather than political events or individuals.

Anomie: The sociological term that Emile Durkheim used to describe the modern urban social experience in which persons feel disconnected from social communities or any sense of shared social values (in contrast to the integrated social life of small villages).

Bloomsbury circle: The writers, artists, and intellectuals who congregated in the London neighborhood of Bloomsbury during the 1920s. They shared a commitment to modern cultural and literary innovations, thus forming a "circle" that included prominent English authors, such as Virginia Woolf and John Maynard Keynes.

Bohemian culture: An imprecise term that refers to unconventional artists, writers, café performers, and others who lived in modern cities but criticized the orderly, routine life of modern workers and bourgeois professionals. Bohemian culture tended to mock respectable behaviors, yet its art and writing could also fascinate the people it criticized.

Bolsheviks: The communists who took power in the Russian Revolution of 1917. They followed Vladimir Lenin in advocating a centralized communist party, state control of the economy, a single-party government, and international opposition to capitalism.

Cubism: An influential approach to art that emerged in early 20th-century Paris among such painters as Pablo Picasso and Georges Braque. The Cubists portrayed objects or people from multiple perspectives that revealed geometric shapes and relations rather than literal images—thus emphasizing subjective visions over objective truth.

Cultural hegemony: The Italian Marxist theorist Antonio Gramsci developed this term to describe the process by which dominant social groups control the education, media, and leading ideas of a society. According to this theory, "hegemonic" cultural power becomes as important as economic power in sustaining the position of ruling groups.

Cultural pessimism: A widespread intellectual response to 20th-century events, such as the two world wars, economic crises, and political upheavals, all of which led many writers and artists to believe that European civilization was in decline and that the earlier confidence in human progress was naïve.

Culture industry: This "industry" consists of the institutions that produce and sell cultural products in modern societies, including publishing houses, newspapers, advertising media, theaters, art galleries, film studios, and even universities. Artists and intellectuals depend on the culture industry rather than the patronage system of older aristocratic societies to support themselves in modern cities.

Dadaism: A radical avant-garde movement that developed in Switzerland and France at the end of World War I. It claimed that Western civilization had lost all rational meaning and that absurd, nonsense literature and art were the only appropriate cultural responses to modern European society.

Empiricism: The philosophical and scientific approach to knowledge that stresses the crucial importance of observable evidence and argues that all reliable truths are based on the collection, analysis, or measurement of such evidence.

Enlightenment: An intellectual and cultural movement in 18th-century Europe led by writers called *philosophes*. The main themes of Enlightenment thought included optimistic beliefs in reason, science, natural laws, or natural rights; religious tolerance; the free exchange of ideas; and the rational advance of human progress.

Epistemology: The term used by philosophers to describe the study of the fundamental structures or categories of human knowledge. The key epistemological question is "How do we know what we know?" This question appears implicitly or explicitly in most intellectual debates (and defies simple answers).

Existentialism: The philosophical movement associated with Jean-Paul Sartre and other 20th-century thinkers who argued that human life has no inherent meaning or essence (except consciousness), that human beings are free to act as they choose, and that the meaning of each individual's "existence" is defined by his or her actions in the world.

Fascism: A right-wing political philosophy that rejects democratic political processes, celebrates the authoritarianism of a powerful leader or political party, praises a mythic national past, represses free speech, endorses violence or warfare as essential expressions of national life, and promotes economic or social hierarchies rather than personal freedom or equality.

Fauves: The term meaning "wild beasts" that critics used to describe early 20th-century Parisian artists who juxtaposed colors and shapes in unconventional images to represent the personal vision of the painter and the fluidity of human movement. Henri Matisse became the most well known member of the Fauves.

Feminism: The political, social, and cultural movement that challenges traditional male privileges, advocates equal legal and political rights for women, and attempts to improve the position of women in education, family relationships, and economic life.

Frankfurt School: Revisionist Marxist social theorists who attempted to link Marx's ideas with other theorists, such as Hegel and Freud. They were affiliated with the "Frankfurt Institute of Social Research" in Germany during the 1920s and early 1930s, but they all went into exile after the Nazis gained power in 1933.

Heisenberg "Uncertainty Principle": The German scientist Werner Heisenberg showed in 1927 that it was impossible to know both the position and speed of an electron at the same time, thus pointing to the limits of scientific knowledge.

Historical sociology: A method of studying society that examines historical patterns and long-developing social values to explain modern social institutions or values. Max Weber and other Germans led the way in developing this sociological method.

Holocaust: The term now used to describe the Nazis' systematic genocidal murder of approximately 6 million Jews and other "non-Aryan" people during the Second World War. Many of these people died in specially constructed death camps, such as Auschwitz.

"Ideal Type": A sociological concept that Max Weber used to designate the traits of persons who shared certain recognizable values (e.g., a typical "capitalist" or "bureaucrat"), even though no single person would embody all these characteristics.

Imperialism: The political, military, economic, and cultural process by which European nations gained control over people in other regions of the world. All major European nations pursued imperialist policies in Africa and Asia during the early 20th century, thereby spreading European institutions and ideas but also provoking anti-imperialist movements that later challenged and displaced the European ascendancy.

Impressionism: The influential artistic movement in late 19th-century France that sought to convey the painter's own vision of people or landscapes or the subtle shadings of light. Artists such as Claude Monet turned away from literal images of reality and used new brushwork and colors to depict their distinctive impressions of what they painted.

Intellectual: A person who writes about ideas, the creative arts, or society. The term "intellectual" emerged during the Dreyfus Affair in late 19th-century France, but the social role developed much earlier. Intellectuals produced (1) new knowledge and (2) new social critiques, thus becoming "experts" or "critics" or both.

Intellectual history: A branch of historical studies that examines systematic statements of human ideas and the people who produce or interpret ideas. In contrast to social or cultural history, intellectual history tends to emphasize the ideas of complex and original thinkers rather than the intellectual themes of popular culture or daily life.

Intuitionism: The philosophical theory of Henri Bergson and others who argued that science alone cannot provide a complete understanding of the fluid realities of personal experience or time.

Such realities must be approached through an "intellectual sympathy" or intuition that exists in the human mind.

Involuntary memory: The experience that Marcel Proust described when he wrote about the ways in which an encounter with a specific smell, taste, sight, or person can provoke a sudden, unexpected remembrance of past experiences or people.

Liberalism: A 19th-century political theory that stressed individual rights, constitutional government, rational legal reforms, religious tolerance, and a free-market economy. Liberals generally favored institutional reforms to protect or enhance equal civil rights and personal freedom—themes that reappeared in 20th-century European "neo-liberalism."

Logical positivism: The 20th-century philosophical movement (centered in England) that attempted to make philosophy more scientific by ignoring metaphysical or ethical questions and focusing instead on the rigorous clarification of language and empirically verifiable truths.

Medieval synthesis: A term used to describe the 13th-century theological fusion of Aristotle's conception of reason with the Christian theological belief in divine revelation. This synthesis argued that there was no conflict between faith and reason.

Metaphysics: The philosophical term used to describe the study of realities or ideas that go beyond the physical world. The metaphysical tradition, which emerged in ancient Greek philosophy, seeks to show the higher meaning of material existence or being.

Modernism: A movement in early 20th-century literature and art that emphasized the inner vision of individual writers or artists; challenged older Enlightenment-era beliefs in a stable, objective external world; experimented with nonlinear narratives or artistic representations; and explored multiple perspectives on time and thought.

Naturalism: A late 19th-century approach to literature that depicted the hard realities of life (e.g., poverty, disease, corruption, bad marriages) through an almost scientific emphasis on the biological heredities and social environments that shaped human actions.

Newtonian science: The late 17th-century scientific theories of Isaac Newton that explained the universal law of gravitation and led to confident modern European beliefs in scientific knowledge, universal truths, and human progress.

Oedipus complex: Sigmund Freud's term for what he described as a psychological triangle in which sons yearn to displace their fathers and love their mothers. Freud used this theory to explain the origin of general social taboos (e.g., the incest taboo), as well as the unconscious tensions in families.

Ontology: A philosophical term that refers to the nature or theory of "being." Such beliefs in a reality or grounding that underlies human existence and thought are often not made explicit in language and daily life, but they shape our understanding of the world.

Phenomenology: The 20th-century philosophical "school" that emphasized the complex relation between human consciousness and objects, phenomena, or experiences in the world. It is the interaction of consciousness and the world around it that creates meaning and human understanding (which are not intrinsic in the world itself).

Positivism: An intellectual movement that developed in 19th-century France and spread across modern Europe. Positivism viewed science as the only "positive" form of knowledge and as the stable foundation for human progress.

Postmodernism: A late 20th-century view of the contemporary world that stresses the fragmentation of social and political life, the relativism or cultural contingency of truth, the multiplicity rather than the unity of human identities and cultures, and the flaws of universal social theories. Postmodernism influenced both the arts and cultural studies.

Poststructuralism: A critical approach to literature, philosophy, and the social sciences that stresses the powerful role of language or discourse in the construction of cultural truths and questions concepts of "unity" in Western thought.

Psychoanalysis: The psychological theory and clinical practice that emphasizes the decisive importance of the unconscious mind and drives in all forms of human activity and conflict. Emerging primarily in the works of Sigmund Freud, psychoanalysis widely influenced 20th-century views of human identities, relationships, and creativity.

Realism: A mid-19th-century cultural trend that rejected the sentimentality of Romantic literature and the arts. It sought to portray life as it is rather than life as it should be, and its critique of the greed and clichés in modern social life continued to influence modern literature.

Relativism: The belief that truth can never be absolute or universal, because all human knowledge emerges in specific cultures, languages, and historical contexts that shape its meaning.

Relativity: The scientific theory that explains why time and space are relative to an observer's position and movement in space. Albert Einstein developed this theory, which stressed that there is no fixed reference point for the study of motion, changed Newtonian physics, and contributed to new cultural beliefs in the relativity of all knowledge.

Romanticism: An influential movement in the arts and philosophy (developing between 1780–1840) that challenged Enlightenment beliefs in reason and science. Romanticism praised human feelings, the mysteries of nature, and the unique creativity of artists, thus contributing to modern beliefs in art as a source of personal or cultural salvation.

Stalinism: The dictatorial form of communist rule that Joseph Stalin (1879–1953) used to control the Soviet Union from the late 1920s until his death. More generally, the term refers to any highly authoritarian or rigid form of communist thought or party.

Stream of consciousness: A literary innovation in the early 20th-century novels of James Joyce and others, who tried to convey the different thoughts, memories, and anxieties that flow almost unconnectedly through the human mind during even the briefest periods of time.

Structural linguistics: An approach to human language that was developed by the Swiss linguist Ferdinand de Saussure in the early

20th century. It examines the grammatical systems that enable speakers to make meaningful statements, and it stresses that infinitely diverse, specific sentences always rely on the same underlying structures.

Structuralism: An influential theory in post-World War II social sciences and literary studies. It drew on structural linguistics to describe human cultures as systems of deep structures that organize human relationships, shape the limits of human thought or action, and create social meaning through binary oppositions.

Surrealism: The literary and artistic movement that emphasized the often disjointed images of dreams, mental "free associations," and automatic writing.

Symbolism: A late 19th-century literary movement that explored the complex symbols in cultures, languages, literatures, and human minds.

Weltanschauung: The German word that refers to the distinctive consciousness of a historical era or culture.

Biographical Notes

Adorno, Theodor (1903–1969). A member of the Frankfurt School of critical theorists in Germany, Adorno tried to reconcile the theories of Freud and Marx as he wrote about the cultural legacy of the Enlightenment, "authoritarian" personalities, music, and Nazism.

Algren, Nelson (1909–1981). American writer who lived in Chicago, entered into a relationship with Simone de Beauvoir in the late 1940s, and contributed at least indirectly to some of the themes and American information in Beauvoir's book *The Second Sex* (which she wrote during the time of her relationship with Algren).

Arendt, Hannah (1906–1975). German political theorist and philosopher who opposed the Nazi regime, went into exile in the United States, wrote an influential critique of totalitarian political systems, and developed a controversial account of the Holocaust in *Eichmann in Jerusalem: A Report on the Banality of Evil* (1963).

Ayer, A. J. (1910–1989). British philosopher and a leading figure in the philosophical school of logical positivism.

Barthes, Roland (1915–1980). French literary and cultural theorist who wrote on semiotics (the study of cultural signs), photography, novels, and popular cultural forms, such as advertising and fashion.

Baudelaire, Charles (1821–1867). French poet who lived in the Bohemian culture of Paris and developed the early themes of the symbolist movement. He said that the world is full of symbols that often carry strange meanings and call for imaginative interpretations.

Baudrillard, Jean (1929–). A postmodern French social theorist whose writings discuss the cultural influence of television, simulated images of reality, consumerism, advertising, and the fragmentation of contemporary personal and social identities.

Beauvoir, Simone de (1908–1986). Existential philosopher in France who wrote novels, political commentaries, and an influential study of woman's position in social and cultural life, *The Second Sex*—a book that helped to shape a new wave of modern feminism.

Bergson, Henri (1859–1941). French philosopher who lectured at the Collège de France, criticized positivism, favored an "intuitionist" approach to knowledge, and emphasized the interior realities of thought, time, and personal experience rather than scientific approaches to the observable external world.

Bloch, Marc (1886–1944). Historian of medieval Europe who co-founded the influential French historical journal *Annales d'histoire économique et sociale*. Bloch examined long-term, deep structures in French social history and was executed by the German Gestapo because of his work for the French Resistance during World War II.

Bonhoeffer, Dietrich (1906–1945). German Protestant theologian and staunch opponent of Nazism who criticized German Christians for supporting Hitler and joined the underground anti-Hitler resistance in Germany during the Second World War. He was imprisoned in 1943 and executed in the last month of the war.

Braque, Georges (1882–1963). French painter and innovative contributor to the new Cubist art that emerged in early 20th-century Paris. Braque's work represented geometric shapes, explored spatial relations, and portrayed objects from multiple perspectives.

Braudel, Fernand (1902–1985). Influential historian and leader of the "second generation" of *Annales* historians in France after the Second World War. Braudel argued that history was shaped more by geography and long-developing social structures than by individual actions or political events.

Breton, André (1896–1966). The most well known French advocate for the literary and artistic ideas of surrealism. Breton wrote two "Surrealist Manifestos" in the 1920s, calling for new artistic explorations of the unconscious mind, dreams, and fantasies.

Camus, Albert (1913–1960). French writer whose novels expressed existential themes, including the importance of taking action in the social world, and whose belief in human freedom led him into the anti-Nazi French Resistance during World War II and into a critique of Eastern Europe's communist regimes during the Cold War.

Cézanne, Paul (1839–1906). A post-Impressionist artist who lived in southern France and developed a distinctive, colorful style in which he painted the shapes he saw in objects, landscapes, and human bodies. Cézanne had a wide influence on 20th-century art.

Cixous, Hélène (1937–). One of the third-wave feminist writers in France. Cixous urged women to draw on their distinctive physical and reproductive experiences as they developed forms of "feminine writing" that would differ from the writing of men.

Comte, Auguste (1798–1857). The French social theorist who developed the ideas of positivism, a sociological theory that promoted the scientific description and solution of modern social problems.

Conrad, Joseph (1857–1924). A Polish-born writer who settled in England and wrote about European encounters with non-Western peoples. His descriptions of European imperialists and economic policies were often critical, but he also implied that the evils he described came from human nature, as well as from the nature of imperialism.

Courbet, Gustave (1819–1877). French artist and critic of Romanticism. Courbet developed a new artistic "realism" by painting common people in non-heroic situations and by rejecting the formalism or elite themes that often defined traditional European art.

Darwin, Charles (1809–1882). English scientist who developed the theory of biological evolution after traveling in South America and after many years of research in England.

Debussy, Claude (1863–1918). French composer who wrote music that evoked the poetic themes of the symbolist movement (he was a friend of Stéphane Mallarmé) and the artistic themes of Impressionist art.

Derrida, Jacques (1930–). A poststructuralist theorist in France whose critique of Western metaphysics and binary oppositions had a wide influence on literary theory and cultural studies.

Dilthey, Wilhelm (1833–1911). German philosopher and historian who stressed that human consciousness makes people different from nature and plays a crucial role in historical change. He said that each era has its own consciousness, or *Weltanschauung*.

Dostoevsky, Fyodor (1821–1881). Russian novelist whose literary works portrayed the complex desires and nonrational drives of the human mind. He defended Russia's distinctive cultural traditions and criticized the optimistic 19th-century faith in science.

Dreyfus, Alfred (1859–1935). The French Jewish army captain who was wrongly convicted of spying for Germany in 1894. Many French intellectuals joined a campaign to overturn this conviction (Dreyfus was exonerated in 1906).

Durkheim, Émile (1858–1917). French sociologist whose method of analyzing religion, urban social life, individual isolation ("anomie"), and suicide helped shape the modern social sciences. Durkheim used "social facts" to support his account of a declining social integration of modern societies.

Eichmann, Adolf (1906–1962). German bureaucrat who organized the deportation of Jews to the death camps during the Second World War. He came to represent the "banality of evil" by claiming at his postwar trial that he was simply doing a job in his government office.

Einstein, Albert (1879–1955). The German scientist whose Special Theory of Relativity (1905) revolutionized modern physics and contributed to a modern cultural emphasis on the "relativity" of knowledge. A Jewish exile from Nazi Germany (1933), he lived the rest of his life in America as the most well known figure in 20th-century science.

Eliot, T.S. (1888–1965). English writer and poet, originally from the United States, whose poetry after World War I described a crisis or hollowness in modern Western culture.

Febvre, Lucien (1878–1956). A co-founder of the French historical journal *Annales d'histoire économique et sociale*. Febvre promoted new forms of social and cultural history and argued that shared cultural assumptions shape the limits of human thought.

Fichte, J.G. (1762–1814). Idealist German philosopher who argued that the human mind shapes rather than simply reflects what it encounters in the external world. Fichte contributed to German nationalism by stressing the distinctive traits of German culture.

Foucault, Michel (1926–1984). French social theorist and historian who analyzed the evolving "discourses" of Western knowledge, described scientific or medical truths as expressions of specific cultural systems, emphasized the relation between knowledge and power, and viewed individuals as exemplars of widely diffused structures of thought.

Freud, Sigmund (1856–1939). The physician and scientist who founded psychoanalysis in early 20th-century Vienna. Freud wrote detailed descriptions of dreams and the unconscious mind (with particular attention to sexual drives), analyzed the conflicting desires and aggressions in human relationships, and extended his theory from the individual mind to the repressive processes that shape civilization.

Gauguin, Paul (1848–1903). French artist who moved to Tahiti, became fascinated with the pre-modern cultures of the South Pacific, and developed a distinctive, colorful style of painting to represent the people and scenes that he encountered there.

Gramsci, Antonio (1891–1937). Italian Marxist journalist and political theorist who spent the last 11 years of his life in fascist prisons. Gramsci's *Prison Notebooks* (published after World War II) revised Marxist theory by arguing that ruling groups exercise power through their "cultural hegemony," as well as their control of economic and political institutions.

Grass, Günther (1927–). German writer who challenged his compatriots to face the painful meaning and legacy of the Nazi era in novels such as *The Tin Drum* (1959).

Graves, Robert (1895–1986). English writer whose account of his experiences in the army during World War I (*Good-Bye to All That*) expressed a typically ironic postwar disillusionment with many of the cultural and political values in British society.

Habermas, Jürgen (1929–). German philosopher and social theorist who criticized Romantic cultural traditions, praised Enlightenment conceptions of reason, rejected postmodernist accounts of "culturally constructed" truths, and advocated a democratic public sphere in which rational debates would shape enlightened laws and public action.

Harvey, David (1935–). Geographer and social theorist who has discussed the themes of postmodern thought and the characteristics of postmodern societies in such works as *The Condition of Postmodernity* (1989).

Havel, Václav (1936–). Czech writer who wrote plays in the 1960s, became a leader of the movement for democracy in communist central Europe during the 1970s and 1980s, and served as president of the post-communist Czech government in the 1990s.

Hayek, Freidrich (1899–1992). Austrian-born economist and political theorist who worked in Britain during the 1930s and 1940s. Hayek defended classical free-market ideas, arguing that government planning undermined both democracy and the economy.

Hegel, G.W.F. (1770–1831). German philosopher who described history as the unfolding expression of a transcendent Spirit. Hegel said that this Spirit could be seen in the progressive development of reason and freedom, which advanced through the dialectical conflicts of world history.

Heidegger, Martin (1889–1976). German philosopher whose work examined the nature of Being—the deep, fluid reality that underlies human existence and makes philosophical thought possible.

Heisenberg, Werner (1901–1976). German scientist and author of the "Heisenberg Uncertainty Principle," which argued that it is impossible to know at the same time both the precise speed and position of an electron. The principle attracted much attention, especially when it was linked to theories of relativity and a general cultural skepticism.

Hitler, Adolf (1889–1945). Leader of Germany's Nazi Party and dictator in the Nazi regime (1933–1945) that launched the Second World War, conquered most of Europe, and murdered millions of Jews and other European civilians. Hitler's extreme form of nationalism included a hatred for democratic political traditions, as well as a virulent anti-Semitism, and his policies provoked an enduring intellectual search to understand how such barbarism could appear at the center of modern European civilization.

Horkheimer, Max (1895–1973). One of the leaders of the Frankfurt School of German social theorists. Horkheimer tried to explain why Nazism gained power in Germany, but he also wrote critically about the culture industry in America and Europe.

Husserl, Edmund (1859–1938). German philosopher who developed the key ides of 20th-century phenomenology (a philosophy that later influenced existentialism).

Ibsen, Henrik (1828–1906). Norwegian playwright whose portrayals of bourgeois family life exemplified aspects of literary naturalism. Ibsen's plays suggested that most families were haunted by hidden conflicts and that women still faced difficult constraints in modern societies.

Jaspers, Karl (1883–1969). German philosopher whose emphasis on the disturbing human awareness of one's own inevitable death, on free will, and on the choices of an active life had an important influence on 20th-century existential thought.

Joyce, James (1882–1941). Irish novelist who lived most of his life as an exile in European cities and used innovative literary methods, such as indirect interior monologues and stream of consciousness, to convey the complexity of human thoughts and experience.

Jung, Carl (1875–1961). Swiss psychologist and designated successor to Sigmund Freud in the Psychoanalytical Association until the two men fell into conflict over various psychological issues, including the role of sexuality, the nature of religion, and what Jung called a "collective unconscious." Jung later developed his own "analytical psychology."

Kafka, Franz (1883–1924). German-language Jewish writer who lived in Prague, worked in an insurance office, and wrote short stories and novels about the alienating, disorienting experiences of modern life. He described a threatening social world and nightmarish limitations on human communications and personal freedom.

Kandinsky, Wassily (1866–1944). Russian-born artist who worked mainly in Germany and France. Kandinsky developed an abstract expressionist style of painting that used vivid colors rather than recognizable objects to convey his personal vision; he said that painting should be viewed as "color music."

Keynes, John Maynard (1883–1946). English economist and advocate for government spending in times of economic crisis. Keynes argued that the government's deficit spending could revive a weak economy because it put more money into circulation, thus fueling demand for more goods and services (and for more workers to produce them).

Kristéva, Julia (1941–). Bulgarian-born literary and cultural theorist who moved to France in 1966. Kristéva called for a new kind of "dialogical" language that would move beyond "phallocentric" linguistic traditions and lead to a more open-ended understanding of all human identities, including the identities of male and female.

Lacan, Jacques (1901–1981). French theorist who sought to unite psychoanalysis and linguistics by describing connections among the body, the unconscious mind, and language.

Le Bon, Gustave (1841–1931). French social psychologist whose analysis of the emotional, violent behavior of crowds exemplified the late 19th-century social scientific attempt to understand the nonrational components of human behavior.

Levi, Primo (1919–1987). Italian chemist and one of the rare Jewish survivors of the Nazi death camp at Auschwitz. Levi wrote about the camp and his own painful memories in postwar books that described the horrors of Auschwitz.

Lévy-Bruhl, Lucien (1857–1939). One of the French "founding fathers" of anthropology. Lévy-Bruhl sought to explain the different ways in which modern and pre-modern people think about nature and human beings.

Mallarmé, Stéphane (1842–1898). French poet whose poems and aesthetic theories conveyed the themes of the symbolist movement.

Manet, Edouard (1832–1883). An early French Impressionist painter, Manet portrayed unconventional scenes, experimented with the representation of light and the "blurring" of human figures, and organized exhibitions of such works with other like-minded artists.

Mann, Thomas (1875–1955). German writer whose novels pointed to various forms of "illness" in European culture. His books, such as *The Magic Mountain* (1924), suggested that Europeans had embraced death over life—a critique that was confirmed for him by the rise of Nazism (from which he fled into exile in America).

Matisse, Henri (1869–1954). French artist who sought to represent the "inherent truth" rather than the literal images of people and objects. He pursued this idea by juxtaposing colors and shapes in unexpected combinations, portraying the movement of human bodies, and encouraging an innovative group of artists called the "Fauves."

Mauss, Marcel (1872–1950). French anthropologist who examined structural similarities in European and non-European societies.

Monet, Claude (1840–1920). French painter whose distinctive brushwork and explorations of light and color helped to shape the methods and themes of the influential Impressionist movement in late 19th-century French art.

Mussolini, Benito (1883–1945). Leader of the Italian Fascist Party and the first fascist dictator to gain power in Europe (1922).

Niebuhr, Reinhold (1892–1971). American theologian at Union Theological Seminary in New York. Niebuhr wrote on the social and ethical dimensions of Christianity and had close connections with European religious activists, such as Dietrich Bonhoeffer.

Nietzsche, Friedrich (1844–1900). German philosopher and social critic who challenged Western philosophical conceptions of reason and truth and stressed what he called the human "will to power."

Nijinsky, Vaslav (1889–1950). Russian-born dancer whose interpretations of music, such as Claude Debussy's "The Afternoon of a Faun," brought a controversial choreography into modern dance and expressed the unconventional attitudes of modernist art.

Orwell, George (1903–1950). English journalist, novelist, and critic of totalitarian governments. Orwell developed his political arguments in popular fictional works, most notably his post-World War II novels *Animal Farm* and *1984*.

Owen, Wilfred (1893–1918). An English "war poet" during the First World War, Owen became an angry critic of what he saw as a naïve and dangerous patriotism on the British home front. He was killed in France one week before the end of the war.

Pankhurst, Emmeline (1858–1928). English feminist and political activist who led the campaign for women's voting rights in early 20th-century Britain.

Péguy, Charles (1873–1914). French poet and writer whose mystical inclinations and intense patriotism led him into the French army and an early death at the beginning of World War I.

Picasso, Pablo (1881–1973). Spanish-born artist who lived mainly in France after 1904. Picasso developed an influential new Cubist style that portrayed the author's personal vision of angular, geometric shapes and provided multiple perspectives on the objects, people, and scenes that he painted.

Pound, Ezra (1885–1972). American poet and critic who promoted modernist literature, befriended numerous writers in modernist literary circles, wrote influential experimental poems, and gained public notoriety because of his support for the fascist regime in Italy.

Proust, Marcel (1871–1922). French writer whose six-volume novel *Remembrance of Things Past* explored the meaning of time, memory, love, desire, and solitude. Proust's work helped to shape the widespread modern literary interest in the psychology and inner experiences of human beings.

Renoir, Pierre-Auguste (1841–1919). French Impressionist painter. Renoir used contrasting colors to represent subtle shadings of light and shadows and to portray the non-heroic everyday lives and leisure activities of middle-class people.

Rimbaud, Arthur (1854–1891). Avant-garde French poet who wrote his famous poems before he was 20 years old, then traveled around Europe and Africa for the rest of his life. Rimbaud's poetic images of personal liberation and his description of the poet as a lonely visionary influenced cultural "rebels" and writers throughout the 20th century.

Russell, Bertrand (1872–1970). English philosopher who contributed to the early development of logical positivism. Russell opposed metaphysical thought and sought a philosophical language that would be as precise and verifiable as mathematics.

Saint-Simon, Henri, Comte de (1760–1825). French social theorist who argued that modern societies should be managed by scientific experts and social planners.

Saussure, Ferdinand de (1858–1913). Swiss linguist who developed structural linguistics. Saussure argued that all linguistic meanings depend on a system of deep grammatical structures and on linguistic processes that link a "signifier" (word or symbol) with a "signified" (the object, idea, or referent that the signifier represents).

Sartre, Jean-Paul (1905–1980). French philosopher and advocate of existentialism. Sartre said that human beings have no fixed essence or eternal spirit, but he insisted that they have the consciousness and freedom to define the meaning of their own existence—if they act on their freedom and refuse to let others define who they are.

Sassoon, Siegfried (1886–1967). English "war poet" and critic of British government policies during the First World War. He wrote about his military experiences and the horrors of trench warfare in numerous postwar poems, memoirs, and novels.

Simmel, Georg (1858–1918). German sociologist who analyzed the impersonal aspects of modern urban life, examined the influence of cities on intellectual work, and described how money mediates the anonymous relations between strangers in modern societies.

Spencer, Herbert (1820–1903). British social theorist and proponent of Social Darwinism. He believed that human progress evolves out of struggles in which the "fittest" people survive (if governments avoid intervention in the process).

Spengler, Oswald (1880–1936). German philosopher and historian whose *Decline of the West* (1918) expressed a popular cultural pessimism that spread across Germany and much of Western Europe after the First World War.

Stalin, Joseph (1879–1953). Communist leader who gradually gained power in the Soviet Union after the death of Vladimir Lenin, promoted the state-organized "five-year plans" for economic development, and imposed a brutal, repressive dictatorship on the communist party and the people of Soviet society.

Stein, Gertrude (1874–1946). American writer who lived in Paris after 1903. Stein collected the paintings of innovative artists, such as Henri Matisse and Pablo Picasso, and tried to apply the nonlinear or Cubist styles of modern art in her complex prose.

Tzara, Tristan (1896–1963). Romanian-born poet and leader of the Dada movement in Switzerland and Paris after World War I. Tzara claimed that European cultural traditions had lost meaning; he mocked traditional culture by writing nonsense poems and staging strange literary performances in cafés.

Van Gogh, Vincent (1853–1890). Dutch-born artist who spent his later years in France. He used bright colors and distinctive swirling shapes to express strong emotions and a personal vision that would influence the later development of expressionist art.

Verlaine, Paul (1844–1896). French poet who had a turbulent relationship with Arthur Rimbaud, associated with the symbolist writers in Paris, and promoted new forms of poetry (including the poems of Rimbaud) in literary journals.

Villiers de l'Isle-Adam (1838–1889). French author whose work exemplified typical themes of the symbolist literary movement.

Wagner, Richard (1813–1883). German composer whose innovative operas combined music and art to produce all-encompassing dramatic experiences. His aesthetic theories had wide influence, but his strong German nationalism provoked political criticisms.

Weber, Max (1864–1920). German social theorist and historical sociologist who analyzed possible links between religion and economic behavior, complained about the "iron cage" of modern bureaucracies, and warned that people might turn to charismatic leaders as they searched for magical powers in the "despiritualized" modern world.

Wittgenstein, Ludwig (1889–1951). Austrian-born philosopher who lived and worked for many years at Cambridge University in England. He contributed to the modern philosophical interest in language, criticized philosophers for using imprecise language, and claimed that many crucial problems must be passed over in silence because language could not always speak truthfully or precisely about the questions that philosophy raises.

Woolf, Virginia (1882–1941). English writer and novelist. Woolf contributed to modernist literature in novels that explored the complexities of time, personal experience, and human communication.

Yeats, William Butler (1865–1939). Irish poet and playwright who supported literary and political movements for Irish independence. His poems expressed a fascination with various mystical symbols and a pessimistic view of culture and politics in modern European societies.

Zola, Émile (1840–1902). French novelist who tried to apply scientific theories about heredity and the influence of environments in a literary genre called naturalism. Zola wrote popular novels about social problems and social classes in French society.

Bibliography

Works by Influential Figures in Modern European Thought

Arendt, Hannah. *The Portable Hannah Arendt*. Edited with an introduction by Peter Baehr. New York and London: Penguin Books, 2000. A useful collection of excerpts from Arendt's most influential works, including her analysis of totalitarianism and *Eichmann in Jerusalem*.

Baudrillard, Jean. *America*. Translated by Chris Turner. London and New York: Verso, 1988. The iconoclastic description of the United States as a fragmented, electronic postmodern society by a prominent postmodern critic in France.

Beauvoir, Simone de. *The Second Sex*. Translated and edited by H.M. Parshley, introduction by Deirdre Bair. New York: Vintage Books, 1989. This book helped to launch a new wave of feminist thought in the decades after World War II by describing women's role in society and calling on women to take control of their own lives.

Bergson, Henri. *An Introduction to Metaphysics*. Translated by T.E. Hulme, with an introduction by Thomas A. Goudge. New York: Macmillan Publishing Company, 1955. The best, most concise summary of Bergson's ideas about the limits of scientific knowledge and the "intuition" that comprehends the flow of human thought and experience.

Bloch, Marc. *The Historian's Craft*. Translated by Peter Putnam, with an introduction by Joseph R. Strayer. New York: Alfred A. Knopf, 1953. Reflections on the nature of continuity, change, and historical understanding by one of the innovative leaders of the *Annales* school of historians in France.

Bonhoeffer, Dietrich. *Writings*. Selected and with an introduction by Robert Coles. Maryknoll, NY: Orbis Books, 1998. This concise collection brings together Bonhoeffer's commentaries on Christian ethical commitments and the nature of evil with some of the letters he wrote from prison before he was executed by the Nazis in 1945.

Breton, André. *What Is Surrealism? Selected Writings*. Edited and introduced by Franklin Rosemont. London: Pluto Press, 1978. This useful edition of Breton's writings includes numerous brief summaries of his theoretical arguments for surrealist literature, art, and politics.

Camus, Albert. *The Plague.* Translated by Stuart Gilbert. New York: Vintage books, 1972. Camus wrote this novel as a parable about the importance of human choices and actions in even the most difficult or apparently uncontrollable situations. It tells the story of a doctor's struggle against illness in a North African city.

Conrad, Joseph. *Heart of Darkness.* New York and London: Penguin Books, 1999. This novel portrays the racism and brutality of imperialism in late 19th-century Africa, but the narrator describes the madness of a lone European "dictator" (the general problem of human evil?), as well as the exploitative policies of a European trading company.

Derrida, Jacques. *Of Grammatology.* Corrected edition, translated by Gayatri Chakravorty Spivak. Baltimore: The Johns Hopkins University Press, 1997. The definitive early work (published in 1967) of "poststructuralist" literary theory. In complex prose, Derrida analyzes the metaphysical components of modern language usage, social science, and writing.

Durkheim, Emile. *Emile Durkheim: Selected Writings.* Edited, translated, and introduced by Anthony Giddens. Cambridge: Cambridge University Press, 1972. A valuable collection of excerpts from Durkheim's sociological work on social relations, anomie, and religious rituals in various cultural contexts; these writings helped to shape the themes and methods of 20th-century sociology.

Einstein, Albert. *The Expanded Quotable Einstein.* Collected and edited by Alice Calaprice, with a foreword by Freeman Dyson. Princeton: Princeton University Press, 2000. This book provides fascinating brief quotations from Einstein's writings and opinions on a wide range of personal, scientific, political, and cultural issues.

Foucault, Michel. *The History of Sexuality,* vol. 1. Translated by Robert Hurley. New York: Vintage Books, 1990. A good example of how Foucault examined cultural "discourses" to show connections among knowledge, power, and the regulation of behavior. He argues that 19th-century scientific experts redefined sexual identities and created a language that still controls the meaning of normal and abnormal behaviors.

Freud, Sigmund. *Civilization and Its Discontents*. Translated and edited by James Strachey, with a biographical introduction by Peter Gay. New York and London: W.W. Norton & Company, 1961 and 1989. This is Freud's influential account of how civilization produces human unhappiness through guilt-inducing demands for the repression of deep sexual and aggressive drives in the human body and mind.

————. *The Interpretation of Dreams*. Translated and edited by James Strachey. New York: Avon Books, 1965. Using evidence from the symbols and complexities of human dreams, this book (first published in 1899) summarizes Freud's theory of psychological repression and the unconscious mind. Its cultural influence extended far beyond the clinical practices of modern psychoanalysis.

The Freud/Jung Letters: The Correspondence between Sigmund Freud and C.G. Jung. Edited by William McGuire, translated by Ralph Manheim and R.F.C. Hull. Princeton: Princeton University Press, 1974. This collection offers the best source for understanding the complex, lively, and ultimately hostile relationship between Freud and Jung.

Geddes, Gary, ed. *20th-Century Poetry & Poetics*. Toronto and New York: Oxford University Press, 1996. An outstanding collection of English-language poetry; it includes poets who responded to the First World War with reflections on violence and death: Wilfred Owen, W.B. Yeats, and T.S. Eliot.

Gramsci, Antonio. *The Antonio Gramsci Reader: Selected Writings, 1916-1935*. Edited by David Forgacs, with a new introduction by Eric Hobsbawm. New York: New York University Press, 2000. This is the best collection of political and theoretical writings by the Italian communist whose analysis of how ruling groups exercise "cultural hegemony" brought new cultural themes to the traditional Marxist emphasis on economic relations.

Graves, Robert. *Good-bye to All That*. Revised edition. Garden City, NY: Doubleday Books, 1957. A classic autobiographical account of how the First World War changed the life and beliefs of a disillusioned English soldier-writer.

Habermas, Jürgen. *The Structural Transformation of the Public Sphere*. Translated by Thomas Burger, with the assistance of Frederick Lawrence. Cambridge, MA: MIT Press, 1989. This historical study describes the emergence and decline of an

Enlightenment-era public sphere (based on reason and free debate). The Enlightenment provided a partial model for the rational democratic political and cultural systems that Habermas promoted in late 20th-century Europe.

Havel, Václav. *Open Letters: Selected Writings, 1965–1990*. Selected and edited by Paul Wilson. New York: Alfred A. Knopf, 1991. This collection shows the evolution of Havel's ideas on writing, politics, and freedom and offers an excellent introduction to his belief in the connections between intellectual work and public action.

Hayek, Friedrich A. *The Road to Serfdom*. Chicago: University of Chicago Press, 1944. This influential book became Hayek's most well known account of his views on the political dangers of government economic planning and the value of classic liberal conceptions of individual rights and the free market.

Husserl, Edmund. *The Idea of Phenomenology*. Translation and introduction by Lee Hardy. Dordrecht and Boston: Kluwer Academic Publishers, 1999. A recent translation of five lectures that Husserl delivered in 1907 to summarize the main themes of his phenomenological philosophy; it is a challenging philosophical work but the best concise statement of his ideas.

Ibsen, Henrik. *A Doll's House*. Translated by R. Rarquharson Sharp and Eleanor Marx-Aveling, revised by Torgrim and Linda Hannas. London and Rutland, VT: J.M. Dent and Charles E. Tuttle, 1993 (volume in the Everyman Library). This play is Ibsen's famous depiction of a woman's struggle to define her own identity, resist social expectations, and declare her personal independence from conventional social roles.

Kafka, Franz. *Metamorphosis and Other Stories*. Translated and edited by Malcolm Pasley. London and New York: Penguin Books, 2000. This collection of short stories is an excellent introduction to Kafka's writing style and distinctive vision of personal alienation in the modern world.

Kristeva, Julia. *The Kristeva Reader*. Edited by Toril Moi. New York: Columbia University Press, 1986. This book includes several of Kristeva's most influential essays, including her reflections on language, gender identities, and the multiple voices of a creative "dialogical" cultural life.

Levi, Primo. *Survival in Auschwitz: The Nazi Assault on Humanity*. Translated by Stuart Woolf. New York: Simon & Schuster, 1996. This moving memoir by one of the rare survivors of the Nazi death camp at Auschwitz is a remarkable description of how the Holocaust was organized and how people responded to the brutal, dehumanizing conditions in which they were confined.

Lévi-Strauss, Claude. *Tristes Tropiques*. Translated by John and Doreen Weightman. New York: Washington Square Press, 1977. Lévi-Strauss often wrote technical anthropological works, but this popular book on his travels in Brazil combined the style of a personal memoir with the research notes of an ethnographer to make his themes accessible to a general audience outside the university.

Mallarmé, Stéphane. *Mallarmé in Prose*. Edited by Mary Ann Caws, translated by Jill Anderson, et al. New York: New Directions Publishing Corporation, 2001. This well-translated collection of prose works provides an accessible introduction to Mallarmé's letters, aesthetic theories, and cultural commentaries. The prose offers an intellectual context for understanding Mallarmé's symbolist poetic aspirations.

Matisse on Art. Edited by Jack Flam. Berkeley and Los Angeles: University of California Press, 1995. This collection, which includes the essay "Notes of a Painter," brings together Matisse's reflections on painting and art from all periods of his long artistic career.

Mauss, Marcel. *The Gift: The Form and Reason for Exchange in Archaic Societies*. New York: W.W. Norton, 1990. The classic anthropological study of the symbolic role that gift giving plays in the creation of social solidarities and in the personal relationships of friends and families.

Orwell, George. *1984*. New York: New American Library, 1983. This fictional portrayal of totalitarian political parties, governments, and language usage (e.g., "War Is Peace") reflected Orwell's political concerns as he wrote about the dangers of totalitarianism after World War II (when he was most concerned about communist regimes).

Proust, Marcel. *Swann's Way* (first volume of *Remembrance of Things Past*). Translated by G.K. Scott Moncrieff. New York: Vintage Books, 1971. This is the classic English translation of the first part of Proust's novel, which begins with the narrator's description of childhood experiences and introduces the famous Proustian themes of time and memory.

Rimbaud, Arthur. *Complete Works, Selected Letters*. Edited and translated by Wallace Fowlie. Chicago: University of Chicago Press, 1966. This translation of Rimbaud's poetry and prose by a distinguished American expert on French literature has long been the best English edition of the poet's complex works; it includes Rimbaud's famous letters on poetic vision.

Sartre, Jean-Paul. "Existentialism Is a Humanism," in Nino Langiulli, ed., *European Existentialism*, pp. 391–416. New Brunswick, NJ: Transaction Publishers, 1997. This volume places Sartre in the context of other existential philosophers and provides a convenient introduction to a wide range of existentialist thought. This essay is one of Sartre's most accessible summaries of his philosophy.

Simmel, Georg. *On Individuality and Social Forms: Selected Writings*. Edited by Donald N. Levine. Chicago: University of Chicago Press, 1971. This useful collection of Simmel's sociological writings includes his influential essay on anonymity and creativity in modern cities, "The Metropolis and Mental Life."

Villiers de l'Isle-Adam, Jean Marie Mathias. *Axel*. Translated by Marilyn Gaddis Rose. Dublin: Dolmen Press, 1970. This translation conveys the mysterious mood and themes of a strange play that expressed symbolist disenchantment with the material realities of modern social life.

Weber, Max. *The Protestant Ethic and the Spirit of Capitalism*. Translated by Talcott Parsons, introduction by Anthony Giddens. London: Counterpoint, 1985. This study of the relation between religious values and the transition to modernity became the most influential example of Weber's historical sociology, and (despite numerous critiques of its thesis) it is still an intriguing, provocative book.

Woolf, Virginia. *A Room of One's Own*. New York: Harcourt Brace Janovich, 1989. First published in 1929, this brief analysis of the constraints that inhibit the creative work of women remains a fascinating critical assessment of gender relations, intellectual hierarchies, and women's writing.

———. *To the Lighthouse*. Foreword by Eudora Welty. San Diego and New York: Harcourt Brace Janovich, 1981. This remarkable novel explores the nature of human relationships, the meaning of time, the struggle to create, and the complex flow of thought in the human mind.

Supplementary Reading

Bell, Quentin. *Virginia Woolf: A Biography*. Two volumes. San Diego and New York: Harcourt Brace Janovich, 1972. A lively, comprehensive account of Woolf's life and cultural milieu by a nephew who had much first-hand knowledge of the writers and artists in the Bloomsbury circle.

Brown, Frederick. *Zola: A Life*. New York: Farrar Straus Giroux, 1995. A detailed, well-written biographical study that describes Zola's cultural context, exhaustive literary work, friendships, public actions, and family life.

Burke, Peter. *The French Historical Revolution: The Annales School, 1929–1989*. Stanford, CA: Stanford University Press, 1990. A concise, well-informed survey of the French historians who developed a new emphasis on social history and the deep structures of social and cultural life.

Butler, Christopher. *Early Modernism: Literature, Music and Painting in Europe, 1900–1916*. Oxford and New York: Oxford University Press, 1994. This book provides a well-illustrated overview of avant-garde innovations in European cultural life during the first decades of the 20th century, stressing the interactions among art, literature, and music.

Calhoun, Craig, ed. *Habermas and the Public Sphere*. Cambridge, MA: MIT Press, 1992. This collection of essays includes diverse commentaries on Habermas's conception of the modern European public sphere and concludes with his own reflections on the theories and history of the Enlightenment that he originally proposed in 1962.

Cohen-Solal, Annie. *Sartre: A Life*. Translated by Anna Cancogni, edited by Norman Macafee. New York: Pantheon Books, 1987.

Cohen-Solal's generally sympathetic biography of Sartre describes his life, his ideas, and his role as a cultural symbol in France after 1945.

Ellmann, Richard. *James Joyce*. Revised edition. New York and Oxford: Oxford University Press, 1982. This comprehensive study by the leading 20th-century expert on Joyce's life and writing is both informative and a pleasure to read.

Eribon, Didier. *Michel Foucault*. Translated by Betsy Wing. Cambridge, MA: Harvard University Press, 1991. One of the numerous studies of Foucault to appear in the decade after his death, Eribon's biographical account is balanced, knowledgeable, and a good introduction to Foucault's evolving intellectual concerns.

Farrenkopf, John. *Prophet of Decline: Spengler on World History and Politics*. Baton Rouge: Louisiana State University Press, 2001. Farrenkopf's book summarizes Spengler's pessimistic views of modern European history and defends many of these ideas as perceptive descriptions of the crises that Europe would face over the course of the 20th century.

Ferguson, Robert. *Henrik Ibsen: A New Biography*. London: Richard Cohen Books, 1996. A useful recent description of the events and relationships in Ibsen's life; it also discusses the influential themes of his plays.

Fussell, Paul. *The Great War and Modern Memory*. Oxford and New York: Oxford University Press, 2000. This is a fascinating study of how English soldiers entered World War I with certain literary expectations about the noble meaning of war, then responded to the horrors of trench warfare in ironic poems or memoirs that expressed the pervasive ironic sensibility of modern European culture.

Gay, Peter. *Freud: A Life for Our Time*. New York and London: W.W. Norton & Company, 1988. Gay's comprehensive, sympathetic biography of Freud provides a wealth of information about the man and his ideas and argues for Freud's decisive influence on modern descriptions of the human mind and behavior.

Heilbut, Anthony. *Thomas Mann: Eros and Literature*. New York: Alfred A. Knopf, 1996. An interesting study of Mann's life and work that argues that the traditional emphasis on Mann's intellectual concerns overlooks the complex emotional and erotic themes in Mann's fiction.

Janik, Allan, and Toulmin, Stephen. *Wittgenstein's Vienna*. New York: Simon and Schuster, 1973. This engaging book exemplifies a "contextual" approach to intellectual history by arguing that the linguistic concerns in Wittgenstein's thought grew out of specific cultural and political debates in late Habsburg Vienna.

Jay, Martin. *The Dialectical Imagination: A History of the Frankfurt School and the Institute of Social Research, 1923–1950*. Boston: Little, Brown and Company, 1973. This book, by one of the best contemporary intellectual historians, is an excellent introduction to the people and ideas of the famous German "school" of leftist cultural critics (who fled Germany after the Nazis took power in 1933).

Kern, Stephen. *The Culture of Time and Space, 1880–1918*. Cambridge, MA: Harvard University Press, 1983. An imaginative study of new trends in science, technology, and the arts that challenged older stable conceptions of time and space to produce a new sense of fluidity and movement in early 20th-century European culture.

LaCapra, Dominick. *Emile Durkheim: Sociologist and Philosopher*. Revised edition. Aurora, CO: The Davies Group, Publishers, 2001 (first published by Cornell University Press in 1972). LaCapra is an innovative intellectual historian who often uses literary theories to interpret influential texts. This book analyzes the displaced religious themes in Durkheim's account of social life and cultural rituals.

Lloyd, Rosemary. *Mallarmé: The Poet and His Circle*. Ithaca and London: Cornell University Press, 1999. An excellent study of Mallarmé's symbolist aesthetic theories and his personal connections with a wide range of creative writers and artists in late 19th-century Paris.

Lottman, Herbert R. *Albert Camus: A Biography*. Garden City, NY: Doubleday and Company, 1979. An older but still valuable and insightful account of the activities and writings that made Camus an international intellectual figure.

Malcolm, Norman. *Ludwig Wittgenstein: A Memoir and a Biographical Sketch by G.H. von Wright*. Second edition. Oxford and New York: Oxford University Press, 1984. An intriguing brief account of Wittgenstein's personal qualities and thought by a philosopher who studied with him and later wrote about his psychological complexities.

Mitzman, Arthur. *The Iron Cage: An Historical Interpretation of Max Weber*. New York: Alfred A. Knopf, 1970. A controversial attempt to analyze Weber from the perspective of psychoanalytical theory, stressing a wider German cultural pattern of authoritarian fathers and "suppressed hostilities" among the sons (which led, in Weber's case, to a mental breakdown).

Moi, Toril. *Simone de Beauvoir: The Making of an Intellectual Woman*. Oxford and Cambridge, MA: Blackwell Publishers, 1994. This study of Beauvoir sympathetically examines the struggle to become an "intellectual woman" in early 20th-century French culture and argues for Beauvoir's crucial influence on modern feminist thought.

Neske, Günther, and Kettering, Emil, eds. *Martin Heidegger and National Socialism: Questions and Answers*. Translated by Lisa Harries and Joachim Neugroschel. New York: Paragon House, 1990. This useful book brings together Heidegger's writings and later reflections on Nazism with commentaries by people who knew Heidegger and later wrote critically about his actions during the 1930s.

Preece, Julian. *The Life and Work of Günther Grass: Literature, History, Politics*. New York: Palgrave, 2001. Preece's study is an excellent recent analysis of Grass's literary work and the main events of his life. It places Grass squarely in the political and cultural contexts of 20th-century German society.

Ringer, Fritz K. *The Decline of the German Mandarins: The German Academic Community, 1890–1933*. Cambridge, MA: Harvard University Press, 1969. This older work of intellectual history remains one of the best accounts of the elite academic culture in early 20th-century Germany, with particular attention to the ways in which professors responded to challenges to their cultural position.

Roudinesco, Elisabeth. *Jacques Lacan*. Translated by Barbara Bray. New York: Columbia University Press, 1997. An excellent biographical and intellectual study of the difficult French thinker. Lacan's writings become more comprehensible when placed in the personal and cultural contexts that Roudinesco describes.

Schorske, Carl E. *Fin-de-Siècle Vienna: Politics and Culture*. New York: Vintage Books, 1981. A classic work of intellectual history that analyzes the architecture, art, music, and crisis of liberalism in a city and era that Schorske calls the birthplace of the "modern."

Seigel, Jerrold. *Bohemian Paris: Culture, Politics, and the Boundaries of Bourgeois Life, 1830–1930*. New York: Viking Penguin, 1986. Seigel's book describes the lively, rebellious bohemian culture that flourished outside the universities, fostered cultural innovation, and created new cultural products or identities for bourgeois consumers.

Sheehan, James J. "Culture," in T.C.W. Blanning, ed., *The Nineteenth Century: Europe, 1789–1914*, pp. 126–157. Oxford and New York: Oxford University Press, 2000. This helpful essay by a well-known historian of modern Germany briefly summarizes the scientific, literary, and institutional trends that would shape the emergence of 20th-century European culture.

Skidelsky, Robert. *Keynes*. Oxford and New York: Oxford University Press, 1996. A brief, informative summary of Keynes's life and ideas by a knowledgeable scholar who has also written the definitive three-volume biography of Keynes.

Smith, Barry, and Smith, David Woodruff, eds. *The Cambridge Companion to Husserl*. Cambridge and New York: Cambridge University Press, 1995. This useful collection provides informative essays on various aspects of Husserl's thought and a good overview of his significance in modern European thought.

Tadié, Jean Yves. *Marcel Proust*. Translated by Euan Cameron. New York and London: Viking, 2000. An outstanding, detailed biographical study by a leading French expert on Proust's life and literary work.

Winders, James A. *European Culture since 1848: From Modern to Postmodern and Beyond*. New York: Palgrave, 2001. This survey of modern European culture provides an excellent overview of general trends and specific intellectuals, including a helpful account of both the faith in science and the modern critiques of scientific thought.